# Executive Teams

# Executive Teams

David A. Nadler

Janet L. Spencer

and Associates

*Delta Consulting Group*

Jossey-Bass Publishers • San Francisco

Substantial discounts on bulk quantities of Jossey-Bass books are available to corporations, professional associations, and other organizations. For details and discount information, contact the special sales department at Jossey-Bass Inc., Publishers (415) 433–1740; Fax (800) 605–2665.

For sales outside the United States, please contact your local Simon & Schuster International Office.

Jossey-Bass Web address: http://www.josseybass.com

 Manufactured in the United States of America on Lyons Falls Turin Book. This paper is acid-free and 100 percent totally chlorine-free.

**Library of Congress Cataloging-in-Publication Data**

Nadler, David A.
  Executive teams / David A. Nadler, Janet L. Spencer. — 1st ed.
    p. cm. — (The Jossey-Bass business & management series)
  Includes bibliographical references and index.
  ISBN 0–7879–1023–6
  1. Teams in the workplace.   2. Executives.   I. Spencer, Janet L.,
date.   II. Title.   III. Series.
  HD66.N33   1997
  658.4′036—dc21                                              97-30446
                                                                 CIP

First edition
*HB Printing*   10  9  8  7  6  5  4  3  2  1

**The Jossey-Bass Business & Management Series**

The Jossey-Bass Business & Management Series

# Contents

# Preface

Leadership is becoming a team sport. In major enterprises and institutions throughout the United States, senior executives are finding that the demands of leadership necessitate the creation, building, and management of executive teams. Nowhere is this trend more dramatic than at the pinnacle of corporate leadership—the chief executive officer. As their jobs have become more complex and demanding, many CEOs have found it useful, if not necessary, to establish corporate-level leadership teams to assist them in the task of running the whole enterprise. Such executive teams are a leadership model for this new era.

During the past several years we have been working closely with more than sixty CEOs who have opted to develop and lead team structures at the top of their enterprises. We participated in and facilitated the development of teams that were clear successes, as well as some that were frustrating, time consuming, and ultimately not productive. Working with these teams on strategy, organizational architecture, change management, and leadership development has given us insights into their unique characteristics and the dynamics inherent in their operation. From this experience, we have developed some observations about the nature of executive teams and the specific requirements for CEO team leadership. *Executive Teams* has been written to pass on some of the knowledge we have both created and gained from these experiences.

## Audience

This book is a vehicle for us to share our insights with others. Perhaps the reader who will benefit most is the CEO who is charged with the responsibility to design and deploy the executive team. This book can better equip even the most enlightened CEO to identify the elusive dynamics at play in the executive team, dynamics that if not effectively addressed can undermine team success. (Note: For simplicity's sake, we have opted to use *he, him,* and so on when referring to CEOs. We recognize and support the fact that there are an increasing number of women in this arena, but we found that referring to both genders was unwieldy.)

We expect that this book will also benefit executive team members who are looking to understand the environment in which they work, their team's role, and how they as individuals contribute to both team chemistry and team performance.

Other readers who will find this book useful are the individuals who deal directly with executive teams: organization development practitioners and other consultants, human resource professionals, academics and graduate students who study this select group, senior managers who report to members of the executive team, board members, and so forth.

*Executive Teams* provides all these audiences with more than just high-level concepts to ponder. It offers both practice-driven learnings and concrete suggestions for applying the knowledge our company, Delta Consulting Group, has derived from its work with the elite of corporate America. Application of the ideas contained in this book will enable CEOs, executive team members, and those who work with them to tap the power of executive teams.

## Overview of the Contents

The movement toward executive teams raises major questions about the composition, organization, chemistry, and function of these teams. What makes them distinctly different from teams at all other levels in the organization? What are the required membership characteristics, behaviors, and group norms? How are differences of opinion handled, and how is conflict surfaced and managed? What unique tasks can the senior team perform that no other individual or team in the organization can perform? It also raises questions about the role and management style of the CEO. How does a chairman of the board or president need to function differently in a team environment? What are some of the unique problems CEOs face in leading executive teams compared with the challenges encountered by leaders at other levels in the organization? What strategies have successful CEOs with effective executive teams employed to effectively lead those teams?

*Executive Teams* is intended to answer these questions of organization, chemistry, and function. It provides both a broad framework with which to think about these issues and exploration of such specific and particular concerns as governance, conflict resolution, and the like.

Part One of the book lays the foundation for understanding the raison d'être of executive teams. It explains specifically what executive teams are, factors that have created the need for them, and characteristics that distinguish them from other senior management groupings in the organization. It also addresses details particular to the organization of executive teams.

Part Two addresses some of the least attended to yet most critical aspects of executive team effectiveness, those revolving around team chemistry: that is, trust, manifestation and resolution of conflict, management of poor performance, distribution and use of power, succession-related competition, and so forth. These chapters outline both what is at play in executive teams and how to deal with their inherent complexities.

Finally, Part Three addresses the function of the executive team, for example, its value-added role. Certain responsibilities lie solely with the executive team: governing within the organization, developing and implementing strategy, leading enterprisewide transformations, and changing the organizational culture. Chapters in this part discuss the nature of these responsibilities and strategies to effectively implement these important executive team roles.

## Acknowledgments

Working with executive teams requires true teamwork on the part of Delta consultants. This book is the result of the work of many Delta teams, and we would like to acknowledge some of the contributions that made this book possible. In particular we would like to thank Delta colleagues Marilyn Showers, Terry Limpert, and Kathy Morris for sharing their experiences with executive teams.

The writing of this book stems out of a project in Delta to collect our knowledge of executive teams. The project was initiated by Elise Walton and David Wagner. The book could not have been written without their efforts. Elise and David have been our partners in this undertaking, and we thank them for all of their tremendous work.

We would also like to express our deep appreciation to our clients who have let us become part of the lives of their executive teams. Our work with CEOs and teams over a period of many years has contributed centrally to our understanding, and we could not have achieved it without their collaboration. While many clients have been involved, we would like to express special thanks to the CEOs and executive teams of Xerox Corporation, Corning Incorporated, Lucent Technologies, and Chase Manhattan Bank.

Delta's operation staff—especially Georgette Patti—deserve recognition for the important contributions they made to producing this book. And finally, a very special thanks goes to Lynn Roberts for her keen editing eye and all the support she provided in pulling this material together.

Although we recognize and thank the individuals and organizations who have helped us in this project, we of course take responsibility for the content and the opinions expressed here.

*New York, New York*                           David A. Nadler
*August 1997*                                        Janet L. Spencer

# The Authors

*David A. Nadler* is chairman and CEO of Delta Consulting Group. He works primarily in the areas of large-scale organizational change, executive leadership, organizational design, and executive team development. He has served on the faculty at the Graduate School of Business at Columbia University and the staff of the Survey Research Center at the University of Michigan Institute for Social Research. He received his B.A. degree in international affairs from George Washington University, his M.B.A. degree from Harvard Business School, and his M.A. and Ph.D. degrees in psychology from the University of Michigan.

*Janet L. Spencer* works in the areas of strategy, organizational design, executive leadership, and executive team development. She received her B.A. degree from Clark University and her M.A. and Ph.D. degrees in organizational psychology from Columbia University.

*David Bliss* specializes in the areas of large-scale change management, collaborative strategy development and implementation, organizational architecture, executive leadership, and governance. He holds a B.S. degree in marketing and finance from Babson College and is a graduate of the executive program of the School of Organization and Management at Yale University.

*Michael V. Collins* works with senior management on the assessment, development, and implementation of strategic organizational change, executive team development, and internal capacity building. He has served as a faculty member at the California School of Professional Psychology and at the NTL (National Training Laboratories) Institute for Applied Behavioral Science. He received his B.A. degree from Vanderbilt University and his M.S. and Ph.D. degrees in clinical psychology from Purdue University.

*Jeffrey D. Heilpern* specializes in working with CEOs and executive management teams on improving their leadership effectiveness in designing and implementing an integrated change agenda. He received his B.A. degree in political science from Tufts University and his M.B.A. degree from Harvard Business School.

*Richard F. Ketterer* works in the areas of executive leadership, executive team effectiveness, organizational change, and strategic human resources. He received his B.A. degree in political science from Wesleyan University, his M.A. degree in human development from the University of Connecticut, and his Ph.D. degree in psychology from the University of Michigan.

*Lilian M. King* specializes in strategy formulation, organizational diagnosis and architecture, and executive team development and leadership. She received her B.Sc. degree from Aberdeen University, Scotland, and her M.P.P.M. degree from the School of Organization and Management at Yale University.

*Mark B. Nadler* is chairman of the editorial board at Delta Consulting Group, where he works in the areas of communications strategies, processes, and functions in the context of organizational change. A journalist and news executive for twenty-two years, he received a B.A. degree in English from George Washington University.

*Daniel Plunkett* specializes in large-scale organizational change, executive team development, CEO and executive development, organizational diagnosis, and culture change. He received his M.F.A. degree from the University of Massachusetts and a Ph.D. degree in human resource development from the University of Texas at Austin.

*Charles S. Raben* works primarily on issues of strategy, transition management, executive leadership, organizational design, and executive team development. He has served on the faculties of the University of California, Berkeley, and the University of Maryland. He received his B.A. degree in psychology from Fairleigh Dickinson University, and his M.A. and Ph.D. degrees in industrial and organizational psychology from Ohio State University.

*J. Carlos Rivero* is responsible for applied research activities at Delta Consulting Group. He works in the areas of organizational diagnosis and change, organizational culture, and action research with emphasis on survey methodology and feedback. He has served on the faculties of George Washington University and Columbia University. He received his B.A. degree from Columbia University and his M.A. and Ph.D. degrees in industrial and organizational psychology from New York University.

*Peter K. Thies* works primarily in the areas of organizational diagnosis, organizational and cultural change, organizational architecture, and information technology strategy. He received his B.A. degree in psychology from State University of New York, Albany, his M.S. degree in educational psychology from the University of Pennsylvania, and both his M.B.A. degree in human resource management and Ph.D. degree in organizational behavior from Rensselaer Polytechnic Institute.

*Roselinde Torres* specializes in organizational diagnosis, organizational architecture, executive team development, and organizational change related to mergers and acquisitions. She received her A.B. double major degree in English and Spanish from Middlebury College and her M.S. degree in human resource development from the American University and NTL (National Training Laboratories) Institute for Applied Behavioral Science.

*David B. Wagner* works primarily in the areas of organizational diagnosis, organizational design, culture change, executive leadership and development, and strategic human resource management. He received his B.A. degree in psychology from Concordia College and his M.A. and Ph.D. degrees in industrial and organizational psychology from New York University.

*A. Elise Walton* specializes in change management, global strategy, organizational design, and quality. She received her B.A. degree from Bowdoin College, her M.A. degree from Columbia University, and her Ph.D. degree from Harvard Business School.

# Executive Teams

# A New Leadership Model

Running a major enterprise today often requires more resources than one person can offer. As a result, the executive team is emerging as an integral part of corporate governance. This set of top executives, most of whom report directly to the chief executive officer (CEO), collectively takes on the role of providing strategic, operational, and institutional leadership for the organization so it can meet increasingly complex internal and external demands.

The effectiveness of executive teams hinges on team members' and other senior leaders' understanding of what they are and what it takes for the CEO to lead them. Chapter One looks at why these teams have emerged, how they differ from other teams, and the unique role the CEO must assume as the team leader.

For an executive team to effectively augment the CEO's leadership in today's demanding environment, it must recognize and master three core processes: work management, relationship management, and external boundary management. Chapter Two examines these processes and demonstrates how their effective implementation makes the executive team a higher risk but also a higher reward model than more traditional organizational designs.

Chapter Three raises CEO leadership issues, many of which executive teams may come to share. In particular it discusses the roles CEOs must play to guide their organizations successfully through *discontinuous change*, periods of substantial and turbulent upheaval and disequilibrium, most often precipitated by a destabilizing event or series of events.

Chapter Three establishes an essential part of the context for executive team leadership, and Chapter Four examines that context further through a detailed analysis of alternative models for allocating responsibilities between the chief executive officer and the chief operating officer (COO) as members and leaders of the executive team. This chapter highlights the importance of a good working relationship between those responsible for leading the team. This relationship is crucial to the success of both the CEO-COO partnership and the executive team. Both traditional and progressive models are discussed, and specific how-to's are provided, along with a worksheet (see the Appendix at the end of the chapter) to facilitate role negotiation between the CEO and COO.

Chapter One

# Leading Executive Teams

*David A. Nadler*

Over the past two decades, at company after company, chief executive officers (CEOs) have begun developing executive teams with leadership responsibilities. As the business environment grows ever more complex and the management of change becomes a standard section of every CEO's job description, CEOs are trying to build executive teams that complement their own abilities with the full range of skills and expertise required for successful leadership of today's organizations and institutions.

This movement toward executive teams raises major questions about the role and management style of the CEO. How have successful CEOs made the transition to team leadership? How have they built and managed their teams to assist in the task of running the whole enterprise? When CEOs become team leaders, what unique problems do they face compared to the multitude of other team leaders throughout an organization?

This chapter provides a perspective on CEO team leadership. I begin by defining teams in general and reviewing the advantages to be gained (as well as the risks inherent) in using them to perform organizational tasks. Then I discuss executive teams: why they have emerged and how they are different from other teams. Finally, I focus on the role of the CEO as team leader, examining why this role is unique and establishing some key requirements for effectively fulfilling it.

## What Is a Team?

Much of the work inherent in managing organizations takes place in group settings. Managerial teams—whose primary purpose is the management or leadership of an organizational entity—are not usually engaged in the actual design, development, manufacture, or delivery of a product. Their work is planning, decision making, and problem solving. The effectiveness of management teams is highly leveraged and has significant implications for the effectiveness of the broader organization.

A team in the organizational context is generally thought of as a group of people who get together to do something. More specifically, a team can be defined as two or more individuals

- Who are aware of and interact with one another
- Who have a sense of themselves as a unit
- Who are jointly accountable for the performance of some activity
- Whose activities are interdependent
- Whose interdependence centers around a work flow or work products

Perhaps the most critical element in this definition is the concept of interdependence. It exists when an individual cannot perform a given task or set of responsibilities without others' assistance. The team's ultimate effectiveness depends upon how well that interdependent work is planned, managed, and performed. The team has more power and potential than an unorganized group of individuals, but the realization of the power requires an investment in team structuring, managing, and motivating.

## Teams Versus Individuals

For years managers and theorists have debated the relative merits of individual effort versus team effort for problem solving. Fortunately, researchers have also done a good deal of investigation in this area; their research, coupled with experience, suggests certain patterns.

| Advantages of Individual Work | Advantages of Team Work |
|---|---|
| Less time | Generation of more ideas |
| Maintenance of control | Increased ownership of |
| Opportunity for individual | product |
| creativity | Increased commitment and |
| Limited awareness of | motivation |
| problems | Wide range of views and |
| Strong individual | perspectives |
| accountability | Baking of ideas |
| Ability to measure and reward | Sharing of risks |
| individual performance | Transfer of expertise |
| Low social overhead | Social support |

On the one hand individual work clearly produces several inherent advantages. For instance, individuals typically perform a given task in less time than teams, which require an assembly and start-up period. Individual efforts allow greater personal control over the work and its outcome. Individual work sometimes provides more opportunities for creative breakthroughs and promotes a strong sense of personal accountability. It limits others' awareness of the task at hand, thus lessening their ability to obstruct it. It is easier to measure and reward, making it easier for supervisors to motivate the desired performance. Finally, there is less *social over-head*—the cost involved in getting people together and organizing their efforts to produce work.

On the other hand there is also significant evidence to support the team approach to problem solving. Team settings may encourage the generation of more ideas and thus enhance the potential for creativity. Using a team may lead to increased ownership of the final product and thus higher quality, increased commitment, and generally higher levels of motivation. Teams can provide a forum for hearing others' views and perspectives. They can serve as a place for refining—or "baking"—raw ideas. They can promote innovation by allowing individuals to share risk. They provide channels for transferring or applying the range of expertise required to solve a problem. Finally, teams can be valuable to the individual as a source of encouragement, motivation, or social support.

Which approach—teams or individuals—is better? The response obviously is, "It depends." In some situations individual action and initiative is clearly the better choice. Involving a team in such situations would not help performance and might even hurt. In other situations the reverse would be true.

How then does one determine when to use a team? The key to the answer lies in the *nature of the task to be performed*. As a general rule the team approach should be seriously considered when more than one of the following conditions are present:

- The work requires a range of different skills, views, or expertise.
- The different components of the work are highly interdependent.
- There is sufficient time to organize and structure team effort.
- There is a need to build commitment for implementation of decisions or execution of plans.
- The problems or issues would benefit from baking.
- The work would benefit from extraordinary creativity or innovation.
- The potential team members can be trusted to be constructive.
- Individuals would respond well to a team experience.

Under these conditions, teams tend to be an effective tool for getting work done. Yet many U.S.-based organizations continue to harbor a bias in favor of individual efforts. The result has been a failure to exploit the full productive potential of the team approach.

## Team Performance

Once the decision has been made to use a team to get work done, then a second problem arises: What makes the difference between effective and ineffective teams? Let's consider two different patterns of team activity and performance. Figure 1.1 graphs two patterns of team performance as individuals are added to the team. The vertical axis represents units of work produced; the horizon-

**Figure 1.1.  Two Patterns of Actual Group Performance.**

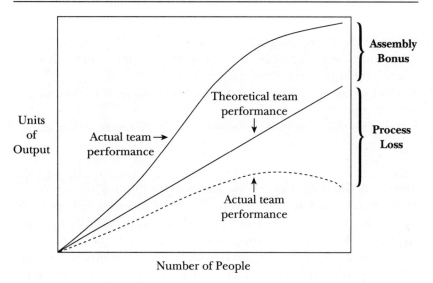

tal axis represents the number of people in the team. Assuming that each individual produced one unit of work, one would expect that each time one person was added to the team, the team would produce an additional unit of work. This theoretical group performance is represented by the heavy straight diagonal line on the graph. But actual performance is different.

One common pattern of actual team performance is represented by the solid curved line. As more people are brought together the performance of the team outdistances the performance one would expect from the same number of individuals working alone. This *assembly bonus* is a direct consequence of bringing people together in a team. But sometimes a second pattern is observed, illustrated by the dotted curved line. As more people are added the team becomes less effective. In fact the team produces less than the individuals would have produced on their own. This productivity gap is known as *process loss*.

If working as a team can lead to either a performance gain or a performance loss, what makes the difference? In general terms several factors are influential. Groups are more likely to be effective when they

- Are performing the *right work* for a team
- Include the *right people*—the appropriate types of individuals and the appropriate number of them
- Exist in the *right context*—a positive environment for working in teams
- Develop the *right work process*—appropriate methods for working together

Teams can be very effective mechanisms for getting work done, or they can be costly and inefficient. The four points listed are a first cut at identifying the conditions that determine the pattern of performance. Yet obviously things are not quite that simple. To truly understand how to create and manage effective teams, we need to understand in more detail what influences a team's long-term effectiveness. This is the subject of Chapter Two, where I examine in depth a model of executive team effectiveness and how to employ the model to build a high-performing executive team. Before addressing this model, however, I will set the context for the rest of this book by defining executive teams and introducing the CEO as team leader.

## What Is an Executive Team?

During the 1960s, the CEO-COO model emerged in the United States as an approach to structuring executive roles and work. This structure typically includes a chairman of the board serving as the CEO, a president serving as chief operating officer (COO) and reporting to the CEO, and a number of executives reporting to the COO, each responsible for the operations of a particular unit.

Work is allocated so that the CEO is responsible for strategic issues, external relations, and overall corporate governance, and the COO has primary responsibility for running internal company operations. The COO might meet regularly with his direct reports, individual executives who manage their own pieces of the organization in ways consistent with the strategies and direction from the top. Although specific roles and assignments vary from company to company, by the 1960s this two-person structure became the dominant form of organizing major U.S. corporations at the executive level.

During the past decade and a half a different type of organizational design at the top—the executive team—has emerged. In this design a team of executives reports to the CEO. This team, in the absence of a CEO, collectively assume the role in managing internal operations and may even take on some of the CEO role of formulating strategy and managing external relations. In organizations that employ a COO, the role of the executive team remains important yet may be managed differently. (See Chapter Four for more on this subject.) In either situation, if set up effectively, the executive team is more than a set of individuals who work together; it is a truly interdependent interacting team. That is, team members have a sense of identity (they perceive themselves as a unit and they are interdependent), they depend upon each other to produce their output, and they have joint outcomes (their rewards and penalties are affected by each other's efforts). The core defining characteristic is the existence of a set of people who collectively take on the role of providing strategic, operational, and institutional leadership for the organization. Thus each member is not only responsible for his own unit or function but also explicitly wears another "hat," that of corporate leadership.

## Why Has the Executive Team Emerged?

The fundamental rationale for establishing any team, including executive teams, is the creation of an assembly bonus (see Figure 1.1)—the essence of which is increasing effective coordination or coupling across functions and activities so that the performance of the whole is greater than the performance of the sum of its parts. Why has the shift to executive teams seemed to accelerate recently? Three factors emerge: external demands, organizational complexity, and succession.

At the broadest cultural level, teams have come to be viewed as a more acceptable form of organizing than they were formerly, particularly because of the effective use of team structures by the Japanese and other foreign competitors. Thus in contrast to the bias toward "rugged individualism" that prevailed for many years in U.S.-based organizations, the idea of managing through teams at the executive level is seen as a more legitimate concept today. One company even talks about "rugged groupism."

External business pressures also have played a role in intensifying the demands on corporate leadership and the demands on the CEO in particular. Increasing global competition, technology-based change, government intervention, and turbulence in financial markets have all added to the burdens of the CEO. The need to spend more time on strategies to meet such environmental instability has had to be balanced with a focus on shorter-term performance, driven by shareholder demands and the emergence of boards of directors as potent forces in setting corporate direction. As a consequence CEOs have found themselves looking for help in both strategic and operational tasks.

In addition to external events, internal requirements of managing diverse yet interdependent organizational units also cause executive teams to emerge. Executive teams may also develop when a CEO needs to manage succession-related issues.

One way of thinking about these various elements is to describe the three distinct scenarios that my colleagues and I have observed for the formation of an executive team. The first is related to the internal management challenges, and the second and third to management succession.

1.   *The business diversity scenario.* This scenario is driven by the diversity and complexity of the parts of the organizations. In those companies where diversification has created multibusiness or multi-industry activities in the context of an unstable and demanding environment, the CEO feels that it would be difficult for one individual COO to provide the needed direction and integration across the diverse businesses and new structures, so the CEO forms an executive team to collectively perform as the COO. The CEO believes that this team will provide him with many heads applied to a problem and that the company will benefit from the team's collective wisdom and intellect. Examples of this scenario are the

Corporate Office that Paul Allaire has created at Xerox and the Management Committee that CEO Jamie Houghton created and led for many years at Corning.

2. *The new CEO scenario.* Executive teams also emerge when new CEOs are designated and first take office. Particularly in situations where they have not been the COOs themselves prior to succession, new CEOs are often hesitant for several reasons to immediately designate a COO. First, they may want to have direct contact with those parts of the business with which they are less familiar. Second, they may not want to put a layer of management between themselves and the major business units during the initial stage of their terms when they are creating their leadership agenda and putting their stamp on the organization. Third, they may not want to implicitly designate a successor through the appointment of a COO, narrowing down their ultimate choices or creating a perception of reduced opportunity for other executives. Therefore new CEOs create an executive team to work directly with them in leading the organization. Examples of this approach can be seen in Bob Allen's structuring of the AT&T senior management after he succeeded Jim Olsen in 1988 and in Walter Shipley's creation of the "three president" structure at Chemical Bank in the mid-1980s.

3. *The executive selection scenario.* This scenario occurs at the end of a CEO's term. As the CEO contemplates the choice of a successor, he or she modifies the leadership structure, frequently by the retirement or removal of the current COO when it is clear that the COO is not the desired successor and by the concomitant creation of an executive team that includes a number of the succession candidates. The team then becomes an arena for assessing, selecting, and preparing successors. It provides an opportunity for the CEO and the board of directors to observe the candidates as they interact around common business problems, or as one CEO has said, "on a level playing field." The CEO is able to test the quality of the candidates' thinking, their leadership skills, and the nature of their relationships with others in senior management. Thus the executive team is created as an environment for a succession "horse race." Notable examples of this scenario can be seen in the structures created by Reginald Jones at GE and Walter Wriston at Citicorp during the early 1980s as part of their executive selection processes.

These scenarios develop and change over time. CEOs may manage and create teams through different scenarios, and they may move in and out of using team approaches.

## How Are Executive Teams Different from Other Teams?

One might reasonably ask whether executive teams are any different from other management teams that might be encountered in an organization. The work my colleagues and I have done indicates some very significant differences. This is important because the members of these teams are often unprepared by their previous experiences in teams for the dynamics they encounter in the executive team. These differences also pose some unique challenges for the shaping, structuring, and managing of these teams. Some of the notable differences are these:

*Salience of the external environment.* Though many teams find they need to deal with the environment beyond team boundaries, the executive team is uniquely influenced by external forces. Several elements of that environment have a major impact on team functioning—particularly customers, competitors, financial markets, the board of directors, and shareholders. The understanding and managing of that environment therefore become central and critical tasks of the team, much more so than in other team settings.

*Complexity of the task.* As noted, the executive team today faces a set of tasks or work requirements that is potentially more complex than the work of most other teams. The combination of internal operations management, external relationship management, institutional leadership, and strategic decision making creates a task that has many more interrelated elements and greater uncertainty than the tasks facing most other teams.

*Intensified political behavior.* The essence of the executive team is power, or the exercise of influence over the behavior of others. In that environment, therefore, the presence of politics is much more pronounced and explicit political behavior appears to be more frequent than in other teams.

*Fixed-pie reward contingencies.* Although there are many rewards for executive team members, the ultimate reward is succession—

who ends up as the CEO, or team leader. By definition, succession creates a zero-sum game and thus a perception of a "fixed pie" of rewards. When one person wins, others have to lose.

*Increased visibility.* As a source of institutional leadership, the executive team has symbolic value, and therefore the team's actions, interactions, and dynamics are carefully watched by many others in the organization. The team becomes a stage upon which dramas are acted out. What might on other teams be small and inconsequential interactions become major events.

*Composition.* Individuals become members of the executive team through a multiyear process of selection. Though it is dangerous to generalize on this topic, in the firms we have observed, individuals selected for the executive team tend to be very high on needs for power and achievement. They also have histories of distinguishing themselves through individual achievement rather than through their work with or through teams. Thus in many U.S.-based companies the executive team ends up composed of people who have been brought up and rewarded for their successes in the rugged individualism model of management and who may be less prepared than their colleagues at lower levels to either lead or participate in effective teams.

*Special meaning of team membership.* Although membership and inclusion is an important issue in many teams, membership has special meaning in the executive team. Because this is the ultimate team in the organization, just being a member has special status and symbolism attached to it. Frequently, people talk about the importance of "sitting at the big table" as shorthand for membership in the executive team. As a result, the questions of who becomes a member, how members are initiated, what it means to lose membership in the team, and so forth become of much more concern than in other teams.

*Unique role of the CEO as team leader.* A key difference in the executive team is that the team leader is the CEO. As a consequence there may be more social distance between the leader and the team members than in other settings.

In light of these factors executive team dynamics are significantly different from those of other teams. Both the work of the team and the relationships in the team are more complex.

## The Uniqueness of the CEO Role

As I have mentioned, one of the unique properties of the executive team is the uniqueness of the role of its leader, the CEO. A number of elements contribute to the social distance between the CEO and team members—distance greater than that normally experienced between team leader and team member. First, the CEO is not only the team leader but the ultimate determiner of rewards, particularly succession. Unlike other teams, this team usually offers no recourse beyond the CEO; if relationship or performance problems arise between individual team members and the CEO, there is no place else to go. Second, the CEO's tenure is more defined than that of other team leaders. It is more finite (because of customary retirement ages) but also of potentially longer term than in other teams. Therefore the CEO is both more permanent in the role and more certain about the point of ending that role. Third, the CEO plays several roles in addition to the role of team leader. In particular the role of institutional leader is important. As representative of the enterprise to the world outside; as symbolic icon of the organization; as focal point for employees, shareholders, and sometimes customers, the CEO has the potential for a larger-than-life presence. As institutional leader, the CEO is also the individual whom the world, including the board, the shareholders, the financial community, and the public, will see as responsible for the success or failure of the enterprise.

The problem then is how this larger-than-life character, this holder of ultimate power, this symbolic leader, can also function as the builder, facilitator, and coach of a team of individuals. These individuals who are often, in turn, institutional leaders for their own segments of the organization.

## Dynamics of Team Leadership

Understanding the CEO's role requires a brief review of some basic concepts of group dynamics and leadership. When we observe and seek to understand a team in action, there are two perspectives we can take. One is *content*—we focus on *what* the team is doing, the nature of the work or tasks the team is undertaking. When we watch an executive team, we might see content related to corporate strategy, resource allocation, management succession, and so on. A second perspective is *process*—we look at *how* the work is being performed by the team. We examine the patterns of interaction, the relationships, and the dynamics of the team as it goes about its work.

Understanding a team involves the observation of both content and process at the same time. Content influences process, and process influences content. For example, how the team members work at making decisions, solving problems, and committing the action will influence the outcomes of their work together. At the same time different content topics (such as management succession, for example) will elicit different process dynamics in the team. I should also point out that although this book talks about the observable behavior of the leader and the team when they are physically in proximity (in team meetings and work sessions), the concepts apply as well to the day-to-day work of the team and its members' interactions—even when they are not all assembled at the same time in the same room.

The role of the effective team leader at the most basic level is to shape and manage both the content and process of the team. The team leader participates in the choosing of content for the team to consider and often takes a position on content—making a strategic decision, for example. At the same time the leader shapes the process, through formal structuring of the team's activities and also through her or his day-to-day activities, both in formal team sessions and in other interactions with team members.

Using these terms and framework, then, there are three issues to consider with regard to the CEO as team leader. The first is the *participative leadership* issue, or how the CEO can create participation without abrogating leadership. The second is the *two-hat* issue, or how the CEO can participate in the work of the team on content and at the same time be the ultimate decision maker. The third is the *team builder* issue, or how the CEO can lead the design and development of the executive team.

## The Participative Leadership Issue

When CEOs form and lead teams, they frequently find themselves in a quandary about how they should lead. This is a process question. They realize that teamwork at the top will require changes in

**Figure 1.2. The CEO's Perceived Leadership Choice.**

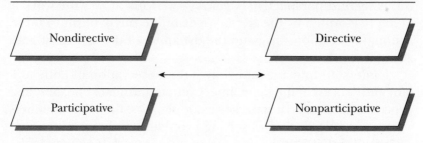

how they lead, and they also recognize that they will need to become more participative.

A classic problem occurs, however, when the CEO confuses participation with a lack of leadership. In discussions with many CEOs it appears that they think of their leadership choice in the terms illustrated in Figure 1.2. They confuse and confound two distinct dimensions of leadership. They desire to move from being nonparticipative (leading alone) to being participative (leading together with a team). But they conclude that this means they must also move as team leaders from being directive toward being nondirective and letting the team manage and decide for itself. This approach frequently leads to ill-structured and nonproductive work sessions and a drift toward ineffective management by consensus.

In reality two different dimensions of leader behavior are at play here. The actual choices that CEOs face are best described as illustrated in Figure 1.3. What typically happens is that CEOs start in quadrant four (directive and nonparticipative) prior to establishing a team. Because they confuse the two dimensions, they then move to quadrant one (participative and nondirective), with the resulting frustrations associated with that approach. In some cases they then do away with the team and return to quadrant four; although in other cases they recognize that they have a role in directing the process of the team, and they move to quadrant two.

In quadrant two, leaders are participative—they involve the team in the *content* of decision making, discussing issues, raising

**Figure 1.3.  The CEO's Actual Process Choices.**

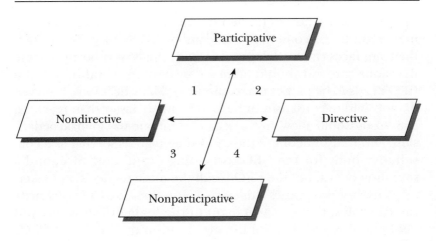

concerns, solving problems, and learning. At the same time they are quite directive about the *process* of the team, shaping and structuring how the team works. Some of the functions these effective CEO team leaders perform include the following:

- Defining the agenda topics
- Clarifying meeting objectives
- Questioning and testing for understanding
- Managing the time allocated to each topic
- "Calling the question"—clarifying when it is time for a decision
- Summarizing discussions and the results of work sessions
- Identifying next steps and accountabilities

This is an illustrative rather than an exhaustive list, but it suggests how the CEO shapes the way the team works by managing the team's work process. In this manner the CEO is very directive and is pushing the team toward high performance, but he or she is exercising direction through management of the process, rather than by taking a position on all elements of the content of the team's work.

## The Two-Hat Issue

There are times, however, when the CEO needs to take a position in relation to the content of the team's work. Some decisions that the team faces can be delegated to individuals or subteams. Some decisions can and should be made by consensus (although the CEO needs to be part of that consensus). Many decisions, however, do not yield to consensus or have to be made faster than reaching consensus would allow. In those cases someone has to make a decision, and that someone is the CEO. The team is serving as a consultative body for the CEO, providing input, guidance, and a sounding board, but the CEO is still the ultimate decision maker.

This, however, raises a dilemma. How does the CEO reconcile the two roles, that of participant in the team's discussions and deliberations and that of ultimate decision maker? Some CEOs choose to become very explicit about those roles. For example, when Jamie Houghton was CEO and chairman of Corning Incorporated (and leader of a very successful executive team for more than ten years), he talked about wearing "two hats." In his terms there were times when he wanted to be a member of the team, to argue, to test ideas, to have people push him, to get into the rough and tumble of the team's work. In those cases he saw himself as "one of the boys," and talked about wearing a "cowboy hat." At other times he was in the position of CEO, making a decision. In these cases he was not looking for testing, push back, or argument. Instead he would say he was wearing the "bowler." His two-hats concept helped his team members understand what he wanted from them and when they should consider him a member of the team and when the institutional leader. It created a language system that all could use to talk about a difficult subject—the CEO's role. For example, Houghton might get to the end of a team discussion and then announce, "I'm going to put on the bowler." Or a person arguing with him during a discussion might ask him, "Is that a cowboy hat comment or a bowler comment?"

## The Team Builder Issue

The final issue is that the CEO needs to see himself as a builder of teams. Teams don't just come into existence and automatically function well. Effective teamwork requires investment in building the team. Specifically, this involves CEO time devoted to answering some of these questions:

- Who should be members of the team?
- What is the charter or mandate of the team?
- What is the appropriate value-added work of the team?
- What are the roles and expectations of different team members?
- What procedures will be used to manage work, to build an agenda, to solve problems, to make decisions, and so on?
- What types of interactions will be required among team members, and what will be acceptable and unacceptable behavior?

In addition to this initial work, the team itself needs to engage in quality assurance, through periodic quality checks and reviews of its performance and through methods to ensure continuous improvement.

This team building and team maintenance can be managed by the CEO or can involve some form of outside help or facilitation, but it must be done to ensure team effectiveness.

This means that the role of the CEO is not just leader and not just team leader but also team builder and developer over time. The CEO needs to invest the time that is necessary with the team and also make the investment needed to develop his own skills in these areas.

## Summary

The era of the executive team has begun. The complexities and demands associated with running an enterprise in today's environment require more resources than one person alone can typically bring to the task. As a consequence, executive teams are emerging as a major fixture of corporate governance, and they are creating a whole new set of requirements for the CEO as a leader.

Of course the CEO is frequently the leader of several teams. The CEO participates in and sometimes leads teams outside the enterprise in business and community activities. Most important, any public company CEO also has one special team to shape, lead, and develop—the board of directors. As boards become more active and more assertive, the skills that the CEO develops to manage the executive team will be transferable to managing the board.

In the era of executive teams the CEO will need to be an effective team leader without giving up any personal effectiveness as an individual leader and as an institutional leader. This is a challenge and a tough one, but when well met, it produces significant rewards for the individual CEO, for the team members, and for the enterprise as a whole.

## Chapter Two

# Executive Team Effectiveness

## Teamwork at the Top

*David A. Nadler*

Chapter One examined the emergence of executive teams as an alternative to more traditional structuring of executive roles and work. The issues that drive the need for such teams—internal demands, organizational complexity, and succession—need to be kept in mind as I discuss in this chapter the nature, effectiveness, and management of executive teams.

Figure 2.1 displays an example of an executive team, in this case entitled a Corporate Management Committee (CMC), of a diversified technology-intensive manufacturing and services company. The CMC is composed of three group presidents, each responsible for a particular strategic sector of the company, and two vice chairmen, one for technology and one for all of the corporate staff functions.

This team was created when a new chief executive officer was named upon the retirement of the existing CEO and chief operating officer, who had been using the traditional two-person structure. The new CEO announced that he was going to run the company differently. He created the CMC and started to spend a good deal of time with it working on developing a shared vision for the company, including a set of strategies and a statement of values and operating principles. The group presidents in particular, as they were asked to take the perspective of "owners" of the

**Figure 2.1. Corporate Management Committee:
Diversified Technology-Intensive Manufacturing and Services.**

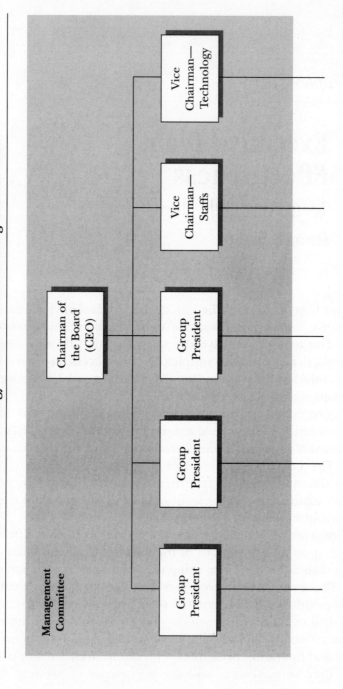

company, found themselves suddenly involved in a whole set of corporate policy and direction discussions in which they had not participated previously.

There are a growing number of companies with organizational charts similar to the example shown here (even though different titles may be used, such as Office of the Chairman, Policy Committee, or Corporate Office). New organizational charts alone, however, do not make an executive team. As stated in Chapter One, the core defining characteristic of an executive team is the existence of a set of people who collectively take on the role of providing strategic, operational, and institutional leadership for the organization. Thus each member is not only responsible for his own unit or function but also assumes a role in corporate leadership. The remainder of this chapter looks in more detail at what it takes to make an executive team.

## What Contributes to Effective Teamwork at the Top?

The work I and my colleagues have carried out supports the way of thinking about executive teams shown in Figure 2.2. This approach is based on some general models of group performance (Hackman, 1983; McGrath, 1984; Shea and Guzzo, 1987). Traditional models often deal primarily with internal processes, however, so we have expanded the model to emphasize the two issues particularly salient for executive teams: external relations and succession. In this model, executive team performance is determined by how three core team processes are managed over time. These processes are, in turn, shaped by certain critical aspects of executive team design.

What are some of the key features of the model? To begin with, team performance is seen as having two dimensions.

- *Production of results.* This dimension reflects the team's ability to effectively meet the demands of its role. At the executive level it includes whether the top team produces consistent positive results (earnings, growth, returns, and so forth) and maintains organizational performance in the face of strategic and environmental challenges. Production of results also includes the quality

**Figure 2.2.  A Model of Executive Team Effectiveness.**

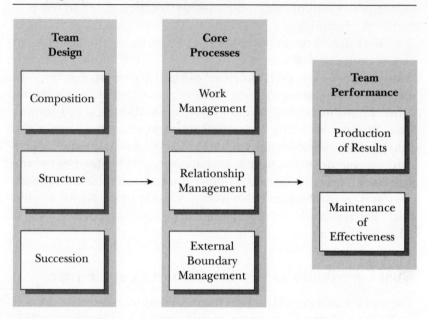

of decision making, the ability to implement decisions, the outcomes of team work in terms of problems solved and work completed, and finally, the quality of institutional leadership provided by the team.

• *Maintenance of effectiveness.* This second dimension of team performance includes the ability of the team to satisfy its members' needs, the ability of the team members to work together over time, and the ability of the team to adapt to new demands, situations, or challenges. Over time, maintenance of effectiveness is required to ensure consistent production of results. The two are necessary and complementary aspects of performance.

Executive team performance is seen as being directly influenced by the quality, effectiveness, and appropriate shaping of these three core processes:

• *Work management process.* This is how the team organizes and manages itself to perform work, including how it shares information, how the work agenda of the team is set, how the team goes about making decisions, how the team coordinates the activities of different individuals and groups, and so forth. In executive teams the work is primarily strategy, policy, and operating decisions. Work management therefore concerns how the team gets those decisions made and implemented.

- *Relationship management process.* This is how the team manages the nature and quality of relationships among team members. Some key elements include the degree of openness between members, how conflicts are resolved, the nature of support expressed among members, the cohesiveness of the group, and the degree of trust. In executive teams the issue is how to manage relationships in the context of the political, symbolic, and succession factors described in Chapter One, particularly when team members may be geographically distant or not in daily direct contact with each other.

- *External boundary management process.* This concerns how the team deals with factors and elements outside the team and largely outside the organization. It is a particularly salient process for executive teams. It includes how boundaries are defined, how key external actors are identified, and how boundary management approaches or strategies are developed. In executive teams boundary management may focus on factors outside the organization such as financial markets, the media, key customers, competitors, and governments, but these teams must also manage the boundary between the team itself and the rest of the organization that it leads.

The effectiveness of an executive team is determined by how well the team manages these three processes to meet the demands and exploit opportunities. Although the three core processes can be directly managed and fashioned by the team leader, they are also highly influenced by several factors that can be shaped ahead of time. I call these elements of *team design*:

- *Composition.* The effectiveness and process of the team are greatly shaped by the selection of team members. The mix of skills and experiences in the team obviously affects the team's ability to work effectively on different types of problems and tasks. In addition the extent to which the team has shared values and shared perspectives also greatly affects the relationship management issues in the team.

• *Structure.* Different teams will have different formal structures. In executive teams, team structure is determined by the organizational design decisions that establish the nature of the positions in the team. Structure also includes the size of the team, the boundaries (who's in and out), the specific formal roles, the goals of the team, and the nature of team and individual rewards.

• *Succession.* A third design element is succession, which reflects the scenario that has been created for the team, the resulting perceptions of team members about succession, and expectations of team members about how their performance and behavior affect their succession prospects.

## What Type of Teamwork Is Needed in Different Situations?

The executive team effectiveness model identifies some of the key elements that strongly influence team performance. Yet we at Delta have shied away from identifying any set of universal characteristics of a "good team." Effective teams facing different strategic environments and created in disparate scenarios will require varying types of teamwork. Investing time and effort in the work management, relationship management, and boundary management processes when there is little potential added value from teamwork does not make sense. The decision to develop and work on the executive team has cost or overhead associated with it, including the time required, the potential slowing of decision making, and the creation of added interfaces and thus coordination costs and an increased burden of managing more relationships.

The more effective executive teams appear to be those that focus their time and thus their coordination efforts on the appropriate core processes given the strategic context of the team. Two contextual factors need to be considered. The first is the environmental context, or the nature of the external demands placed on the organization by the environment. These demands are determined by the degree of threat from the environment, the pace and rate of change in the environment, the complexity of the environment, and the degree to which important environmental factors are outside the executive team's control. Obviously, the greater the demands of the environment, the more attention the team needs to pay to external boundary management processes.

A second factor is the structural context of the executive team, or the degree of interdependence (and therefore coordination requirements) among the major organizational units. There are at least two determinants of the degree of interdependence.

One determinant concerns the organization's strategic choices regarding its portfolio of businesses and the resultant strategic interdependence among them. For example, a vertically integrated company typically has higher interdependence at the top level than one following a strategy of unrelated diversification (Michel and Hambrick, 1988; Rumelt, 1974). Another determinant is the set of organizational design decisions that results in major organizational units that are more or less interdependent. If a company is grouped into business units, there is typically less interdependence than if it is grouped by function. The greater the internal coordination requirements, the greater the demands for focus on internal work management processes and the greater the requirements for a focus on relationship management in support of effective work management.

This identification of possible types of teamwork leads to a way of thinking about which processes to focus on and manage in different executive contexts, as shown in Figure 2.3. Those situations with low coordination requirements and low environmental demands (context one, the upper-left-hand cell of Figure 2.3) require relatively little team process management. What is required is the most minimal level of work management around the broadest institutional issues where there is some common fate or interdependence. In practice this means that the executive team merely needs to focus on information exchange among members.

Organizations in this category might be holding companies in industries with relatively low levels of market and technical change. Here the top team is more like a set of portfolio managers, pushing managerial decisions down to the diversified businesses at a lower level in the organization. High levels of integration are not needed in these teams, and therefore studies have shown that the work of building a cohesive group is not related to performance (Michel and Hambrick, 1988; Song, 1982). Teams facing low coordination and environmental demands need develop only such

### Figure 2.3. Critical Processes for Executive Team Performance: A Contextual Approach.

| | | Structural Context (Internal Coordination Requirements) | |
|---|---|---|---|
| | | Low | High |
| **Environmental Context** (Complexity/Instability of External Demands) | **Low** | 1. Minimal Work Management (information exchange) | 2. Internal Work Management and Relationship Management |
| | **High** | 3. External Boundary Management | 4. Multiprocess Management |

rudimentary group process skills as the ability to call meetings, follow agendas, and surface information relevant to the few joint decisions team members must make. Meetings can be formal and infrequent in this condition.

Context two—with high internal coordination requirements but low environmental demands—is best typified by the large integrated business in a relatively stable industry. Among large organizations there are fewer and fewer that fall into this category. Currently, only those companies that hold monopolies, are in "protected" industries, or are part of an oligopoly find themselves facing environments that are stable and that do not make significant new demands on the organization. Consequently, many organizations that used to face context two now face a different set of conditions and must change their processes accordingly.

For those teams that remain in this context, the focus is on the internal work management and relationship management processes. In contrast to organizations in context one, companies in this condition are often functionally organized, thus decisions are not easily delegated to lower levels, and organizational units need to be more tightly coupled. Top management teams end up making major decisions about products to produce, markets to serve, technologies and structures to employ, and stance toward the competition.

To accomplish these tasks, teams need to develop cohesiveness, engage in frequent and open communication, and have well-managed meetings. Coordination across members is key to success. The smooth work and relationship management processes needed in this context can be facilitated through a relatively homogeneous and long-term top team.

In situations with low coordination requirements but high environmental demands (context three), most of the team effort should be focused on the external boundary management process. Academic institutions, professional service firms, and diversified companies in dynamic heterogeneous environments are exemplars of this condition. In these cases much of the operational work is delegated to the executives responsible for particular groups, businesses, sectors, or segments of the organization. These groups have relatively little operational interdependence and sometimes little strategic interdependence. Examples include industrial companies that have developed significant financial services businesses that are separate from the core manufacturing-based business.

In context three the team does not need to be involved in coordination or management of the interdependent work among the units. The focus is on the corporation as an entity: its strategy and policies and the relationships that it has with various external organizations, groups, or bodies. The key process involves managing external relationships—including alliances, joint ventures, arrangements, and the like—and deciding how those will be handled over time. Team members in this context must represent the corporation externally, negotiate agreements with outsiders, promote the organizational image to competitors and allies, work with the media, scan and monitor key external groups, and ward off unwelcome advances from other corporations.

Finally, in those situations with high internal coordination requirements and high environmental demands (context four), the team needs to be able to manage all three core processes effectively at the same time; it must engage in multiprocess management. Computer firms and other high-technology companies, for example, face turbulent markets and are often integrated businesses. Here teams face the difficult challenge of adapting to a changing set of demands as they also exercise internal leadership in setting priorities and direction that keep people mobilized.

External monitoring and communication with outsiders who have different values, priorities, and viewpoints are needed to meet environmental demands in both contexts three and four, even though these actions breed conflict within the team as the multiple perspectives are juxtaposed and evaluated (Dougherty, 1987). This conflict can be easily managed in context three because these teams have relatively low coordination demands. In context four, however, the conflict requires more complex management, and the team must exhibit sophisticated processes. Teams in context four must bring together members with high social skills and be able to negotiate and compromise, to pool information from multiple sources, and to blend analysis and action (Bourgeois and Eisenhardt, 1988; Quinn, 1982). Team members must meet more frequently with each other and with outsiders than in the other conditions. Team members must always be working multiple agendas, trying to pull disparate individuals together toward an ever-changing target.

It is important to keep in mind that effective teams do not completely ignore any of the core processes. The bulk of the team's time and energy will be focused on making sure that the critical processes for the team's current context are developed and managed. However, when the prospect of strategic change faces the organization, the team may also work on developing competencies that although not critical now, may be critical in the near future as the organization's context changes.

## Team Building for Executive Team Effectiveness: Applying the Model

Many CEOs experience tremendous difficulty in creating and managing executive teams. The team effectiveness model discussed in this chapter provides a framework for thinking about the factors that contribute to team performance, and can assist in ensuring that the basic elements of team design are determined—the type of teamwork that is needed and the composition, structure and succession issues. Once these have been addressed, however, the "real" work begins: *designing the executive team's work process* is perhaps the most critical and problematic step in creating an effective executive team, and it frequently requires significant investments of time and energy. It is also the step in team development CEOs most frequently ignore when establishing new teams. I therefore discuss designing the work process in more depth in this section.

The task of designing and implementing the right work process is frequently called *team building*. There are a number of ways of thinking about how to do effective team building (see, for example, Schein, 1988; Dyer, 1977). The particular approach outlined here builds on methodology developed by Beckhard (1972) as part of his work with health care teams but used widely in a range of different settings. The team-building framework is shown in Figure 2.4.

The starting point for team building is to clarify the context and charter for the team members so that they have a shared understanding of the elements surrounding and defining the team's work process. Several specific features are important in clarifying the specific role of this team in the larger system: the team's performance requirements, the team's key relationships with other groups, and rewards or consequences related to team performance.

## Four Elements of Team Building

At the core of this team-building approach are four elements that are leverage points for defining how an executive team functions, or what its work process looks like in practice. These elements are *goals, roles, procedures,* and *interactions.*

Although each of these elements is important, I tend to think of them in the order given because, for example, problems related to interactions among group members frequently are reflections of problems in goals or roles. Working the issues that are earlier in the list frequently prevents problems in the later issues.

Each of these elements raises questions the CEO and the team must consider.

**Figure 2.4.  A Team-Building Framework.**

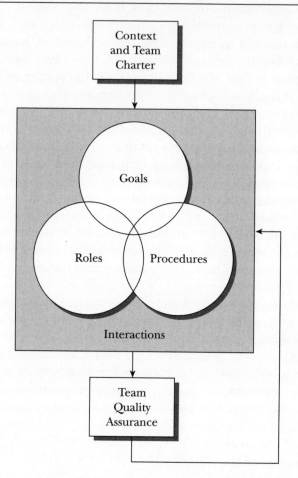

*Goals.* The fundamental question is, What is the value-added work that this team can and should perform? In most cases it is safe to assume that the time of executive team members is valuable and that the marginal cost associated with working in the team (as opposed to doing something else) is relatively high. The team needs to define the work activities with the potential for adding value that is greater than the marginal cost of the team. Based on this analysis the team then needs to determine the core agenda content—what will it work on when the members are together? Finally, the team needs to determine what constitutes success and what measures will be used to assess the effectiveness of the team.

*Roles.* A second set of questions has to do with individual team members' specific expectations or their individual roles in the team. The core question is, What are the requirements that team members are expected to meet? Also, do those requirements come from the work, the context, the leader, or from other group members? A related question is, What are the specialized roles within the group? One key specialized role is the role of the CEO, which needs to be defined and understood. There are, however, other types of specialized roles that may be structured or may evolve in different settings.

*Procedures.* Procedures include the mechanisms by which the group does its work, particularly when it is together. Questions here concern the structure of meetings or work sessions (time, location, purpose), the management of team agendas, the management of information flow to and from the team, how the team makes decisions, and finally how the output of the team is managed—how it is captured, what form it is in, and how it is distributed.

*Interactions.* The final core element concerns the interactions among the individual team members. Here the question is, What team members' patterns of behavior toward one another are required for the team to function effectively? Typically, this involves the identification of operating principles or "rules of the road" that the team can use as guidelines for members' actions. In some cases teams may also engage in detailed analysis of patterns of interactions to help team members learn patterns that can aid the group's work and avoid patterns that can get in the way of group effectiveness.

## Quality Assurance Processes

A final element in team building is to create a set of quality assurance processes that enable the team to be self-corrective, that help it prevent errors and promote continuous improvement. Several features are important in team quality assurance. First, team quality can be designed in by investing the time to launch the team well, usually through initial team-building sessions that focus on charter and context, goals, roles, procedures, and interactions. Second, each time the team works together, it can spend time reviewing the agenda, clarifying expectations and requirements, and planning how the time together will be used. Third, at the conclusion of each work session, the team can spend time in a *process review*, a discussion of how the team has worked together. Such reviews usually focus on what went well, what went less well, and what improvements can be made for the future. Finally, the team can plan to engage in periodic process reviews where the team steps back and reflects upon how it is doing and makes improvements in its design. The important idea here is that the team will continuously improve its effectiveness over time if it invests in its own capacity to learn, both from success and from failure.

## Common Problems in Executive Teams

The approach presented here suggests how to design, establish, and manage an executive team in different contexts, but implementing the appropriate team process is often difficult. In our work with executive teams, my colleagues and I have encountered seven common problems that are related to either the setting up of the executive team or the management of core processes.

*Synthetic teamwork.* Many so-called executive teams do not actually engage in teamwork. The group is not a real team—it is synthetic. The leader of the team does not want or require increased coupling and coordination, and therefore nothing more than information sharing happens in the team. There is no coordinated effort and no synergy. Thus the team is formed and presented as being in context two or four but is really in context one.

Synthetic teamwork has several negative consequences. The creation of a team leads to expectations that the team will take action, make decisions, or lead. When this does not occur, a leadership vacuum is often perceived, a loss of executive credibility and frustration throughout the organization. To the extent that there is no one performing the COO function and coordination is indeed required, the lack of true teamwork may cripple decision making and implementation.

*Cosmetic teamwork.* In certain executive teams, although the trappings of teamwork and cooperation are created, the day-to-day behavior of the team members not only indicates lack of teamwork but frequently reveals intensely negative relationships among these individuals. In cosmetic teamwork, surface behaviors—particularly in formal team meetings—affirm the team, the value of teamwork, and the importance of trust, openness, and collaborative effort. In truth, however, effective relationship management processes are absent. Team members are apt to interact in subgroups between meetings and in other settings, complaining about other members or planning noncollaborative, and in some cases destructive, actions (Eisenhardt and Bourgeois, 1988).

Cosmetic teamwork often occurs when an executive team structure is created to enhance collaboration and coordinated effort, but the underlying scenario (including issues of rewards and succession) is one that motivates people to work in competitive as opposed to collaborative modes. Similarly, cosmetic teamwork occurs when the CEO claims to want teamwork but is unwilling to give up any control. Because teamwork is often articulated by the CEO as the socially desirable behavior, the trappings of collaboration occur in the presence of the leader but do not carry forward into members' day-to-day interactions.

*Under-designed teams.* Frequently executive teams run into trouble because they are under-designed; the team has been established, but composition has not been thought through, the structure (size, boundaries, goals, roles, rewards) has not been adequately or appropriately developed, and the succession scenario has not been clearly defined. Team members gather together but are incapacitated. In the worse cases the wrong people are at the table, attempting to do the wrong work, with unclear goals and roles, few rewards for true teamwork, and ill-defined succession scenarios creating relationship problems. In these cases the CEO has not taken the time and effort to develop the needed design of the executive team and has not worked with the team to implement the design.

*Consensus management.* Many CEOs have limited experience

and skills in team leadership and management. Having created an executive team, they do not hold an image of how to effectively harness the energies of the team to create coordinated action. In particular they do not know how to create effective work management and relationship management processes. This is particularly problematic for teams moving into a multiprocess mode. Not wanting to dominate the team, the CEO mistakenly shifts to the other side of the spectrum and ends up providing no direction for the team, resulting in consensus management. Although there are some situations where consensus is an appropriate method for decision making, the more effective teams we have observed tend to make different decisions in different ways—choosing the decision-making process most appropriate for the issue. Some decisions are made in a consultative mode, with the CEO getting input and discussing options with the team but retaining the role of ultimate decision maker; other decisions are made through a negotiation between the individuals most directly involved in the decision and the CEO; and in yet other cases consensus is appropriate. When all decisions become consensual, however, the team usually gets bogged down and loses effectiveness.

In consensus management the CEO mistakes lack of direction and structure for participation and collaboration. The resultant laissez-faire work process results in slow and ineffective decision making, risk aversion, and a sense of a leadership vacuum. The problem is usually not the team but rather the inability of the leader to create effective work management and relationship management processes.

*Good plow, wrong field.* Another common problem is that the team is engaged in positive activities, but the effort is misplaced—the wrong processes are being developed and managed. For example, an executive team facing major environmental challenges that works on the internal work management processes to the neglect of the boundary management issues is a team that is doing things right but not doing the right things. This contextual misalignment results in an executive team that does not have the capacity to accurately understand and competently manage the processes that are responsive to the most critical strategic challenges facing the team.

*Inertia.* Frequently executive teams run into trouble because they become very comfortable with the set of team processes that fit their context but take those processes to an extreme. For example, teams in context two may excel in work and relationship management processes, but when member cohesion is too high, negative consequences can ensue. When they have high cohesion, group members want to maintain high agreement, so they do not critique each other and often continue to follow decisions that as individuals they think are wrong. No one wants to start a conflict. Similarly, high cohesion leads to insulation from the environment and the inability to detect warning signals and change in that environment (Dutton and Duncan, 1987; Janis, 1982). In contrast, team members in context three may excel at boundary management but become so engaged in external activity that they lose loyalty to the team. These teams have a harder time getting members to commit to team decisions.

*Succession overhang.* Succession is a fundamental issue that can hang over the team, shaping the nature of the relationships in the team and thus the relationship management processes. Once relationship management processes are poisoned, they can incapacitate the team's work management and boundary management processes. Each of the two succession scenarios has a different potential impact, but each is fundamentally negative. In the executive selection scenario, the horse race creates an inherently competitive win-lose situation that motivates individuals to not collaborate. This scenario creates the exact opposite of what is required for effective teamwork—team members now perceive that the stakes for them individually overwhelm the stakes deriving from the success or failure of the team as a whole—at least in the short term. Thus competitive, noncollaborative, and in some cases destructive behavior is motivated. At the least, cosmetic teamwork starts to occur. Similarly, in the new CEO scenario the aftermath of the succession decision (or the social psychological hangover experienced the morning after) can create interpersonal dynamics that make teamwork difficult or impossible. Losing candidates may be team members and may feel wounded or attempt to prove (consciously or not) that the choice made was incorrect. Team members may be anxious about their position in the new administration and their evolving relationship with the new CEO who so recently was a peer and perhaps a competitor. Despite the statements of the new CEO, individuals may perceive that a COO will be named, so a secondary succession scenario begins. All of these factors may contribute to significant problems in team members' relationships.

These seven problems, although not all inclusive, are fairly common and can severely undermine team effectiveness. Most of them, however, can be prevented through thoughtful design of the team and deliberate management of the team's core processes.

## Summary

The executive team has emerged as a viable alternative for organizing work and roles at the most senior levels of complex organizations. As I have emphasized throughout this discussion, these teams have emerged as a result of three distinct sets of demands: external demands posed by the environment, internal demands posed by the requirements of running diverse but interdependent organizations, and a unique and powerful set of demands created by the problem of executive succession. Not surprisingly, effective executive teams need to be able to manage the three sets of issues raised by these demands. They must organize to manage external complexity, and they must manage internal work requirements and relationships—and they need to do all this while coping with both the reality and perceptions associated with succession.

Teams in different situations face varying degrees of intensity and different combinations of these demands. As I have illustrated through the contextual approach presented in this chapter, the more effective teams appear to be those that can focus their time, energy, and resources on managing the issues that are most critical given the team context. Using the composition, structure, and succession scenarios to determine the core processes that will meet internal and external requirements is clearly the most critical single challenge for those creating effective executive teams.

The executive team therefore emerges as a higher-risk–higher-reward structure than the traditional CEO-COO model. The rewards come when an effective team provides a quality of leadership, decision making, and implementation that no single individual COO could ever hope to replicate. However, CEOs run significant risks of incurring the problems I have listed when not enough thought and care are given to the design of the team and the management of the team over time. The implication is that executive team structures make sense in many situations although not all. A second implication is that the CEO who seeks to employ this approach needs to be ready to invest the time, effort, and energy required to understand the requirements of the particular situation, to develop an appropriate team design, and to work on nurturing the evolution of the right core processes in the team. When this effort is made, the rewards of teamwork at the top can be very significant.

## Chapter Three

# The World of the CEO

*David A. Nadler*

*Jeffrey D. Heilpern*

To better understand the growing importance of the executive team, it is helpful to understand the ways in which organizational leadership itself is becoming more complicated. In this chapter, therefore, we look more closely at the work and world of the CEO, at the CEO's personal characteristics, and at the entire range of demands on today's leadership. It is within this complicated context that the executive team is evolving and that it must sometimes be an extension of the CEO's personal leadership as it deals with an organization's constituencies.

The past decade has been characterized by an unprecedented increase in the public visibility of corporate and institutional chief executive officers. The collective anonymity that once enveloped the leaders of major commercial and not-for-profit institutions has given way to intense public attention. Today, with increasing frequency, the men and women who lead important organizations are seeing their names and faces on television, in newspapers, on magazine covers and book jackets. They are being subjected to a barrage of publicity that testifies to a growing recognition of their central role in U.S. life.

This heightened visibility can be a mixed blessing. CEOs are alternatively portrayed as visionaries, gurus, saviors, villains, and even "killers," to use the term employed on the cover of one news magazine (*Newsweek,* Feb. 26, 1996). The fact that so many of the depictions amount to nothing more than superficial caricatures does nothing to lessen the importance of this trend.

The question CEOs ought to be asking themselves is what is behind this profound change in the public's perception of their power and social impact?

The answer, we believe, lies in the increasing rate at which corporate and public institutions are finding themselves forced to undergo massive, fundamental, and inherently disruptive change. Driven by a host of competitive forces, those changes increasingly translate into headlines trumpeting mergers, acquisitions, spin-offs, break-ups, and ultimately the job loss and downsizing that so often accompany the pursuit of greater efficiency and productivity. At the same time the press is awash in stories reporting the impressive results achieved by many of these same companies and the seemingly staggering compensation awarded to those who drive that performance.

To the general public the result is a confusing and sometimes disturbing picture of economic dislocation accompanied by endless reports of rising profits, booming financial markets, and lavishly paid executives. At the center of this maelstrom is the CEO, the single most pivotal—and visible—individual associated with each new instance of organizational change and disruption.

Some CEOs, through a combination of vision, skill, luck, and smart public relations, are able to emerge as corporate heroes; Bill Gates of Microsoft, Jack Welch of General Electric, and Roberto Goizueta of Coca-Cola are the latest to inherit the mantle of corporate superhero first bestowed upon Lee Iacocca. Less fortunate, but much more common, are the CEOs who either fail to produce the necessary change or fail to meet the critical needs of their key constituencies while implementing change and who end up either ridiculed or demonized.

Obviously, the determination of success or failure is not that simple. Numerous factors contribute to a CEO's effectiveness in the midst of dramatic change. Any meaningful assessment of the CEO's role requires a basic understanding of both the nature of the changes being experienced by today's major organizations and of the unique and complex world of the CEO. In what follows, then, we look at leadership largely from the viewpoint of the necessity to manage change, suggesting why an effective CEO and executive team are so crucial in guiding organizations through phases of instability and describing some major elements that characterize effective leaders, especially those who can bring about productive internal change in relation to expected or existing external change.

## A Perspective on Change

Without question today's society is in the midst of a period of protracted and repeated large-scale change in its major organizations. This current period started in the mid-1980s, driven by competitive pressure on U.S. companies to reshape themselves in order to improve quality, increase productivity, and heighten overall efficiency. But what began as a belated and somewhat desperate response to competition from abroad has continued unabated through the mid-1990s and seems likely to remain a fact of organizational life into the next century. To a certain extent, organizational change has always been present. But the type of change experienced in the past decade is qualitatively different than that seen in the past.

Chapter author David Nadler has written elsewhere about the altered nature of change and about the environmentally driven *change imperative* that has emerged (Nadler, in press). His basic proposition is that periodically every industry experiences a phase of substantial upheaval and disequilibrium, generally precipitated by a destabilizing event or series of events. Such events include the emergence of a new technology, of major judicial or legislative action, or of a new player who somehow alters the basis of competition.

Unlike the ongoing changes that incrementally alter every industry during normal periods, these destabilizing events are major mutations, radically reconfiguring the size, shape, and pace of change. It is during such periods of disequilibrium that the change imperative surfaces. Those companies that make the appropriate fundamental changes in their strategy, work, people, formal organization, and operating environment stand a good chance of weathering the storm and emerging as healthy players, well positioned for the next phase of industry development. Those that fail to make the necessary changes cease to continue in their traditional form and often disappear.

These periods of upheaval require *discontinuous change* (Tushman, Newman, and Nadler, 1987; Nadler and Tushman, 1994), a step function change that affects practically every major variable in the equation of the enterprise. This form of change responds to environmental discontinuity through a carefully designed, deliberately led period of organizational discontinuity.

This view of change implies three basic challenges for those entrusted with leading organizations during these inherently unstable times. The first challenge is recognition—the ability to understand the environment and recognize at an early stage the massing of forces likely to create disequilibrium and require discontinuous change.

Second is the challenge of strategy—the need to make the appropriate strategic choices that will reposition the organization as a strong competitor in the context of the disequilibrium reshaping the industry.

Third is the challenge of reshaping the architecture of the organization—the capacity to creatively design and deftly implement the changes that will enable the organization to function successfully in the new environment.

## Change and the World of the CEO

In any institutional change at the enterprise level the CEO, by definition, is the most pivotal person involved. Indeed, it is practically impossible to conceive of major change proceeding without the CEO's vital personal engagement. Our experience and observation bear this out: without the active committed involvement of the CEO in a central role, successful discontinuous change is simply impossible.

The reason is obvious. Fundamental change requires the focused and aggressive exercise of power. And within any organization the levers of power are uniquely concentrated in the hands of the CEO. Yet CEOs frequently admit in private to a sense of powerlessness. We often hear CEOs compare their situation to that of the captain who issues orders but gets no response from the engine room. In part, that problem is inherent in the size and complexity of large corporations. But it also has to do with the multiple constituencies each CEO is required to serve.

That perspective suggests that rather than thinking of the CEO as the captain on the bridge unilaterally setting a course and issuing orders, a more realistic view sees the CEO positioned at the center of a collection of constituencies, each of which acts as a *role sender*. More specifically, each constituency periodically transmits a set of expectations regarding the behavior and performance it expects from the CEO, whose job is to constantly find the proper balance among those varied, and sometimes conflicting, expectations.

Depending upon the size, scope, and nature of the organization, each CEO will have a varied set of role senders. However, some important and fairly universal constituencies can be identified. Figure 3.1 maps these constituencies with a 360-degree view of the world of the CEO. The CEO has two sets of external constituencies; one group, including the financial community, suppliers, and customers, is clearly related to the organization's value chain. The other external group can be described as the social constituencies and includes the government and official regulators, communities where the organization operates, and society at large. The social constituencies can send equally pressing messages about their expectations of the CEO.

Of most immediate concern are the constituencies at the top and bottom of the map. The shareholders, institutions and individuals with an economic stake in the firm, convey their expectations through their proxy, the board of directors, an infinitely important constituency in itself. Similarly, the CEO manages and regularly interacts with only a small number of employees, though all the employees together form another key constituency; in this case, the executive team is the key linkage between the CEO and the enterprise as a whole.

Taken together, the various role senders correspond to what are often referred to as corporate *stakeholders*. In reality, the orga-

**Figure 3.1. The World of the CEO: 360-Degree Map.**

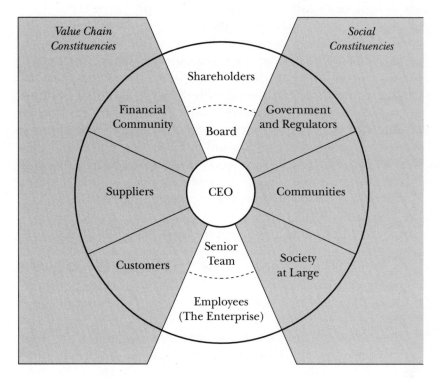

The World of the CEO—360° Map

nization's stakeholders become the CEO's constituencies (Heilpern, 1994).

Now consider how this perspective on the world of the CEO intersects with the idea of discontinuous change. During periods of discontinuous, or radical, change each constituency experiences seriously heightened uncertainty, or lack of clarity, about the future. Accordingly, each compensates by making increased demands upon the CEO. Although all the constituencies are important, we would argue that it is absolutely essential for the CEO to focus personal energy and attention on the demands of a limited group of constituencies—those that no one else in the organization can adequately address.

Customers, for example, represent an essential constituency for any organization. And in some situations, particularly those involving industrial marketing, the CEO might have an important personal role to play with customers. But in the final analysis, the CEO's personal involvement is not a truly essential component of the transaction; the customers might like to meet and greet the CEO, but their real business is with the sales and service representatives. So if during a time of major change the CEO decides his time can better be spent elsewhere and makes fewer customer visits, it is unlikely that business will suffer. In consumer businesses the CEO's connection to customers is even more abstract; the truth is that most customers neither know nor care who heads up the company that makes their laundry detergent and VCRs.

The same holds true for most of the other constituencies, where the CEO's personal role is normally limited to ceremonial visits and public rituals. Although those activities are an important part of the CEO's role in normal times, we suggest they should be considered peripheral and secondary during periods of discontinuous change, when the organization's very future may be at stake.

Instead, we believe the CEO must concentrate during these turbulent periods on the *hot spots*—critical areas of tension where the CEO, and only the CEO, can play a decisive role. There are three of these hot spots. The first is the board of directors, because no one in the organization but the CEO has the legitimate standing from which to deal with them. The second is the executive team, because only the CEO, as its immediate supervisor, can shape, manage and lead this group of top executives. And third is the employees and the enterprise at large, because no one but the CEO can speak to them as the single institutional leader.

Given the pressures of change and the requirements change imposes on the CEO in terms of dealing with key constituencies, the real issue is how CEOs can remain effective leaders of their organizations and their teams over time and particularly during periods of dramatic change. To properly address that issue, we first examine several perspectives on what constitutes effective leadership in the world of the CEO.

## CEO Effectiveness: A Static View

A static view, a snapshot in time, of CEO effectiveness, reveals numerous styles and approaches that work for different individuals. Nevertheless, there are some common characteristics that are shared by nearly all effective CEO leaders of change, regardless of their stylistic differences (Nadler and Tushman, 1989). These fall into three broad categories:

- *Envisioning.* Successful CEOs share an ability to articulate and communicate a vision of the organization that captures the imagination of the people they lead. Typically, that vision challenges people to meet seemingly unattainable goals by committing themselves to a superior level of performance.
- *Energizing.* Effective CEOs energize their people by constantly and publicly demonstrating their own sense of personal excitement and total engagement. They consistently convey a sense of absolute confidence in the organization's ability to achieve the most challenging goals. And they actively energize people by highlighting examples of success as a way of building a sense of confidence and accomplishment.
- *Enabling.* In addition to envisioning a set of goals and energizing people to pursue them, effective CEOs then find ways to give people the confidence, authority, and resources they need to work realistically toward those demanding objectives. At the same time truly effective CEOs understand the need for strong operational leadership—the development, management, and control of essential structures, systems, and processes. Because it is generally difficult, particularly in change situations, for a CEO to play the roles of institutional leader and operational manager simultaneously, substantial responsibility for operational leadership can be delegated to the executive team. Nevertheless, the successful performance of those duties remains part of the CEO's ultimate responsibility.

Beyond these major roles, our experience suggests there are some personal characteristics that are particularly valuable for CEOs in building and managing relationships with their various constituencies during periods of change. These traits include:

*"Towering strength" balanced by other strong capabilities.* Typically, CEOs are particularly strong at some aspect of the job—making bold moves perhaps, or managing operational performance or articulating an inspiring vision. But they must also be able to do other things well, so that when change alters the rules of the game and it no longer plays to their towering strength, they can comfortably switch gears rather than become immobilized or incompetent.

*Emotional strength and perspective.* As they deal with numerous constituencies, all of whom may be anxious, impatient, and demanding, CEOs must be *grounded,* a quality that prevents them from getting rattled by pressure and adversity. They avoid losing touch with their own sense of perspective and common sense.

*An ability to convey the sense of acting and responding as genuine people.* That impression is practically impossible to fabricate; it requires the CEO to open up to people to an unusual degree. Effective CEOs avoid giving the impression that they are cloaking themselves in the role of chief executive to shield their true thoughts and emotions.

*A sense of humor.* As obvious as it may seem, a sense of humor—particularly one that allows for occasional and gentle self-deprecating remarks—plays a key role in helping all concerned maintain perspective during pressure-filled periods.

*A capacity for empathy with a broad range of people.* Although President Clinton's constant evocation of the phrase "I feel your pain" became a source of derision among politicians, journalists, and late-night TV-show hosts, he has been immensely successful in face-to-face situations in convincing people that he not only understands their problems but is somehow sharing their experience and emotions. Particularly in difficult times, members of each key constituency constantly look for signs that the CEO truly understands the depth of their concerns.

*Connectedness, the ability to make a deeply personal connection with individuals emotionally or intellectually.* This is the capacity to leave people feeling that even a brief exchange was a meaningful interaction, not a perfunctory ritual.

The truly effective CEOs possess these capabilities for managing difficult relationships. And it is worth noting that we chose not to discuss *charisma*. In our experience the characteristics popularly associated with so-called charismatic leaders have relatively little to do with long-term success in leading complex organizations. Few of the most successful CEOs rely on movie-star looks or celebrity appeal. Instead, their capacity to achieve long-term results rests upon the more subtle and complex traits we have just described.

## CEO Effectiveness: A Dynamic View

The preceding elements are essential to a CEO's success but form only a first layer of analysis. They do not encompass the more dynamic view of how CEO effectiveness is likely to change over a substantial period of time. A more complete perspective involves the intersection of two concepts: the frequency of discontinuous change and the notion of the CEO life cycle. It involves the assumption that in general—given variations from one industry to another—there is a movement today toward greater frequency of periods of disequilibrium and discontinuous change.

Through the mid-1980s, a CEO could easily serve out a normal tenure without ever experiencing a true period of discontinuous change. From the mid-1980s to the early 1990s, with the restructuring of U.S. business and the growing intensity of foreign competition, there was a high probability that a CEO would encounter one cycle in which he would have to manage discontinuous change. Particularly in industries undergoing fundamental change such as health care, financial services, and information technology, there is every likelihood that the CEO will have to manage more than one period of discontinuous change.

That in itself presents major challenges to CEOs and their organizations. David Kearns, the former chairman of Xerox Corp., once described the job of managing discontinuous change as "all consuming." The toll this responsibility takes on CEOs, on a very personal level, should not be underestimated. In the early 1990s, a Fortune 500 company whose board had just removed a CEO for failing to initiate sufficiently radical change was having great difficulty finding a successor. When asked why the job search was taking so long, the CEO of another major corporation told us, "Because of what they're facing, their ideal candidate is somebody who has already managed a major change. But anybody who's done it once doesn't want to go through it again."

A closely associated issue is addressed by the work Donald Hambrick and Gregory Fukutomi (1991) of Columbia University have done in investigating the CEO life cycle, or the "seasons of a CEO's tenure." Essentially, they contend there is a predictable pattern of activity and behavior that encompasses five discernible periods throughout the normal tenures of most CEOs.

On one hand the pattern describes a learning curve, as CEOs actively seek information and advice, shape their view of the organization and their leadership style, and learn the multiple roles inherent in the job. On the other hand CEOs also become increasingly isolated as time goes on, more rigidly fixed in their views about strategy and organization, and less inclined toward risk, experimentation, and instability.

This view of the CEO's life cycle has tremendously important implications for the management of change at the top of the organization. When overlaid upon the patterns of industry evolution and the unavoidable periods of disequilibrium, it raises some serious issues that should be considered by anyone concerned with the management of organizational governance.

To begin with, it is common to find discontinuous change taking place during the early stages of a CEO's tenure. Frequently, the new CEO has been hired for that express purpose and handed an explicit mandate to initiate and manage the kind of major change the previous CEO, for whatever reason, failed to undertake. Presumably, the new CEO was hired because his experience, abilities, and organizational perspectives were well suited to the kind of change the board believed was necessary. The CEO enters the job with considerable energy, a genuine desire to be open-minded and inventive, and a compelling drive to put a personal stamp on the organization.

A problem arises, however, when the need for discontinuous change develops during the latter phases of the CEO's tenure. As Hambrick and Fukutomi make clear, the CEO's later years are marked by diminished energy and openness; moreover, considering the CEO's huge investment of emotional capital in current structures, processes, and people, it is unlikely that the CEO will suddenly turn into an agent of radical change.

Similarly, what happens when the need for a *second round* of discontinuous change becomes necessary late in the tenure of a CEO who has already managed a round of major change earlier in his tenure? Given the time, energy, and personal commitment devoted to the first change, it is unreasonable to expect any but a few unique individuals to enthusiastically take on the challenge of starting all over again.

Clearly, there is a critical relationship between the timing of change and the length of the CEO's tenure. When the need for change coincides with the appropriate phase of the CEO's tenure—as often happens in the early years—the results are often quite successful. But when the need for change—either a first or second round—becomes evident late in the CEO's tenure, the situation becomes much more complicated. CEO responses vary from the truly constructive to the highly dysfunctional. There are four, in particular, that we have observed:

*Denial.* Convinced that the people, structures, processes, systems, and operating environment they put into place are sufficient to meet any challenge, CEOs insist that sufficient change can be accomplished through incremental moves.

*Avoidance.* Rather than subjecting themselves to the arduous task of leading radical change involving every element of the organization, some CEOs attempt to make dramatic personnel changes among top executives or major structural moves, such as spin-offs, in a search for a less painful quick-hit approach to change.

*Bowing out.* Some CEOs, recognizing the situation demands radical change and accepting the fact that they no longer have the interest, energy, or appetite for such change, simply leave. After nineteen years as chairman of Corning Inc., for example, Amory Houghton Jr. gave up the job and went on to a successful career in politics, leaving his younger brother, Jamie Houghton, to lead the company through a period of sweeping change in the mid- and late-1980s.

*Succession management.* In some situations where CEOs have recognized the need for discontinuous change and their own lack of interest in managing it, the change effort has been closely linked to management succession. The CEO supports the change effort but does not lead it with the same degree of personal involvement he invested in that first round of change. At the same time, the CEO delegates significant responsibility for directing the change effort to the heir apparent, paving the way for the heir's ascension to the CEO's job as architect of the newly redesigned organization he is now empowered to lead.

## Questions for Today's CEO

A few years ago we prepared a confidential memo for the CEO of a major corporation whose industry was clearly entering a period of unprecedented upheaval. It was obvious at that point that massive change of one kind or another would soon become unavoidable if the company was to maintain its role as an industry leader. So we posed a number of questions to the CEO, who earlier in his tenure had led the organization through a series of historic changes. We asked him:

- Do you believe that major change will be required?
- If you are to lead that change, what do you think will be required of you?
- At this point in your life and your career, are you capable of leading this change?
- Do you want to do it?

We suggest that all CEOs facing the likelihood of major change ought to ask themselves these same questions, even though they are unsettling to contemplate. To begin with, most CEOs, by their very nature, are driven by action rather than introspection; their jobs demand the ability to make decisions and then plunge ahead without reservations or self-doubt. Perhaps more important, an admission that they might no longer be up to the challenge carries the implication of professional mortality and a recognition that it might be time to hand over the reins to someone else.

Few CEOs can easily come to grips with that realization; like everyone else, they're less than eager to pursue a line of questioning that's likely to arrive at that conclusion. But the awesome responsibility they owe to their various constituents both within and outside the organization requires that at some point each CEO must give serious consideration to these deeply personal questions.

The willingness, preparation, and ability of the CEO to lead major change is far more than a theoretical concern. As we said earlier, it is not unreasonable, particularly in industries undergoing fundamental change, to see waves of severe disequilibrium following as closely as every five years—a time frame considerably shorter than the average tenure of most CEOs (Vancil, 1987, for example, found that one out of four Fortune 500 CEOs served for ten years or more). Consequently, as the pace of change in markets, technology, and competition continues to increase, so too does the likelihood that organizations will face multiple periods of turbulence calling for leadership of discontinuous change during the tenure of any given CEO.

## CEO Relationships with Key Constituencies in Times of Change

The CEO's role in discontinuous change is central and critical, and clearly the CEO's attitude toward taking on and managing such change will deeply affect the composition of the executive team and its structure and tasks. It will be a large part of the context in which the team operates. Indeed, the intersection of the demands of change with new perspectives on the life cycle of the CEO's career has profound implications for all three key constituencies. We now begin to sketch out a general landscape of these implications with some initial observations about the CEO's relationships with the institution and its employees, the board of directors, and the executive team in times of change. We also look at the demands on the CEO from the board's viewpoint and at the board's responsibility to ensure effective CEO leadership before and during periods of discontinuous change.

### The CEO, the Institution, and the Employees

During periods of turbulent change, the CEO assumes the role of institutional icon. Although others on the executive team can—and should—assume much of the operational responsibility for managing change, it is the responsibility of the CEO to *lead* change. To a great extent, the CEO does that by articulating the change agenda in simple memorable terms that challenge, inspire, energize, and reassure the people employed by the organization.

During these unstable periods, only the CEO has the combination of formal and informal power—of legitimate institutional authority coupled with the character traits of an experienced leader—that can slice through the cacophony of cluttered messages and speak to the entire organization with a clear voice. Only the CEO has the standing to gain a consistent *share of mind* among the employees and to have a ready audience for practically any public utterance.

Given that standing and opportunities to use it during times of change, CEOs should deal with this particular key constituency by delivering constant repetition of closely related themes—what Paul O'Neill, chairman of ALCOA, describes as "consistency and connectedness." Successful leaders understand that as instability breeds anxiety, people's ability to hear and process messages is seriously diminished. Consequently, the important messages have to be communicated time and time again before they truly begin to have an impact. Moreover, the varying messages have to be clearly and closely linked to the change agenda, so that people understand there is a unifying logic to the changes taking place all around them.

Jamie Houghton, the recently retired chairman of Corning Inc., offers another perspective on the CEO's relationship to the enterprise and its people. Houghton argues that the best CEOs adopt a contrarian emotional perspective in relation to their organizations. In other words, during downturns or periods of change and instability, the CEO's proper role is to be confident, upbeat, and reassuring. When things are going smoothly, the CEO is skeptical and concerned, warning subordinates to remain ever vigilant to the dangers that so often accompany arrogance and complacency. This contrarian perspective requires the CEO to sensitively walk a fine line—neither appearing to be a Pollyanna during rough times nor failing to recognize and celebrate success when times are good.

## The CEO and the Board

It is imperative that the CEO, in the role of chairman of the board, assume the lead role in ensuring the selection of an active non-ritual board, similar to what Millstein describes as a "certifying board" (1993). It is the CEO's responsibility to help shape a board that is truly engaged and involved in the direction of the organization, one that works closely with senior managers. It is important that the board include a sufficient number of people who are currently active (rather than retired) and who are in possession of a range of experience and expertise involving markets, strategy, management, and appropriate technologies in order to be helpful in dealing with the issues related to change.

Moreover, the board should be active in the strategic process and be brought in early enough to play the role of strategic early warning system. The CEO should make sure that board members are provided with a comprehensive understanding of the strategic issues facing the organization, reinforced and updated by continuing education efforts. That information, when filtered through their collective experience and insight, should enable them to recognize and alert the company to the early signs of impending disequilibrium.

Finally, CEOs should recognize the importance of actively and explicitly seeking the board's assessment and feedback regarding their own performance. Only the board, in effect the CEO's supervisor, can fulfill this feedback role. As we suggested earlier, CEOs pass through each phase of their tenure improving in certain areas and weakening in others. Yet as CEOs' tenure grows longer and they become more powerful, self-assured, and comfortable in the job, they are less likely to feel the need to seek out the board's assessment of their performance—even though that might be the time when they most need it.

CEOs need to realize that regardless of whether they seek assessment, the board will indeed be judging their performance, either with or without their knowledge and participation. Consequently, it is infinitely preferable for the CEO to structure a formal appraisal process, with both opportunity for helpful feedback and opportunity to modify performance. The alternative is the kind of informal "hallway talk" that board members sometimes engage in as momentum builds toward some drastic action—and possibly dismissal.

In this chapter, we have largely assumed that the CEO recognizes not only the potential for change but also the likelihood that with the passage of time he may have to draw upon the insights and energy of others to anticipate and drive the change effort—something that might not have been quite so necessary early in the

CEO's tenure. But it would be naïve to assume that all CEOs can realistically assess their own limitations, and we want to give some consideration to the board's role in situations where the need for change is obvious but the CEO's response is inadequate.

The responsibility for ensuring appropriate action by the CEO falls squarely on the board and no one else. To exercise this responsibility the board requires a thorough understanding of the nature of change, especially discontinuous change, and CEO life cycles. It is incumbent upon the board to recognize that the energetic deeply engaged CEO who eagerly led the organization through an earlier period of change has experienced a gradual transformation and cannot realistically be expected to respond precisely the same way the second time around.

Although we have suggested that soliciting board feedback is a CEO responsibility, it cannot be assumed that the CEO will always take the lead. If the initiative does not come from the CEO, then it is up to the board to develop a systematic process for conducting regular in-depth CEO appraisals and for delivering feedback in timely, constructive ways. In too many situations boards have failed to become actively involved until a crisis has already erupted. At that point faced with pressing business concerns, the board tends to demand that the CEO make immediate and dramatic changes, usually with unsatisfactory results. Ideally, the board's dissatisfaction with the CEO should never come as a surprise, and performance problems should be recognized and raised early enough for the CEO to have sufficient time to demonstrate improved performance.

As part of that process it is essential that the board devise a mechanism for discussing these issues in the CEO's absence. Given the CEO's traditional role as chairman of the board, that is not always easy or comfortable. Nevertheless, a candid discussion with the CEO out of the room should be incorporated into the board's routine process, with a committee or one or two board members assigned to discuss the substance of those discussions with the CEO at a later date.

Furthermore, given the implications of the CEO life cycle, it is important for the board to become more actively involved in decisions involving strategic choices and major change in the later years of the CEO's tenure. That is more easily said than done. The need for the board's involvement may be greatest exactly when the CEO is at the height of individual power and influence. Moreover, the number of board members selected with the CEO's active participation will have been increasing over time, and these people are likely to find themselves conflicted by feelings of personal loyalty or friendship.

Yet this is the time when the board must be at its most vigilant in assessing the appropriateness of the CEO's response to the need for change. The board has the responsibility not to accept at face value the CEO's denial of the need for major change or the CEO's avoidance in the form of structural or personnel moves that fail to address the fundamental issues. Indeed, it may well become the board's duty to decide that the best way to handle change is by managing succession, either gradual or immediate.

## The CEO and the Executive Team

The functions of the executive team and its relationship to its leader, the CEO, are of course the focus of the remainder of this book. The observations here apply specifically to management of the team in times of discontinuous change. Much as is the case with the board of directors, the key to the CEO's relationship with the executive team during times of change is largely dependent on the kind of team the CEO has put together and the nature of the relationship already in place between the CEO and the other senior executives. Particularly in large complex organizations, it is literally impossible for the CEO to be everywhere, see everything, and manage everyone. To be successful, particularly during times of major change, the executive team must effectively become an extension of the CEO's personal leadership, a force that projects the CEO's vision, values, objectives, and requirements out into the organization (Nadler, 1996).

Consequently, part of the CEO's responsibility is to build an executive team whose members possess the skills, experience, and personal characteristics to satisfy two needs. First, they must collectively share the technical and managerial expertise required to enable the organization to meet its strategic objectives. Additionally, the mix of individuals in the team should balance and complement the professional skills and personal characteristics of the

CEO. One of the most rudimentary rules of management training is that supervisors should avoid surrounding themselves with subordinates who duplicate their own strengths and weaknesses. At the executive team level that issue becomes critical to the organization's success. There is no CEO who is equally adept at every aspect of the job; the role of the executive team, in part, is to fill the gaps and offset the weaknesses. Keeping in mind that CEOs' energy levels, interests, and areas of emphasis change over the course of their tenures, effective CEOs will periodically take stock and reassess whether the composition of the executive team adequately plays to the kinds of changing strengths and weaknesses illuminated here.

Second, the CEO can take the initiative in developing the executive team's role as a vehicle for institutional learning. Through the delegation of specific responsibilities and the structuring of both formal and informal activities, the CEO can use the executive team as a sophisticated form of institutional radar, constantly scanning the external environment for evidence of destabilizing events or trends that might signal the onset of turbulence and discontinuity. Late in the CEO's tenure, when the CEO's personal antennae might be less acute than in the past and when he is more predisposed to discount evidence indicating the necessity of change, the executive team can be actively engaged in its own search for vital clues.

Once change becomes inevitable, the CEO has the ultimate responsibility for developing an integrated change agenda. But effective CEOs will build that agenda through a process that recognizes the executive team's crucial role in collectively implementing and managing that agenda. To that end the CEO must proactively provide for team members' active participation in agenda development in order to create a collective sense of ownership.

Ideally, members of the team will become champions of particular aspects of change, taking on aggressive leadership roles that serve to further project the team's collective vision. They become partners with the CEO in articulating that vision and assume the hands-on responsibility for deploying the organization's resources in the service of that vision. Just as they are extensions of the CEO's leadership, they in turn extend their shared vision and objectives throughout the organization by constructing concentric circles of involvement for lower-level managers and supervisors and sometimes through chartering strategic change teams (SCTs)—temporary executive task forces convened to generate innovative solutions to integrated change issues (SCTs are examined in more detail in Chapter Thirteen).

## Summary

Our purpose in this chapter has been to look at some realities of the CEO's job and the characteristics required to lead organizations effectively, especially in relation to discontinuous change. In that process we have also looked at the context in which the executive team must function, again particularly in regard to leading change.

First, we described how periodic phases of fundamental instability require organizations to respond with major discontinuous change, and we examined the set of constituencies to which CEOs must always be responsive.

Following a discussion of the static and dynamic views of the CEO as a leader of change and the personal characteristics CEOs need to employ as they guide an organization through discontinuous change, we moved to a deeper level of analysis, laying out a theory of how CEOs evolve during their tenures—a process with many implications for the successful management of change—urging CEOs to engage in serious, albeit uncomfortable, reflection about their current capacity for leading change.

Finally, we considered the general ways that change management also influences CEOs' interactions with their three key constituencies, especially the need for CEOs and their boards to proactively develop plans and strategies for change at periods in CEOs' careers when they might be least inclined to acknowledge the need for massive change, and the ways change may require executive teams to respond as extensions of the CEO.

## Chapter Four

# Designing CEO and COO Roles

*J. Carlos Rivero*

*Janet L. Spencer*

Over the past twenty years there has been a shift in the strategic distribution of leadership roles at the top of corporate organizations. As the previous chapters have described, part of this shift has entailed the movement toward design and deployment of the executive team. With the increasing emphasis on the executive team's responsibility for governance a need has emerged to more clearly define and structure the role of the team leader. The leadership responsibilities typically reserved for the chief executive officer have changed, and different leadership forms have evolved. In many organizations the position of chief operating officer has been created to directly manage internal operations. In others, the executive team functions as the COO. Increasingly, however, companies employ both an executive team and a COO. Neither governing role precludes the importance of the other; instead, designation of a COO opens the door to dual management of the team.

Where both CEO and COO roles are employed, an effective working relationship between the two executives is increasingly critical to successful governance. This chapter describes design options for structuring this CEO-COO working relationship. We begin with a taxonomy of corporate leadership roles and related behaviors that together define the collective executive team leadership responsibilities of the CEO and COO. We then present some alternative models based on the strategic role distribution for structuring the CEO-COO relationship, along with a comparative analysis of each model's relative advantages and drawbacks. The chapter concludes with a discussion of two critical concerns that need to be addressed regardless of structure—management and governance processes and partnership issues.

We present the design options in the context of the following four key assumptions concerning the relative roles of the CEO and COO, whose working relationship is aptly described as a balancing act on the threshold of power:

- Although structural schematics are useful tools for discussing CEO-COO roles, the crux of the issue lies in determining *who does what*. Titles, lines, and boxes should promote, not replace, discussions of leadership roles and responsibilities.
- The balance of unique versus shared responsibilities at the top of the organization will change over time in accordance with the performance and comfort level of key executives.
- Severe hazards are inherent in the CEO-COO relationship and can easily be exacerbated by rivalry and corresponding defensiveness. Focusing on the assignment of specific responsibilities provides an opportunity for a constructive role discussion.
- The working relationship between the CEO and COO is crucial to the success of any structural arrangement. Clear reporting relationships and role differentiation will be of little help if the individuals involved are unable to confront and resolve their relationship issues.

## Corporate Leadership Roles and Responsibilities

We have identified a set of roles and behaviors that are essential to governing a large complex organization. For example, someone, either alone or in partnership with other senior executives, must set strategic vision and direction. Someone must establish organizational structures that ensure the achievement of those strategic objectives. Someone must serve as the external representative of the organization. These roles—strategist, architect, ambassador—and others can be thought of as key categories in the job description of corporate leadership. In Figure 4.1, we define eleven specific roles that together constitute both the strategic and operational responsibilities of corporate leadership.

**Figure 4.1. Corporate Leadership Roles.**

| Role | Activities |
|---|---|
| *Strategist* | Shapes corporate strategic direction |
| *Architect* | Establishes organizational structure and operating systems to ensure achievement of strategic direction |
| *Ambassador* | Serves as principle external representative of the company |
| *Keeper of corporate image* | Sets tone and direction for relations with key external constituencies |
| *Policy management* | Translates corporate vision and strategy into organizational policies, directives, and procedures |
| *Performance management* | Sets and reviews corporate management performance targets |
| *Operations management* | Manages operations of company, in ways consistent with strategic goals and performance targets |
| *Functional management* | Manages functional staff, such as HR, legal, PR, and finance |
| *Process management* | Ensures that core business processes are in place and working effectively |
| *People management* | Develops and leads senior management |
| *Information management* | Serves as internal spokesperson for corporate messages |

# Design Options

Our design options for corporate leadership roles reflect two basic models for structuring leadership at the top of an organization: first, the traditional hierarchical pattern and, second, a partnership structure (embodied in the notion of a corporate office). Multiple variations on these models are possible, based on the relationship of corporate staffs to the CEO and COO, and we describe seven of them.

Readers will recognize of course that organizations are rarely structured in the pure, strict fashion described in this chapter; these diagrams for purposes of illustration only hint at the complexity of the reporting relationships often found in today's corporate environments. Similarly, the real-world manifestations of these models are dynamic; roles and structures evolve over time, shaped by such factors as succession, external pressures, internal reorganizations, and mergers and acquisitions.

## Traditional Designs

Options $A^1$ and $A^2$ in Figure 4.2 represent traditional views of the relationship between the CEO and COO. They reflect a clear hierarchy and division of labor, with the CEO responsible for strategic issues, external relations, and overall corporate governance, and the COO primarily responsible for running internal company operations. Each of the executives reporting to the COO manages his or her own piece of the organization in ways consistent with strategies and policies from the top.

In Option $A^1$ the entire corporate staff reports directly to the CEO. In Option $A^2$ staff functions are divided into two groups—strategic and operational—that report to the CEO and the COO, respectively. Strategic staff manage processes such as corporate policy and resource allocation and often include the distinct roles of corporate strategy officer, general counsel, chief financial officer (CFO), and so on. In contrast the responsibilities of operational staff often have shorter time horizons, focusing on current-year priorities, performance management and integrated operations of

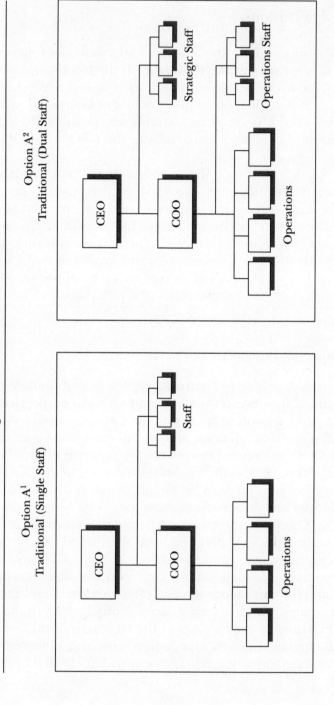

**Figure 4.2. Traditional Models.**

Option A[1]
Traditional (Single Staff)

Staff

CEO

COO

Operations

Option A[2]
Traditional (Dual Staff)

Strategic Staff

Operations Staff

CEO

COO

Operations

business units. For example, human resources and information technology are often (but not always) part of the operational staff.

Although specific roles and responsibilities vary from company to company, this two-person structure has been the dominant leadership model since it emerged in the 1960s. Corporations employing the traditional CEO-COO leadership dyad include Eli Lilly & Co. (Tobias/Taurel), Corning Inc. (Houghton/Ackerman), and previously, PepsiCo (Kendall/Pearson).

The traditional model offers distinct advantages. The well-delineated, clearly understood chain of command is typically associated with equally clear role differentiation. There is little ambiguity about who sets the organization's strategic direction and, by extension, who is ultimately accountable for the organization's success or failure.

The clarity of a single voice and vision at the top of the organization comes at a price, however. The leader-manager distinction characterizing the traditional model frames the exercise of power and influence as a zero-sum game. Within this context, relatively mild personality differences between CEO and COO, exacerbated by insecurity, may develop into intense rivalry and full-blown power struggles. Historical examples include the Brophy-Vanderslice disputes at GTE and the O'Neill-Fetterolf conflicts at ALCOA. In addition, a large power differential between CEO and COO jeopardizes succession planning. Without stretch leadership responsibilities for the number two executive, it is difficult to assess his potential as a future chief executive.

## Corporate Office Designs

As demands for speed, simplicity, customer focus, and cost reduction make governance processes more and more complex, the concept of the corporate office (also executive office, office of the chief executive, and so forth) has received increasing attention. In effect this is a structure with permeable boundaries that speeds the flow of strategic and operational information among executive decision makers. The primary difference between variants of this model and the traditional leader-manager model lies in the increased emphasis on shared responsibility, or partnership, at the top. Roles are less distinct than in a zero-sum perspective and are *blended,* in the sense that more responsibility is jointly owned by the CEO and COO. (There is one exception: the operations staff still report directly to the COO.) This partnership can provide greater flexibility, with leaders less constrained by rigid and static job descriptions (resulting in such perspectives as "that's your job, not mine").

The next set of design options identifies the two top executives as members of a Corporate Office that oversees the entire organization. Within the Corporate Office the COO participates in many of the strategic leadership activities traditionally reserved for the CEO, and the CEO may have more involvement in key operational decisions than the traditional model.

Increased partnership and sharing of leadership responsibilities at the top offers several important advantages:

- It sends a message of trust in the COO.
- It provides "stretch" assignments for the COO.
- When developed through a thoughtful allocation of roles and responsibilities, it allows each individual to maximize personal preferences and strengths.
- It serves to reify the corporate team—the Corporate Office creates a strong sense of team identity and unified leadership at the top.

At the same time this design has several points of vulnerability:

- Partnership requires intensive and continuous work on "chemistry" and "personal style" issues.
- True partnership requires a high degree of trust between the individuals.
- Without a high degree of formal structure, the design has potential for ambiguity in reporting relationships.

The Corporate Office design variations offer alternative reporting relationships for staff functions. In the simplest Corporate Office design (B[1]) (Figure 4.3), staff functions report to the Corporate Office as an entity rather than to any specific individual. The staff can therefore be thought of as reporting *into the box*. No formal distinction is made between strategic or operations staff.

In the dual staff model ($B^2$) (Figure 4.4) there are two sets of corporate staff. Some staff members report to the corporate office, while others report directly to the CEO. The CEO's role as the primary driver of long-term corporate strategy is so fundamental that even within these partnership models, the strategic staff continue to report directly to the CEO. Those staffs reporting to the corporate office, on the other hand, are not clearly aligned with either the CEO or COO, both of whom share the responsibility for managing those staff functions.

**Figure 4.3. Simple Corporate Office Model.**

Option $B^1$
Corporate Office (Staff to the Box)

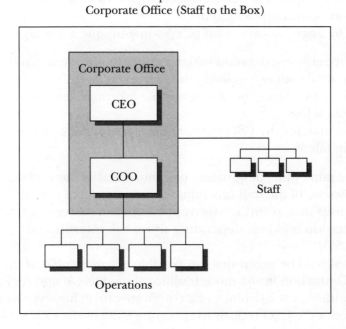

The designated staff model ($B^3$) (Figure 4.4) offers clearer reporting relationships between the staff and the corporate office than are found in the staff-to-the-box model ($B^1$). In the designated staff model individual staff functions are aligned with a primary contact, either the CEO or the COO. This is essentially a traditional staff structure with solid-line (primary) and dotted-line (secondary) reporting relationships. At any given time actual reporting relationships are determined by the current business context. This avoids the ambiguity inherent in pure in-the-box reporting relationships.

## Aggregated Staff Designs

Another set of corporate office designs entails the aggregation of key staff functions under the direction of a chief staff officer (CSO), who brings staff representation to the leadership table. In Option $C^1$ (Figure 4.5) the CSO, CFO, and COO form an executive team, residing in the corporate office with the CEO as team leader. In Option $C^2$ (also Figure 4.5) the CFO and CSO operate outside of the corporate office.

The aggregation of staff offers some unique advantages:

- More efficient decision making. All corporate staff can be represented with two individuals (CFO and CSO).
- Lower overhead, more manageable meetings, less chance of process loss.
- Potential for the CSO to foster development of other leadership talent.

At the same time, designating one individual as the spokesperson or advocate of the staff functions for the purpose of executive team meetings may result in overrepresentation of certain interests in decision making, depending upon the interest and focus of the CSO.

It should be noted that it is possible to aggregate staff through a CSO function in the more traditional models ($A^1$ and $A^2$; Figure 4.2) without the existence of a corporate office; however, in these situations the CSO reports to either the CEO or the COO, thereby simply adding another layer to the structure. In contrast, adding

**Figure 4.4. Dual and Designated Staff Models.**

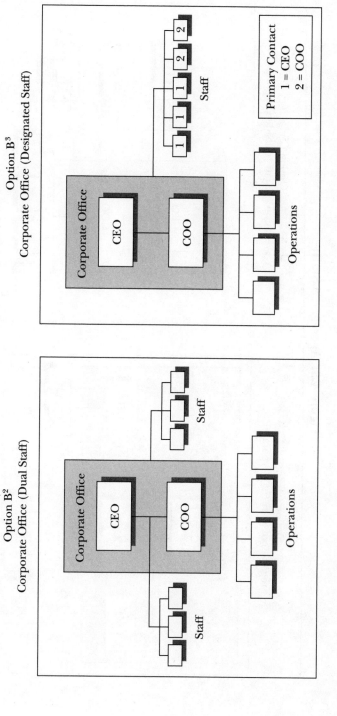

Option B² 
Corporate Office (Dual Staff)

Corporate Office

CEO

COO

Staff

Staff

Operations

Option B³
Corporate Office (Designated Staff)

Corporate Office

CEO

COO

Staff

Operations

Primary Contact
1 = CEO
2 = COO

**Figure 4.5. Aggregated Staff.**

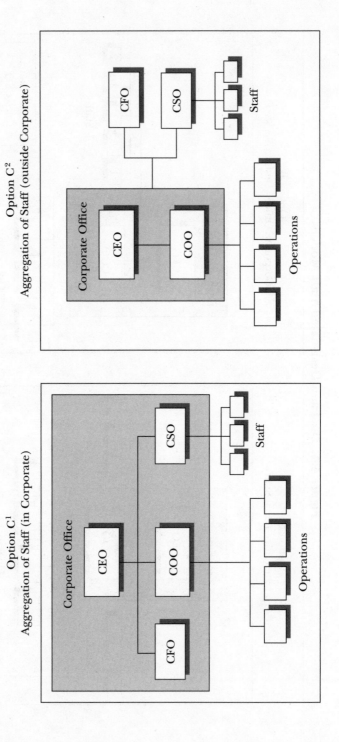

Option C¹
Aggregation of Staff (in Corporate)

Option C²
Aggregation of Staff (outside Corporate)

the CSO function to a corporate office expands the executive team, enabling corporate decisions to include, by representation, the voice of all corporate staff.

The $C^1$ design, as we said earlier, basically creates an executive team, and these are the general advantages associated with this team-at-the-top design:

- Benefits derived from team synergies, such as better-informed decision making
- Development of other executives and future leaders through their participation in executive activities and decisions
- Increased coordination across functions

However, the following points of vulnerability must also be considered with the team model:

- Intensified political behavior
- Potential loss of individual accountability
- Potential for team dysfunction, such as process loss, group-think, diffusion of responsibility, and the like
- Special requirements for the CEO as team leader

## Comparative Analysis of Design Options

Although no design option is inherently correct or incorrect, the selection of a particular option should be guided by how well the model *fits* the current business context and the capabilities, styles and needs of the individuals involved. Toward that end we have evaluated the seven options just presented on the basis of the following high-impact criteria:

- Clarity of CEO and COO roles
- Support of succession plans through validation of COO role
- Provision of stretch assignments for COO
- Effective governance in terms of coordination of various staff and operational functions
- Efficient governance procedures in terms of numbers of meetings, streamlined decision-making processes, and so forth
- Use of governance process as a way to model and drive the desired operating environment from the top

After 'applying these criteria to the options available (Figure 4.6), it becomes apparent that the aggregated staff designs have greater benefit. Clearly, the final choice of option will be influenced by a number of contextual factors, such as players' personalities and styles, the CEO's assessment of the COO's competency, the organization's historical roles for the CEO and COO, and so on. However, all things being equal, partnership-oriented approaches to governance are preferable.

In addition to the structure and role issues raised when evaluating alternative CEO-COO design options, relationship and management process issues demand attention.

## Management Processes

Whatever the organizational structure selected, to ensure organizational performance corporate leadership must design and manage three sets of processes:

1. *Core business processes.* Developed to manage the core work of the organization, such as product development and delivery, innovation, order fulfillment, and customer support.
2. *Management processes.* Developed to help guide the enterprise, allocate resources, and ensure performance, such as strategy development, operating plan development, portfolio management, and performance management.
3. *Support processes.* Designed to support the other management and core business processes and develop and manage infrastructure, such as information management and human resource management.

In a large and complex corporation the core business processes are managed by the operating units and at times may be championed by a senior executive. However, the core management processes and selected support processes are the exclusive responsibility of the executive leadership. The leadership of these processes happens in various forums (committees, teams, or groups and regular meetings) at the executive level.

Typically, the executive level has two primary forums for the management of processes: one devoted to the strategic management of the enterprise and usually a second devoted to the near-

**Figure 4.6. Evaluation of Design Options Against Criteria.**

| Design Options / Criteria | Traditional | | Corporate Office | | | Aggregate Staff | |
|---|---|---|---|---|---|---|---|
| | $A^1$ Single Staff | $A^2$ Dual Staff | $B^1$ Staff to the Box | $B^2$ Dual Staff | $B^3$ Designated Staff | $C^1$ Inside Corporate Staff | $C^2$ Outside Corporate Staff |
| Clarity of role | High | High | Low | Moderate | Moderate | Low | Moderate |
| COO role validation | Low | Low | Moderate | High | High | Moderate | High |
| COO development | Low | Low | Moderate | Moderate | Moderate | High | High |
| Effective coordination | Moderate | Low | Moderate | Low | High | High | High |
| Efficient governance processes | Moderate | Low | Moderate | Moderate | High | High | High |
| Driver of desired operating environment | Low | Moderate | Moderate | Moderate | Moderate | High | High |

*Note:* Cell entries denote the degree to which each design option enables achievement of a given criterion.

term (current year and next year) operations of the company. Critical issues include determining the appropriate forums for managing processes, who has responsibility for the leadership of each forum (the CEO, the COO, or another executive), and how these forums will function.

## Relationship Issues

A genuine partnership between the CEO and COO can be hard to achieve. Rivalry, defensiveness, and issues of control often exacerbate an inherently intense alliance between two powerful individuals responsible for running an organization. Consequently, attention and effort must be dedicated to building a bond of mutual respect and trust. It is imperative that both parties feel not just comfortable enough but absolutely compelled to raise difficult issues with one another in a timely and constructive manner. Their sharing of information must go beyond "due diligence" to a rapport that is characterized by a strong sense of interdependence and joint responsibility.

There are two very important strategies for building this type of unique relationship. First, as early as possible in the development of the partnership, the parties must discuss in explicit terms the distribution of roles and responsibilities. One of the greatest sources of stress between the CEO and the COO is ambiguity about who is in charge of what. Second, the CEO and the COO must candidly express their individual wishes and aspirations concerning both the roles under discussion and their long-term career goals. In addition they must address their feelings and concerns regarding the partnership. This open, honest discussion is essential if the parties are to confront and deal with any potentially destructive interpersonal dynamics that might, over time, undermine the relationship. Due to the sensitive and often awkward nature of such discussions, outside facilitation might be necessary.

The CEO and COO share the responsibility for successfully resolving most partnership issues. However, two areas of responsibility are solely incumbent upon the CEO: empowerment of the COO and the positioning and development of the COO as CEO successor. To carry out these responsibilities, the CEO must

- Give guidance to the COO by sharing the insights and wisdom gained through experience as CEO.
- Work with the COO to develop a shared approach to shaping the future direction of the organization.
- Work diligently to validate and support the COO's role through high-impact assignments and symbolic activities.
- Provide timely and thorough performance feedback to the COO.

Just as the CEO has some unique responsibilities for strengthening the alliance, the COO also has several corresponding responsibilities. He must

- Provide upward feedback.
- Push back on the CEO by testing assumptions, questioning decisions, and disagreeing when necessary.
- Seek high-impact stretch assignments.
- Actively support the CEO in all forums and situations where anyone other than the two of them is involved.

Clarifying structural, process, and relationship or role issues demands significant time and focused attention on the part of the CEO and COO, possibly with third-party support. To aid discussion, a worksheet is provided in the Appendix at the end of this chapter that details the collective responsibilities of the CEO and COO. The worksheet is intended to facilitate determination of which responsibilities are shared, which unique and primary, and which secondary. We also suggest that much of this work be done off-site in order to devote enough uninterrupted time to discuss these important issues. Their discussions should have the goal of producing clear documentation of the agreements reached and an explicit communication plan for start-up and implementation of the desired model.

We believe that in many organizations the partnership-at-the-top model is not only workable but potentially highly productive. But its success will depend on both the CEO's and COO's commitment to the alliance. True partnership involves more than lines and boxes on a piece of paper; in the end it will be the attitudes and behavior of the individuals involved that will determine the arrangement's ultimate success.

## Summary

This chapter has investigated the advantages and drawbacks of seven options for designing a CEO-COO working relationship that can meet the modern organization's governance needs. These models are based on a taxonomy of corporate leadership roles and related behaviors that together define CEO and COO responsibilities. We also addressed the management process and relationship issues that members of an executive team must deal with openly to form an effective partnership.

Although a number of considerations will affect a CEO's design choice, including his views of comparative personalities and management styles, of a COO's competency, and of the way CEO and COO roles have been patterned in the organization's past, we conclude that typically the partnership models of governance are preferable to the traditional model.

# Appendix
# Roles and Responsibilities for CEO and COO: Worksheet

| Instructions: For each responsibility, assign one of the following options in each column: Unique, Shared, Primary, Secondary | | |
|---|---|---|
| *Strategic Responsibilities* | *CEO* | *COO* |
| *Strategist* | | |
| • Sets corporate strategic direction (vision & strategy) | | |
| • Shapes the company's long-term aspiration | | |
| • Makes decisions on key strategic issues facing company (for example, market entry, acquisitions) | | |
| • Communicates and builds commitment to corporate strategic direction among external constituents (board, analysts, customers, and so on) | | |
| • Communicates and builds commitment to corporate strategic direction among internal constituents (management, associates, and so on) | | |
| • Periodically reviews the company's overall strategy to ensure organization anticipates and responds to changing business conditions | | |
| *Architect* | | |
| • Establishes organizational structure and operating systems to ensure achievement of strategic objectives | | |
| • Defines desired corporate philosophy, values, and operating environment | | |
| • Defines core business processes | | |
| *Ambassador* | | |
| • Serves as principal external representative of the company | | |
| • Develops successful alliances and joint ventures | | |

| Strategic Responsibilities | CEO | COO |
|---|---|---|
| *Keeper of the corporate image* | | |
| • Protects and builds brand integrity | | |
| • Sets strategic marketing direction | | |
| • Sets tone and direction for relations with key external constituencies (clients, shareholders, analysts, and so on) | | |
| • Sets tone and direction for relations with key internal constituencies (board, senior team, management, employees, and so on) | | |
| *Policy-Related Responsibilities* | | |
| • Translates corporate vision and strategy into organizational policies, directives, and procedures | | |
| • Develops guidelines for use of corporate assets (people, brand, information) | | |
| • Communicates and builds commitment to organizational policies, directives, and procedures among key external constituents (board and so on) | | |
| • Communicates and builds commitment to organizational policies, directives, and procedures among key internal constituents (management, associates, and so on) | | |
| • Integrates organizational policies, directives, and procedures into coherent corporate framework | | |
| • Ensures implementation of policies, directives, and procedures | | |
| • Monitors effectiveness of policies, directives, and procedures | | |

| *Operational Responsibilities* | *CEO* | *COO* |
|---|---|---|
| *Performance management* | | |
| • Sets corporate performance targets (balanced scorecard) | | |
| • Translates corporate vision, strategy, and performance targets into business unit plans and performance targets | | |
| • Deploys corporate vision, strategy, and performance targets into business unit plans and performance targets | | |
| • Reviews and approves business unit strategies | | |
| • Reviews business unit process performance against world-class criteria (for example, Baldrige National Quality Award) | | |
| *Operational management* | | |
| • Manages operations of the company in ways consistent with strategic goals and performance targets | | |
| • Monitors operational progress against performance targets and organizes countermeasures when required | | |
| • Manages infrastructure required to support operating units | | |
| • Manages resources (including people and capital) across lines of business | | |
| • Resolves critical shared resource issues | | |
| • Manages corporate staff resources | | |
| • Resolves issues of conflict between business units and staff functions | | |
| *Functional management* | | |
| • Manages financial information and compliance activities | | |
| • Manages the attraction, retention, and development of a high-performance workforce | | |
| • Manages public relations | | |

| *Operational Responsibilities* | *CEO* | *COO* |
|---|---|---|
| *Process management* | | |
| • Ensures that core business processes (for example, time to market, integrated supply chain, customer service, and so on) are in place and working effectively | | |
| • Integrates companywide business processes | | |
| • Ensures that effective management processes (for example, decision making and conflict resolution) are in place at all levels | | |
| • Ensures that quality tools and methods are used in managing the business | | |
| *People management* | | |
| • Ensures the right leadership team is in place, with complementary skills represented | | |
| • Leads senior team | | |
| • Develops and monitors succession-planning process for top leadership positions | | |
| • Ensures all critical executive positions are adequately staffed | | |
| • Develops top leadership through selection, coaching, and reinforcement | | |
| • Ensures replacement personnel are suitably trained and developed | | |
| *Information management* | | |
| • Transmits top-level decisions throughout organization | | |
| • Serves as internal spokesperson for corporate messages | | |

# Managing the Executive Team

Part One outlined how internal and external business pressures have intensified the demands on corporate leadership, particularly CEOs. It examined the emergence of the executive team as an approach to extending the CEO's capability in both strategic and operational tasks, how the executive team differs from other teams, how team members can effectively manage the special role the CEO must assume in executive team leadership, and various governance structures that can facilitate performance of the CEO and the executive team.

An understanding of these concepts is helpful before reading Part Two, which explores the elements—both tangible and intangible—that contribute to the effectiveness of an executive team. The executive team has unique characteristics that strongly affect the chemistry among its ambitious, political, and powerful members. It is crucial to understand and manage these dynamics appropriately to ensure the ultimate success of the team and, therefore, the organization.

In Chapter Five we show how management of the team's interpersonal dynamics has an impact on the entire organization. To be successful, the CEO must be mindful of the factors that distinguish this team from others, specifically the distribution of power between the team and its leader, the psychological characteristics of the members, and issues of succession. In addition to identifying problems inherent in executive teams, the chapter suggests effective ways to deal with them.

Chapter Six emphasizes how critical the composition of the executive team is to its ultimate success. Although this is intuitively obvious to most, taking action to remove a dysfunctional team member paralyzes many CEOs. This chapter offers insights regarding why this subject is both so pervasive and so problematic. Beyond their analysis, the chapter authors provide concrete advice on how to improve the CEO's ability to handle these difficult situations.

Chapter Seven deals with a dynamic that is often a source of frustration and failure in executive teams. Lack of trust can prevent teams from accomplishing the task at hand: working on and solving problems. This chapter explores the underpinnings of trust and discusses explicit steps that can be taken to develop this within the team.

The next two chapters take on an inevitable feature of an executive team: conflict. Chapter Eight describes three levels of conflict: behavioral, emotional, and perceptual. An understanding of these levels is necessary before a team leader can determine whether intervention is needed to correct destructive team conflict. The chapter also provides tools to help the reader determine the need for intervention and then demonstrates how intervention can resolve differences.

Chapter Nine takes the concept of conflict a step further by looking at the team leader's role in confronting and managing executive team discord. Cohesive team performance is not easy to come by, and conflict is a constant threat. The roles a CEO can play to resolve the conflict and the competencies necessary to do so are described in detail.

Finally, Chapter Ten explores the use of data and feedback for enhancing the quality of executive team functioning. The chapter illustrates two feedback tools and related processes that can be used to diagnose opportunities for improving team dynamics and to build the team's capacity to self-correct.

## Chapter Five

# The CEO and the Executive Team

## Managing the Unique Dynamics and Special Demands

*David A. Nadler*

*Jeffrey D. Heilpern*

Some time ago we received a call from a chief executive officer who was leading his organization through a difficult period of massive change. Clearly, the fellow was frustrated and perplexed. "I've got more than 100,000 people who are motivated, excited, and moving in the right direction" he explained. "But I still have a big problem with one particular group of eight people—the eight who report directly to me."

He is not alone.

Over the past decade the growing use of executive teams has underscored the unique problems involving this most senior team of all. This group of powerful men and women—the senior executives who report directly to the chief executive officer of their enterprise—encounters the full range of problems and challenges that face every other team. Above and beyond those universal issues, however, this team's performance is complicated by the unique dynamics that exist only at the very top of the organization. Those dynamics, in turn, create a set of special demands on CEOs in the role of leader of the executive team.

Much of what has been written about executive teams has focused primarily on their structure and function. Without question those are important issues. Yet they fail to come to grips with the gritty reality of what goes on when these ambitious, powerful, and political people assemble behind closed doors. Indeed, both *in the room* and when they are apart, team members' behavior plays out a complicated web of relationships—relationships among the members themselves, relationships between the CEO and individual members, and the relationship of the CEO to the group as a collective entity. The degree to which the CEO understands, shapes, and successfully manages the interpersonal dynamics of this pivotal group invariably has a major bearing on the ultimate success of the entire organization.

Our perspectives on this subject are based on more than a decade of experience in which we and our colleagues have worked closely with over sixty CEOs and their direct reports. Moreover, our experience has the benefit of continuity; in some cases we have worked with the same team over the course of thirty or more off-site executive sessions and scores of operational meetings spanning the reigns of two or more CEOs and three or four generations of executive teams. Over the years some distinct patterns have developed; certain patterns of dynamics, and the problems that come with them, are virtually unavoidable. Our intent in this chapter is to describe these predictable problems and challenges and then to suggest some proven approaches to dealing with them in ways that will enhance the executive team's chances for success.

## The CEO as Team Leader

It is important to keep in mind that although the CEO is, by definition, the chief executive of the entire enterprise, he must also shoulder the responsibility of leading his own team. In general terms the CEO plays this role in three basic venues: as the designer of the team, as the active leader in the room when the team is together, and as the leader, coordinator, and shaper of dynamics when the team is not in session.

First, the CEO is, again by definition, the designer of the team. The CEO makes the initial decision whether or not to have an executive team and then goes about creating it in whatever form he deems useful. It is the CEO who determines the composition of the team and its structure. The CEO determines who plays which roles. The CEO decides on the team's work processes, the specific ways in which the team members will work together. Typically, these decisions are made early in the life of the team. Sometimes they are entirely conscious decisions on the part of the CEO; frequently, things fall into place on the basis of implicit understandings.

Second, the CEO is the leader of the team when it meets *in the room.* The CEO convenes the group, wields the gavel, and plays the primary role in shaping the team's dynamics. He serves as both participant and leader and makes the crucial decisions about both content and processes—what the team will work on and how it will go about its work.

Third, the CEO is also the leader of the team *out of the room.* For a host of reasons the most powerful team in any organization is also the team that tends to spend the least time meeting face to face. In comparison think about the average self-managed team at a manufacturing plant. Individuals on that team tend to spend upwards of 90 percent of their work day in close proximity to each other. They do their jobs together. They routinely get together at both formal and informal team meetings. They spend more time with each other at meals and breaks.

The executive team's routine is a far cry from that. Certainly, team members spend some time together, both in regularly scheduled and periodic off-site meetings. But they might get together only weekly or even monthly. In the physical sense, you will rarely find all members of the executive team working near each other; in fact the more they operate as a cloistered team, the less effective they are likely to be in their roles as leaders of their respective operations. Consequently, they tend to be separated by geography, both in micro and macro terms; the operating head of a division or business unit might be located on a different floor of the corporate headquarters than the CEO or COO, whereas the head of operations on the West Coast or in Europe could easily spend most of his time literally thousands of miles from other executive team members.

Consequently, the CEO's leadership of the team has to extend beyond the time they spend together in the room. He must also shape the team through individual interactions and by managing the team's structures and processes. This is not simply a matter of maintaining relationships and making sure everyone is getting along. The fact of the matter is that the executive team's work processes—planning, budgeting, designing strategy, for example—are the organization's work. In order for the organization to operate successfully, the members of the team must perform each of their respective roles effectively. So it is the responsibility of the CEO to do all the things necessary to oversee those team processes—including those that go on even when the team is not working face to face—that have tremendous implications for the rest of the organization.

## Special Aspects of the Executive Team

As CEOs pursue these various functions as leaders of their executive teams, they have to keep in mind those factors that differentiate this team from all others to which they have been exposed over the course of their careers. To be sure, the executive team exhibits all the manifestations of any other team and has to be understood first and foremost in the overall team context (Schein, 1985). To see the similarities and differences, we can examine how the team operates from three perspectives.

The first perspective is *content*—what topics the team discusses, what kinds of decisions it makes, what kinds of actions it takes. A second perspective is *process*—the patterns of interactions between team members, who initiates discussions, who participates and how, who calls the questions, who shapes the agenda, who influences decisions, who engages in conflict with whom, who dominates the proceedings. The third perspective is often described as the team's *affect*—the excitement, anger, frustration, and other emotions that are experienced or unspoken during the course of the team's interaction.

Obviously, all three—content, process, and affect—exert powerful influences upon each other and upon the effectiveness of any team. However, for purposes of identifying the dynamics that differentiate the executive team from all other teams, our main interest is in the team's process and affect—what goes on and how it is dealt with. In that context there are three fundamental differences between the executive team and other senior-level teams.

The first difference has to do with power and more specifically the relative distribution of power between the team leader and the team members. There is always some imbalance of power between leaders and members, but in the case of the executive team the distribution of power is disproportionately tilted in favor of the leader. Unlike any other team leader, the CEO wields power that is virtually absolute. There are several reasons for this.

To begin with, the CEO differs from any other team leader in that virtually all the CEO's decisions are final; there are no avenues of appeal. As the organization's ultimate administrator of sanctions and rewards, the CEO enjoys tremendous flexibility with fewer external controls than any other manager. Obviously, there are innumerable forces and restrictions that constrain any CEO's exercise of power. What is important, however, is the general perception among team members that the CEO possesses unlimited power—and the perception of power is tantamount to reality. If team members believe the CEO has absolute power, and act accordingly, the actual limits on CEO power become inconsequential.

At a particularly stressful executive team meeting at one company, one team member who was at odds with the CEO complained, "You have absolute power over us. You could just fire any one of us, and there's not a thing we could do about it." The CEO, it turned out, was thinking, "Why in the world would I do that?" From his perspective the CEO was well aware that the arbitrary dismissal of any executive team member would result in all sorts of unpleasant consequences. That was the objective reality. The perceived reality, however, was that he could do anything he wanted and get away with it.

The second factor that skews the distribution of power in executive teams involves the tenure of the CEO, which tends to be longer and more determinate than that of other team leaders. On most teams, senior or otherwise, the members really have no idea how long the leader is liable to be around. Leaders might be due for a promotion or transfer, they might be job hunting, or they might be on the way out—there is really no way of knowing. That is usually not the case with the CEO. Based on how long the CEO has already been in the job, his age, and the company's traditional tenure for CEOs, team members can usually make some fairly safe assumptions about how much longer the CEO is likely to remain on the scene. Moreover, CEOs tend to stay in the same job longer than most managers, who are still in the process of moving up, down, sideways, or out. So if the team is formed fairly early in a CEO's regime, the team members can probably assume that the CEO is going to be around for years—in some companies, perhaps a decade or more. That fact has a major impact on the dynamics of the team relationship. Building a good relationship with the CEO becomes an absolute necessity, because this powerful person is about to become a permanent fixture in your life—or as close to permanent as you are likely to get in the business world.

The third factor that gives the CEO disproportionate power is that executive team members have few low-cost outs. Typical managers who decide they do not like working for someone and want to make a move can usually figure out some lateral shift to another division or business unit. But for those reporting directly to the CEO the alternatives are severely limited: they can either move down or out—and ultimately both end up meaning out. For an executive who has reached the top ranks of an organization the costs of leaving are enormous. On one hand there is the loss of benefits—pension, restricted stock, and all the other "golden hand-cuffs" that go with membership in the exclusive senior club. On the other hand starting over somewhere else presents huge risks involving a new job, new colleagues, a new culture, possibly even a new industry. That is a lot of insecurity for anyone, and particularly for an executive who has become accustomed to being a major player in a secure setting. The upshot is that when the CEO's direct reports become restive, they review their options, begin to feel trapped, and convince themselves that the only logical option is to continue to satisfy the boss.

The outcome of these three factors—the power implicit in the CEO's position, the CEO's unique tenure, and the limited exit options for team members—is that the CEO enjoys both real and perceived power in relation to the executive team far in excess of anything experienced by other team leaders. Simply put, the CEO can do things no other leader can in terms of shaping the agenda, setting the rules, declaring issues off limits, and making decisions.

Along with this unusual distribution of power, the executive team is unique because of the psychological characteristics typically found among any group of people who have risen to the top ranks of a major institution. Not surprisingly, these people tend to have unusually high needs for power and achievement. Many are driven by ambition and the desire to succeed in a public arena. What is more, they tend to have well-honed interpersonal skills when it comes to "playing the game," maintaining public facades, and waging office politics. These are not rookies; on the whole, these are smart, ambitious veterans of the corporate wars, and they are immune to the typical team leader's normal bag of tricks.

In addition to the distribution of power and the makeup of the team, there is a third factor that sets the executive team apart from all other teams: succession. Within this team, those who are actively playing the game are all jockeying for the only prize that really counts—the CEO's job. All the team members are aware that they are engaged in a zero-sum game; there can be only one winner.

There is just no way around it; sooner or later, every organization has to confront the fact that its CEO is not immortal. Sooner or later, someone else is going to be sitting in the big chair. And on every executive team, the succession issue is a fact of life. As the CEO grows older and approaches the organization's customary retirement age for top executives or the end of the typical tenure for a CEO, succession increasingly becomes an overarching source of conflict and competition with the team. The leading players maneuver for position; the secondary figures constantly handicap the outcome, trying to guess the right moment to choose sides. All this politicking naturally exacerbates the power distance between the CEO and the team. In this situation as in others, CEOs hold an unusual degree of power; more than any other executive or team leader, they exert enormous influence over the selection of their successors. Certainly, the board of directors has the final say, but unless the organization is undergoing a major downturn or a period of radical change, the CEO's hand-picked successor is almost certain to win board approval.

## Issues and Implications

Take the unbalanced distribution of power between the team and its leader and the psychological characteristics commonly found in executive team members, then superimpose the combustible ingredient of succession, and the result is a volatile set of dynamics that complicates the work of virtually every executive team (See Figure 5.1). On the basis of our experience and observation, we can predict that nearly every executive team will experience at least some, and possibly all of the six issues we are about to discuss. The good news is that there are effective ways to address and cope with each of these problems, and we present those solutions as well (summarized in Figure 5.2).

### Issue 1: Bloated Membership

The cachet associated with the executive team inevitably leads top managers to imbue a seat at the big table with special importance and immense symbolic value. The result is enormous pressure for inclusion. There is constant pressure from those who are clamoring for an invitation to join and also pressure from those already on the team who are lobbying for the inclusion of friends and supporters.

That pressure for expanded membership is being exacerbated in many organizations by the move toward flatter hierarchies and broader spans of control. Instead of having four or five direct reports, as in the past, the CEO now might have ten or twelve. Along with those increased direct reports comes the assumption that anyone who is a hierarchical peer of a team member ought also to be a member. Too often membership on the executive team is extended in the interests of maintaining symmetry; that is not a goal that necessarily ensures the right people are included and the extraneous ones are left out.

All too often membership on the executive team becomes an end in itself, rather than a means to an end—like getting work done. We have all heard executives complain loudly that the executive team eats up valuable time that they would rather be spending on their "real" work. Maybe so; but the fact is that the only thing they would consider worse than being on the executive team is not being on the executive team. It is like one of those parties to which you really want to be invited, as long as you do not have to

**Figure 5.1. Executive Team Dynamics.**

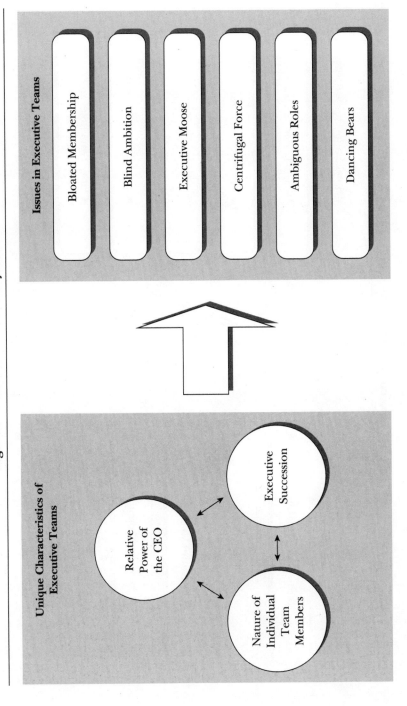

**Figure 5.2. Executive Team Issues and Actions.**

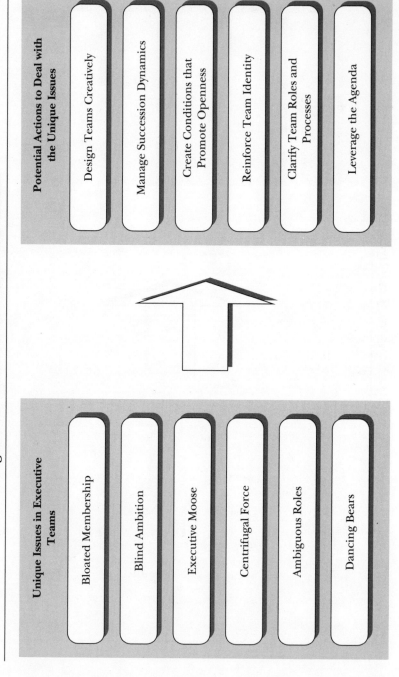

Unique Issues in Executive Teams

- Bloated Membership
- Blind Ambition
- Executive Moose
- Centrifugal Force
- Ambiguous Roles
- Dancing Bears

Potential Actions to Deal with the Unique Issues

- Design Teams Creatively
- Manage Succession Dynamics
- Create Conditions that Promote Openness
- Reinforce Team Identity
- Clarify Team Roles and Processes
- Leverage the Agenda

go. In fact it is a lot like that; once many of the people who lobby long and hard to be named to the team are appointed, they then go out of their way to find excuses not to attend meetings.

In reality lots of people attend executive team meetings for all the wrong reasons. They are more concerned about what might transpire in their absence than in what might be accomplished through their presence. The key to attendance in many cases hinges on whether or not the CEO is likely to be there. When word gets out that the CEO is off on a road trip or tied up with a customer, attendance at the team meeting is likely to drop dramatically. In too many teams the primary motivation for showing up is to fulfill the ritual and to maintain visibility with the CEO, rather than to accomplish important work.

The result of expanded, diluted, and ritual membership is a team that is too big and largely dysfunctional. Research suggests that the optimal group size for real problem solving and decision making ranges from seven to nine, yet it is not uncommon to see executive teams with fifteen or twenty members. Not only is the group too big to work efficiently, with so many aggressive and ambitious people in the room the competition for limited "airtime" can become fierce and counterproductive. There are just too many people jockeying for their moment in the limelight, resulting in a constant progression of performances rather than substantive give and take.

Finally, as the group gets bigger, a natural division develops between operating and staff people. In some teams there is an unspoken distinction between those members who feel they have a very real, personal stake in the outcome of the team's work and those who become relatively passive spectators—and over time come to be perceived as dead weight. Deep divisions gradually separate members in terms of knowledge, credibility, legitimacy, and influence. At a certain point that gap implicitly creates a first team and a second team within the same team, creating a situation in which true teamwork is enormously problematic.

## Implication 1: Design Teams Creatively

One way to avoid bloated, unproductive teams is to think in terms of different teams for different tasks. There is nothing that says there can be one and only one executive team. Some CEOs design concentric rings of executive teams—for instance, a policy team involving the entire executive team and an operating team consisting of a small subset of the full team. The policy team on the one hand would meet periodically and deal with matters suitable for large groups, such as communications, information sharing, gaining alignment around new policies, or building ownership of new strategies. The operating team on the other hand would meet frequently and handle issues requiring problem solving or decision making.

At Lucent Technologies, CEO Henry Schacht meets regularly with his Business Council, which includes the president, the chief financial officer, the chief staff officer, and the heads of the company's four business units. That eight-member group rolls ups its sleeves and deals with the day-to-day operating decisions required to run a $23 billion corporation. Schacht also meets periodically with the full team, which includes the Business Council members plus operating managers at the next level down and key staff or functional people, such as the head of research.

Unilever also has two overlapping teams, but they are structured differently than Lucent's; the Unilever Executive Committee consists of the heads of each of the corporate business segments, and the Executive Council, which meets less frequently, also includes senior operating executives from all over the world. In both cases the underlying principle of team design is the same: the creation of a large inclusive executive team implies permission to set up smaller subgroups designed to handle routine operational responsibilities.

The subsets of the executive team do not have to be permanent groups. Many CEOs frequently use ad hoc subgroups of the executive team to tackle specific issues and then disband these groups once the matter has been resolved. Another technique currently gaining the interest of CEOs concerned about their oversized executive committees is the appointment of a chief staff officer. The specific responsibilities vary from one organization, but in general the CSO is a senior executive whose direct reports include the managers responsible for critical staff functions, such as strategy, information technology, human resources, public affairs, communications, and legal affairs. Xerox, for example, has used this structure for some time. It allows the interests and expertise of senior staff people to be represented on the executive team as it keeps membership to a manageable size.

## Issue 2: Blind Ambition

As we noted earlier, executive teams typically include individuals who are unusually ambitious and achievement oriented. A few join the team in their thirties, but by and large most come aboard in their early forties to early fifties. These days they are extremely conscious of the probability that they have only a limited amount of time in which to realize their career objectives; it is not unusual to hear these people wonder, "How much runway do I have left?" Their career clocks are ticking, intensifying the competitive atmosphere within a naturally competitive group.

Yet within any executive team only a few members are realistic candidates to succeed the CEO. By the time a sitting CEO has reached the tenure stage where succession is a paramount issue, team members typically fall into one of these five categories:

*The contenders.* These are the people who are determined to climb to the top—sooner rather than later, if not here, then somewhere else. Their career paths, their record of success and the positive signals they have received all lead them to believe they have a strong shot at becoming the CEO. They pay serious attention to internal time frames; generally speaking, if they have not been promoted to the top job by the time they reach their early fifties, they are prepared to make a move that will position them to become CEO somewhere else.

*The past-their-prime-time players.* Their moment in the limelight has come and gone; one way or another these executives have been given unmistakable signals that they are no longer in the running for the top job. Their reactions vary: some feel intense disappointment; some are largely reconciled; some are still trying to sort out their feelings. And some continue to hope, against all odds, that somehow lightning will strike: the leading contenders will self-destruct, the CEO will suddenly come to his or her senses and realize how wrong that initial judgment was, and the story will have a happy ending.

*The good soldiers.* These are the executives who fully understand that their careers have topped out, and that is all right with them. They have achieved their personal goals; they have climbed higher in the organization and are making more money than they had ever dreamed was possible, and they do not entertain any real aspirations to go any higher. Often—but not always—they tend to be senior staff people or technical specialists who spent much of their careers on the periphery of the organization's core work. They are motivated in large part by their desire to be valued by their boss and their peers, to maintain a sense of pride and dignity even though they are not bona fide contenders.

*The young and restless.* These executives are the new kids on the block, relatively speaking. They are fully aware that they are not in the generation from which the next CEO will emerge, so they are not immediate contenders for the job. Their immediate mission is to impress their elders, deftly maneuver through the political mine-fields, and generally demonstrate that they possess "the right stuff" that qualifies them for future consideration.

*The over-the-hill gang.* Most executive teams have at least one or two of these members—people who for all intents and purposes have retired but for various reasons are still hanging around, await-ing the day when their retirement becomes formal. They are living out their Golden Years in the warm cocoon of senior management, largely content to sit on the sidelines and watch others get blood-ied in the succession skirmishes. Their exclusive goal is survival. What they dread most is some risky and demanding new assign-ment at which they might fail, ending up being carried out on their shield rather than walking away on their own terms at a time of their own choosing.

As the anticipated date of the succession decision draws near, this entire cast of characters can easily be swept up in a tidal wave of political behavior. The maneuvering, positioning, and competing intensify. Frequently, contenders decide it is not enough to present themselves in the best light; they feel compelled to go after their competitors, sometimes head-on, other times through subtle feints and sneaky subterfuges. Depending on the intensity of the com-petition and the personalities involved, the behavior can easily become irrational and self-destructive. We are familiar with a situ-ation in which one of the contenders was so obvious and heavy-handed in his campaign for the CEO's job that everything he did was seen as self-serving. Before long he had generated so much hostility than even when he tried to do something for the right reasons, everyone assumed he was merely pursuing his personal agenda. In the end he succeeded only in making himself so ineffectual that the CEO asked him to leave.

The issue here is that the anticipation of a succession fight is a major spectator sport; onlookers love to watch what they perceive as competition, even when it is not in fact there. When it really exists—particularly when it is positioned as an outright horse race—matters can get completely out of hand. The competition has a corrosive effect on relationships within the team, weakening and sometimes even demolishing the trust that is crucial to productive teamwork (see Chapter Seven). What is more, the dysfunctional drama can easily continue after the new CEO is named, as people lick their wounds and try to position themselves for second-tier jobs. Depending on its depth and duration, that kind of political activity can easily cripple the team.

## Implication 2: Manage Succession Dynamics

Let us be honest: to one degree or another the succession dynamics we just described are unavoidable. They flow directly from powerful forces of human nature—power, control, competition, self-esteem, survival. What the CEO can do is, to the extent possible, manage the dynamics in ways that soften their impact on the team's effectiveness.

The primary challenge is to avoid the appearance of a public horse race. Time and time again we have seen CEOs create situations in which the leading contenders are pitted against each other with the clear expectation that it is up to each of them to demonstrate the desire, ambition, drive, and know-how to pull ahead of the pack. Perhaps that satisfies some internal notion of the dog-eat-dog nature of corporate natural selection. In reality, placing top executives in a position where they are actively and explicitly competing against one another is misguided, destructive, and detrimental to the organization's long-term interests.

Moreover, a succession horse race is inherently inconsistent with the goal of an effective executive team. In any situation the success of the team relies on each member's belief that the greater good is more important than immediate self-interest and the conviction that in the long run, individual success will be determined by collective triumph. In most situations that is absolutely true—but not when it comes to succession. Once a team member has been designated as an active contender and lined up in the starting gate, there is no way to make that person feel good about losing. So the challenge to the CEO is to keep as many options open for as long as possible and to actively discourage the perception of a head-to-head contest.

For example, timing and the management of expectations are important. We typically counsel CEOs to avoid any announcement, public or otherwise, of a specific time frame for their departure and the naming of a successor. David Kearns once reflected that one of his worst mistakes was made in late 1981, right after his appointment as CEO of Xerox; having just assumed his new position, he announced to the executive team that he planned to retire on August 11, 1990. Kearns had no intention of pitting his potential successors against one another in an eight-year winner-take-all contest and so spent considerable energy over the ensuing years in actively discouraging overt competition. Nevertheless, unless the CEO chooses that same moment to name a successor, the announcement of a retirement date is tantamount to firing a starting gun; the warm-ups are over and the race is on. The longer the race, the greater the damage to the executive team and the organization as a whole.

It is interesting to note what happened at Xerox. One after another the contenders who threw themselves into the race and actively lobbied for the job ended up being disqualified. In turn each one left the company. In the end it was Paul Allaire—the executive whose behavior was least political, who never made any public declaration of his interest in the job, who shunned the horse race and just kept doing his job, and who in fact never even suggested to Kearns in private that he would like to be CEO—who ultimately was named to succeed Kearns.

That is not unusual. In what we consider to be healthy situations—those where CEOs discourage the perception of a horse race and avoid pitting people against one another—the people who actively campaign and openly go after the top job frequently self-destruct. Obviously, there is nothing wrong with ambition. But more often than not, it is private ambition linked with consistently outstanding public performance that wins the big prize. Of course we all can think of exceptions; but by and large, hyper-competitive contenders end up on the sidelines.

The implication is for CEOs attempting to manage succession dynamics to be as explicit as possible—as early as possible—about what kind of behavior is acceptable, both inside and outside the room. As Paul Allaire began talking to his team about the way in which his successor would be chosen, he made a point of telling them about his own experience. In great detail—and naming names—he described the battle to succeed Kearns and ticked off the list of contenders who actively fought for the job and, in the process, crippled their Xerox careers. His message was clear: if you start competing for the job in ways that disrupt the team, not only are you likely to disqualify yourself as my successor, you are probably going to be gone from the company.

## Issue 3: Executive Moose

Virtually every team, regardless of its position in the organization, faces the problem of "undiscussables" (Argyris, 1990). These are sensitive, volatile issues that are on everyone's mind and generally have a direct bearing on the team's work, and yet the group will go to incredible lengths to avoid discussing them—or even mentioning them for that matter. Our colleague Dennis Perkins has developed the inspired metaphor of "the moose on the table" (Perkins, 1988) to describe this phenomenon. He likens these embarrassing, touchy, or unpleasant issues to a huge, hairy, smelly moose that is standing on the conference table—but not one member of the team will acknowledge its existence. The team goes about its business, people talk to each other between and around the moose's legs, but nobody makes any reference to the massive animal standing on the table. By unanimous but unspoken agreement, people decide to ignore the moose.

When the executive team gets together, there is likely to be a herd of moose crowded on top of the big table; some of them embodying the points of tension we have already discussed. In general, you can expect to see at least four of these shaggy beasts on the table.

The first is the distribution of power between the CEO and the team. Where are the boundaries, both for the CEO and the team? What kinds of issues are negotiable, and which are off limits? How far can team members go in attempting to lead or influence the group without encroaching on the CEO's turf? How broad are the limits of dissent, and how deep is the need for consensus?

The second moose—and a huge one—is succession. In some situations, depending on the timing and circumstances, the succession issue may be uppermost in everyone's mind, coloring every statement, vote, presentation, and expression of support. Nevertheless, the group may go for months on end without acknowledging what is going on.

The third moose is the relationships among team members—their relative power, influence, competence, and performance. In most executive teams there are certain unspoken taboos involving criticism of peers and open conflict among them. In most cases such criticism is simply off limits. Everyone around the table may be fully aware that a peer is running his operation into the ground or has been placed in a difficult situation and is clearly in over his head; even if other team members would like to raise the issue to see if there is a way they can offer assistance, there is no acceptable method for bringing it up.

The fourth moose is failure—failure of individuals and failure of strategies, projects, or initiatives. In too many executive teams any open discussion of failure is also simply off limits. Long-time members of the team can disappear like discredited Kremlin bosses, their departure marked solely by a note that the executive has decided to pursue other interests. Naturally, all the team members talk about the dear departed in private, but all too often there is no serious discussion of why the person was asked to leave or what lessons the others might learn from that experience. Similarly, if pet projects of the CEO or other powerful executives crash and burn, they are never referred to again around the table for fear of embarrassing someone.

Any or all of these moose can seriously hamper the executive team's ability to work together effectively. Over time the failure to confront the moose creates an implicit conspiracy of silence. Important issues are sidestepped; vital concerns remain unsurfaced, unspoken, and unresolved. Dark emotions and destructive conflicts fester and worsen. Meanwhile the team wastes extraordinary amounts of time and energy as people posture to talk around the issues sitting between them on the table.

## Implication 3: Create Conditions That Promote Openness

The key to openness is trust—an often scarce commodity at the executive team level, where the stakes are so high and competition so intense. We are not advocating some New Age concept of warm and fuzzy acceptance based on spiritual affirmation of each member's intrinsic worth. The issue here is performance and competence; those who demonstrate their continuing value should be consistently validated and supported.

A sense of trust and openness is more essential at the executive team level than anywhere else in the organization. Day after day these are the people who are asked to mount the high-wire and perform death-defying acts for all to see. Consequently, it is up to the CEO to provide a safety net by building and sustaining supportive relationships with each individual and with the team as a whole. It is up to the CEO to create a fundamental platform of assurance of team members' validity. Even more than the members of other teams, the executive team members have to feel they enjoy sufficient support to gamble on speaking out and being wrong or out of line.

It is not enough for team members to feel confident about the CEO's support. In order for the team to honestly tackle the most sensitive issues, there has to be a sense of trust and respect among the team members as well. Again, the CEO can play a crucial role, supporting people when they take risks, exercising sanctions when others try to undercut the risk takers through open attacks or peripheral potshots. In addition the CEO can drive a process of *appreciative inquiry*—making it more evident to the team members what each of the others brings to the table. As they gain appreciation of each other's insights and capabilities, they become more comfortable about raising difficult issues in front of the team.

From a practical standpoint CEOs can start to tackle the moose through the rules of engagement that they lay out for the team. At the outset of each meeting they can be explicit about what kind of meeting it is—information sharing, problem solving, decision making, and so on—and what issues can and cannot be raised. That is critical; in the absence of any clear instructions a team's default position is to avoid addressing the difficult issues. The CEO needs to make that clarification a normal part of the team's work process, declaring at the outset what the ground rules are.

Finally, the CEO can design specific ways to aggressively go after the moose, through *moose hunts, roundups,* or whatever name you want to attach to a variety of techniques for shattering the wall of silence. The CEO can call special meetings for the express purpose of addressing one or more of the moose issues. The CEO can deal with these issues in small groups of team members or even one-on-one. In the case of particularly uncomfortable or risky issues, the CEO might call in a third party from outside the organization to help the group confront its moose. Whatever technique is chosen, it is important for the CEO to act aggressively; no moose has ever been known to wander off the table of its own volition.

## Issue 4: Centrifugal Force

Complicating the work of any executive team is a set of factors that exerts an inexorable pull on each team member, a centrifugal force drawing him or her farther and farther apart from other team members and from the team's collective responsibilities. To begin with, each team member, by definition, is an institutional leader in his own right, heading up an operating unit or major staff function. Each holds a job that imposes tremendous demands in terms of time, energy, and attention. Members' interests and areas of expertise differ widely. They feel themselves subject to constant pressure, and time spent with the executive team working on other people's problems is frequently viewed as time that could be better spent on the job at hand.

There is often a very good reason for that kind of single-minded attention to the job. In most instances it is how you perform your own specific job that is the major determinant of rewards or sanctions; it is generally how the boss decides whether to give you a big bonus or an invitation to outplacement. If you are the president of Business Unit X and its performance craters, your career at this organization could well be over. If Business Unit X has a fabulous year, your stock is bound to rise in the eyes of the

CEO and your peers. In fact your unit's performance probably has more to do with your professional standing in the organization than any other single factor.

Although job demands are the biggest force pulling teams apart, there are others. Obviously, geography can present major obstacles to maintaining close contact. Another issue is the relatively weak *task interdependence* that exists at the top of the corporation. In self-directed teams in the factory or office, each team member is directly and clearly dependent on the others for getting the job done. By the time you reach the team at the top, each team member is responsible for running his or her own operation. The situations in which team members are directly dependent on each other for getting their work done are minimal, particularly on the operational side. Finally, executive team members tend to be subject to huge external demands; they spend considerable amounts of time with customers, suppliers, and all the other outside constituencies that come into play in a major organization. What is more, executives at this level often serve on outside boards, both of business and philanthropic organizations, and these time commitments can easily balloon out of control.

Taken collectively, then, the internal and external forces tearing at the fabric of the executive team can be enormous. They are constantly at work, eroding the time, energy, and commitment of each member of the collective entity.

## Implication 4: Reinforce Team Identity

It is essential for the CEO to create conditions under which the team members are spending time together, doing the right work. This can be either formal time in conventional work settings or informal time at off-sites or social events or when traveling together, for example. When Lucent Technologies laid the groundwork for its record-breaking initial public stock offering in early 1996, a good deal of thought went into deciding the composition of each team that went with the road show to sell Lucent's story to potential investors. There was a determined effort to team executives from different parts of the company who normally would not spend much time together; as a result it was amazing to see how many of them gained a new appreciation for colleagues with whom they had worked only superficially in the past. Along the same lines, teams benefit from the value of casual serendipitous encounters. The cohesiveness that results from these routine interactions ought to be a goal in decisions about the physical layout of executive offices, so that the resulting design brings key people together.

In addition the CEO ought to employ rewards as a powerful tool for reinforcing the importance of the team. More and more companies are attaching greater weight to overall corporate performance in determining individual compensation. These rewards have to be large enough to be meaningful. They have to provide tangible, significant compensation for placing the greater good ahead of self-interest. At Corning Inc., for instance, executive team members are rewarded in ways that make it worthwhile for them to sacrifice some of their own resources—and in turn their own unit's performance—in the interests of meeting the company's overall objectives. Token rewards will not do the trick; enlightened self-interest requires more than a hearty handshake and a slap on the back. To be effective the entire executive-level compensation program has to be structured to support the collective goals of the team.

## Issue 5: Appropriate Roles

Assuming the executive team members have been convinced to devote the necessary time and attention to their responsibilities as a team, there is still the problem of figuring out precisely what defines appropriate participation. We are referring here to participation beyond mere physical presence at the table. In one situation after another we have witnessed confusion and frustration on the part of team members who are totally in the dark about the role they are expected to play once they are at the table.

On one level team members are trying to discern their proper roles in the context of the politics, interpersonal dynamics, and power distribution we have described. They often feel they are in the dark about what kind of behavior the CEO and the other team members will consider acceptable. What are the real boundaries for argument, dissent, pointed questioning, and direct conflict? How will the CEO and team members react to any attempt to exert leadership or overt influence? How passive are team members expected to be? In the absence of clear signals, team members will tend to hang back and lie in the weeds because the potential cost of overstepping some unstated boundary is so incredibly high.

A second level of ambiguity is uncertainty about agenda items. One of the most serious problems we see crop up time and time again on executive teams is a basic misunderstanding about the nature of the work on the table, resulting in ambiguous roles and inappropriate participation. This can and does happen in teams at every level, but again, the stakes are infinitely higher in the executive team.

Think of it this way. In any team situation virtually all the items that show up on an agenda can fit into one of a very few categories. The same holds true for the executive team's agenda as well. We describe the categories as follows:

- *Giving information.* Someone in a leadership position—the CEO, COO, or CFO, for example, briefs the team on monthly or quarterly performance results.
- *Getting information.* Conversely, the CEO might be putting together a presentation for the board and asks team members for their input regarding major achievements and failures for the past year.
- *Making a decision.* As we will explain shortly, there are different ways teams can make decisions, depending on the relative roles the CEO lays out for himself or herself and the team. Regardless of the type of decision involved, some of the team's work inevitably falls into this category.
- *Solving problems.* In some cases the team has to wrestle with an issue before members are ready to make a decision. First, members have to go through the work of identifying problems, causes, alternative solutions, and possible ramifications.
- *"Chewing over."* In some situations the CEO or other team member brings to the table some issue just to toss out for comment and discussion. The person is not necessarily looking for any decision; he would just like to benefit from the collective insights and perspectives of the rest of the team.

In each of these situations team members are expected to play very different roles. Sometimes, they might be expected to simply listen and occasionally ask questions for purposes of clarification. At other times they might be expected to articulate a strongly held point of view. What happens when people are confused about the nature of the work on the table? They may engage the CEO in debate or start offering divergent opinions when all the CEO wants is for them to sit and listen. Or they may hold back and seem stupefyingly passive at a time when the CEO is looking for ideas and alternative opinions.

The confusion, frustration, and occasional anger that these misunderstandings create show up more dramatically at the executive team level than anywhere else. In some executive teams the ambiguity about roles, exacerbated by political and interpersonal dynamics that permeate this group, leads to wholesale reticence to become involved and risk crossing the line with an autocratic CEO. At the other end of the scale some CEOs think the way to engage the team is to disengage themselves and "just be one of the guys." They mistakenly confuse participation with a lack of leadership. Effective participation does not magically happen on its own; a leadership vacuum tends to be filled by pointless noise and aimless activity. Rather than sitting back and letting events follow their own course, the CEO should be thinking about how to structure the team's processes in order to invite broad, active, and meaningful participation.

## Implication 5: Clarify Team Processes and Roles

The key to generating purposeful participation is for the CEO to make sure everyone is absolutely clear about how the team will operate, what kinds of decisions it will make, and what roles each member will be expected to play. This is not a new concept; it has been discussed, literally, for decades (Tannenbaum and Schmidt, 1958). Both research and experience illustrate that within teams, not all decisions should be made the same way (Vroom, 1976); consequently, we frequently counsel CEOs to be extremely careful about how they go about making decisions in the team setting, because different kinds of decisions will demand different decision-making processes.

In general the CEO and the team will encounter four different decision modes. Some decision making is *unilateral:* the CEO will make the decision on his own and then, in a timely manner, share with the team the decision and the reasoning behind it. The second kind of decision making is *consultative:* the leader seeks input from the team but makes the final decision alone. The third form of decision making is *consensus:* the CEO participates as a team member rather than team leader, and the group works toward a collective decision. The final form of decision making is *delegation:* others are empowered to make the decision as long as this process clearly falls within the CEO's comfort zone.

It is not enough for CEOs merely to recognize these different kinds of decisions; they need to be absolutely clear with their teams about what kind of decision is on the table and the ground rules for getting it resolved. Jamie Houghton, the retired chairman of Corning, used to be very specific with his executive team. He would announce at the outset of a discussion that the matter on the table was a "Type 1" decision, for example, and the team members would know immediately whether they were being asked to help make a decision or simply understand one that Houghton would make on his own. Similarly, during key episodes of corporate decision making, Jack Creighton, the CEO of Weyerhaeuser Company, has made a point of being extremely explicit about the kinds of issues on the agenda and about his role and team members' roles in reaching critical decisions. The clearer he has been up front, the more productive the team has been, both from their standpoint and from Creighton's.

One key to maintaining clarity in the process, as demonstrated by Houghton's technique, is to develop a common language system. It really does not matter what terms are used, as long as everyone in the room knows what the terms mean and is thus completely clear about what kind of work the team is about to do and what role it is expected to play.

A final note: the team's role in making decisions should never be allowed to become a moose on the table. CEOs should create a situation in which team members feel comfortable about stepping forward and asking the CEO to clarify precisely what kind of decisions are on the agenda.

## Issue 6: Dancing Bears

It is practically unavoidable that the executive team periodically becomes a stage for all kinds of performances. Invariably, one of its functions is to act as a review committee, the place where other managers and teams come to present their cases for new projects or expanded budgets or simply to share information and provide updates and status reports. Ideally, these ought to be working sessions in which the executive team extracts necessary information and acts accordingly.

That is what ought to happen. Unfortunately, the opportunity to perform in front of the organization's most influential audience is too much for most people to pass up. As a result, the executive team is treated to an endless spectacle of *dog and pony shows,* carefully staged presentations marked by posturing, positioning, and an obsession with scoring points rather than solving problems and making decisions.

Moreover the most shameless performances tend to come from certain members of the executive team. Like dancing bears in a circus, conditioned by the promise of fresh meat, they lumber into the center ring and go through the predictable and decidedly ungraceful motions of throwing their weight around rather than conducting themselves as thoughtful and deliberative senior managers. Some feel compelled to show the CEO how tough and incisive they can be in questioning the unfortunate supplicants who come before the group. Because most teams frown upon outright confrontation between senior executives, competitors within the team often play out their conflict through surrogates. Even though a team member might be reluctant to launch an open attack on a peer, he will gleefully rip into that colleague's subordinate who has the misfortune to come before the committee. Ridiculed and humiliated before the CEO and the team, the proxy becomes the innocent victim of some flanking maneuver in the succession battle.

If you put it all together, it is a fairly ugly picture. The poor unfortunates chosen to make presentations before the committee quickly learn that their only chance for survival is to get into the room, dump their data, keep their heads down, and make a run for it. The fundamental goal is to get out of the room alive. Few are fast enough; even before they have finished the first overhead, the executive shark attack has begun. And the feeding frenzy can easily go on all day.

That may be the extreme scenario, but even more subtle versions of this common conflict are not much less aggressive or less painful to their victims. And the consequence of all this misdirected activity is that gatherings of the organization's most valuable and highly paid executives, people whose time is an incredibly scarce resource, become wasteful exercises in self-aggrandizement, with precious little value created for the organization.

## Implication 6: Leverage the Agenda

For executive teams caught in the grip of dancing bears and shark attacks, the answer is clear: the CEO has to manage the agenda process in ways that ensure the team is engaged in value-added work. The first step in this agenda management is understanding the balance of costs and benefits involved in the team's work.

Assuming that each member of the executive team holds a responsible job that is critical to the organization's performance, there is a serious opportunity cost associated with the time these executives spend with the team. Obviously, there are other things they could be doing, and presumably, the time spent with the team represents time that is not being spent on other important tasks. Some of the things the team members do together as a group are of discernible value; in other cases the value is harder to determine.

The job of the CEO as team leader is to identify how the marginal value of the team members working together is greater than the marginal cost of taking them away from their primary jobs. If the marginal cost is greater than the marginal value, then there is no added value of having them work together. We constantly urge CEOs to weigh this equation, and figure out other ways to accomplish those tasks that offer no added value. Typically, the value-added group tasks concern strategy decisions, major moves involving people, large resource allocation issues, portfolio moves, and issues involving the management of the organization's values and ethics. These are concerns that have to be handled in the executive team setting, with this group of people at the table, and that

cannot be done anywhere else. Issues that fall outside these concerns should be handled outside the group setting, leaving most
of the team members to go back to their offices and do their jobs.

So the first issue involves the content of the agenda. The second issue deals with process—the kinds of work the team is being
asked to do. To some extent process involves the proper balance
of agenda items. If the preponderance of items simply transmit
information, you probably do not need to bring the team together;
just send them the information and eliminate most opportunities
for showboating and dancing bears. If enough items do require
the team to meet, then it is important to employ some strict rules
of engagement. Some examples:

- Limit presentations to no more than twenty minutes.
- Any time the team is being asked to make a decision, require
  the presenter to provide members with background material
  in advance of the meeting, hold that material to a limited
  length, and not repeat it during the live presentation.
- Make the first slide in the presentation the same as the last; in
  other words the discussion is to begin by specifically identifying what form of action the team is being asked to provide.
- Carefully manage the presence of outsiders: hold them to
  strict time limits to avoid grandstanding and to allow for serious deliberations without an audience.

Those are just a few examples of the kinds of rules that can be used
to manage the agenda and the team's process. The critical point is
that this group, more than any other, requires absolute clarity
about the kinds of items on its agenda and how it is going to deal
with them. Just as CEOs should be explicit about the kinds of decisions on the table, they need to set the ground rules for each piece
of business on the agenda. That requires rigorous management of
the agenda, both before and during the meeting.

Someone has to decide who really needs to be present at each
meeting, who will play what role, and what the outcome should be.
At some organizations the CEO designates a staff person to take
responsibility for assembling and managing the agenda prior to
the meeting. CEOs must also decide whether they can adequately
manage the agenda inside the room and still be a full participant

or whether that role too should be delegated to someone else. There is no right or wrong way to handle it; the important point is for the CEO to think through the process in advance and manage it, rather than just letting each meeting take its own course.

## Summary

It is safe to say that over the past ten years or so, the executive team has come into its own right as a valuable component of organizational governance. It has become a more visible and widely accepted feature of the management world (Nadler and Ancona, 1992). That development involves both good news and bad news.

The good news is the steady increase in the active use of these teams. Work that used to be handled unilaterally and arbitrarily by one or two top executives is now being processed by teams, with the advantages of wider input, broader perspective, and greater opportunities for building support among key constituencies.

The bad news, however, is that in too many organizations, the use of executive teams remains haphazard and unproductive. As we have suggested in this chapter, the unique power relationships, membership, and dynamics of the executive team require special roles and processes. In their absence, executive teams can become enormous black holes for senior time, energy, and talent.

In the end it is the CEO who is critical to the team's success. The CEO must seriously pursue his role and responsibility as the designer of the team, its leader in the room, and the shaper of its dynamics outside the room. Beyond that, the CEO must act as the quality assurance officer for the team. If left to their own devices, these teams will invariably run out of gas: their processes will deteriorate, and their dynamics will become dysfunctional. It is up to CEOs to constantly assess what is working and what is not, to bring in a fresh set of eyes when his have gotten too close to an issue and to make the continuous improvements that are vital to the team's continued success.

## Chapter Six

# Performance on the Executive Team
## When to Pull the Trigger

*David A. Nadler*

*Mark B. Nadler*

Picture, if you will, the chief executive officer of a Fortune 500 company slumped over a conference table, holding his head in his hands, anguishing over whether the time had come to pull the plug on one of his most senior executives. "Tell me," he pleaded with us, "is it this hard for everybody?"

Yes, it is.

Of all the complex, sensitive, and stressful issues that confront CEOs, none consumes as much time, generates as much angst, or extracts such a high personal toll as dealing with executive team members who just are not working out. Billion-dollar acquisitions, huge strategic shifts, even decisions to eliminate thousands of jobs—all pale in comparison with the anxiety most CEOs experience when it comes time to decide the fate of their direct reports.

To be sure, there are exceptions. Every once in a while, an executive fouls up so dramatically or is so obviously incapable of carrying out his duties that the CEO's course of action is clear. However, that is rarely the case. More typically, these troublesome situations escalate gradually; early warning signs are either dismissed or overlooked entirely. By the time the problem balloons into a near crisis, the CEO has become deeply invested in making the situation work. He procrastinates, hiding behind a host of superficially sound reasons for avoiding any dramatic action. Meanwhile the cost of inaction mounts each day, exacted in ineffective leadership and lost opportunities.

This issue is so critical because it is so common. Embedded in the unique composition and roles of the executive team are the seeds of failure; it is virtually inevitable that over time a substantial number of the CEO's direct reports will fall by the wayside. The stark truth, as David Kearns of Xerox once said, is that the majority of executive careers end in disappointment. Nowhere is Kearns's observation more poignant than at the executive team level. Of all the ambitious young managers who yearn to become CEOs, only a minuscule number will achieve their ultimate dream. Even among the relative handful who achieve the second tier, only a few possess the rare combination of intelligence, competence, savvy, flexibility, and luck to go out on top, feeling they have achieved their ultimate career goals. The pyramid is awfully slippery; the closer you get to the top, the harder it is to hold on.

There are lots of ways for senior executives to stumble, and poor performance at the top sends ripples, even shock waves, across the enterprise. At this level the performance and behavior of each executive are magnified; one dysfunctional individual can stop the entire executive team in its tracks and wreak havoc throughout the organization. Consequently, decisions about replacing executive team members are highly leveraged, with far-reaching consequences involving thousands of people and perhaps billions of dollars.

Yet despite the far-reaching consequences, the decision by any CEO to remove a direct report is, in the end, intensely personal and invariably painful. This is not a matter of reasoning your way through a strategic problem or even of deciding to lay off thousands of workers halfway around the globe; this is face-to-face recognition of failure by a powerful, successful member of the inner circle, quite possibly a long-time colleague. There is no way to make these decisions easy; our intent in this chapter is to suggest ways to make them somewhat more rational. There are processes and techniques that can help the CEO deal with executives who are in deep trouble and ways to sort out the conflicting considerations that inevitably muddle the final decision. When the time comes to pull the trigger, however, there are no slick processes or decision trees that can take the place of character and courage.

The process typically plays out along these lines (see Figure 6.1). At some point the CEO recognizes there is a serious problem with a direct report. Those problems come in all shapes and sizes, and we will describe some of the common warning signs that something is seriously amiss. These signs are merely symptoms; the next step is for the CEO, either alone or with help, to spend some time diagnosing the source of the problems, and to that end we offer a diagnostic framework for determining where the problem really lies. At that point the CEO reaches the first fork in the road; he must decide whether the problem is fatal—a decision rarely reached at this early stage—or whether it is coachable. If coaching proves successful, that is fine. If it does not, then the CEO faces the ultimate decision. We describe some of the specific reasons that CEOs fall back on as they put off their decision, and then we explain why many of those reasons are not quite as compelling as they sometimes seem. Finally, we offer some closing thoughts on things to keep in mind while performing the deed and on ways to reduce the chances of encountering similar crises in the future.

## Executive Teams and the Seeds of Failure

Our approach to the replacement of senior executives is grounded in some basic notions about the composition and role of the executive team. To begin with, it is essential to appreciate the complexity of senior-level jobs and the awesome consequences that can befall both the team and the organization when a top executive proves to be deficient. Beyond that, it is essential to understand why the composition of the executive team virtually guarantees that some of the team's members will fail.

For purposes of this discussion the central point is that each member of the executive team is required to play multiple, complex, and essential roles and to play them in concert with the CEO and with each other. That is why it is so difficult—and at the same time so crucial—to create and maintain the right cast of senior characters. Basically, each member is expected to play these seven roles:

1. *Individual contributor,* providing specialized analysis, perspectives and technical expertise to the rest of the team

**Figure 6.1. A Thought Process for Executive Replacement.**

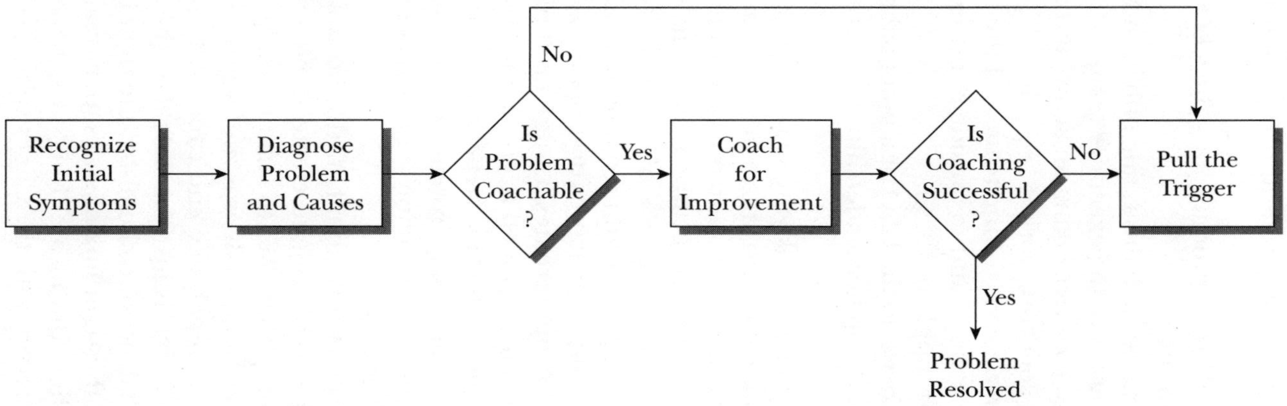

2. *Organizational leader,* holding responsibility for the performance of an enterprise segment and representing that segment's interests in the corporate setting

3. *Supporter of the CEO,* promulgating the CEO's agenda both publicly and privately

4. *Colleague and peer,* demonstrating public and private support for fellow members of the executive team

5. *Executive team member,* taking an active and appropriate role in the team's collective work

6. *External representative* of the team and the organization to the workforce at large and to outside constituencies such as customers and suppliers

7. *Potential successor* to the CEO or a potential member of the next generation of top-tier leadership

With each team member playing so many vital roles, just one ineffective, unqualified, or disruptive member can damage the team and the organization in countless ways. The consequences can range from an impotent executive team to the breakdown of a key operating unit to the alienation of essential customers. Within the organization the CEO's continued tolerance of a senior executive who is failing to meet objectives or is openly flaunting the organization's stated values creates a huge credibility problem. The longer the situation is allowed to go on, the less people believe the CEO is really walking the talk. Depending on the situation the cost of retaining an inadequate executive team member can be measured in millions or even billions of dollars or a stalled attempt at organizational change.

If you stop to think about it, the odds are heavily stacked against a CEO who is trying to create an effective executive team; the equation simply involves too many variables. It would be hard enough if all you had to do was find a group of people each of whom has the competence and capacity to satisfactorily fill all seven roles. But that is just the start. For the team to succeed it requires both balance and chemistry: the right balance of skills and expertise and the right mix of styles, personalities, and relationships. To further complicate things, the balance and chemistry have to be consistent with the CEO's strategic agenda and leadership style.

## The Realities of Staffing

That is a lot to ask. If you as the CEO were starting out in a perfect world—with a clean slate, a bottomless pool of qualified candidates, and all the information you wanted about each of those candidates—you might have a chance of assembling the perfect team. But you do not; no CEO does. And even if you could put together the all-time executive all-star team, it would only be a matter of time before the shifting dynamics of the situation—changes in your strategic environment as well as the playing out of relationships within the team—would throw the equation out of kilter.

In reality the unique circumstances that shape the composition of executive teams invariably lead to the replacement of a substantial portion of their members. If you look at just about any executive team, you will find members who through no fault of their own or of anyone else fit into at least one of these high-risk categories:

*Holdovers.* Unless you are talking about a start-up company or there has been a complete house cleaning, it is probable that new CEOs will inherit all or part of their predecessors' executive teams. Every CEO wants the chance to form a team to fit his own agenda, priorities, personality, and leadership style. It is unreasonable to expect that the old team will remain intact; to the contrary, it is more reasonable to assume that a majority of these teams will not last for any significant period of time.

*Overachievers.* Because executive team roles are unique, past performance is an unusually unreliable predictor of future performance. Time after time, people who have distinguished themselves in jobs just below the executive team level are bewildered and overwhelmed by the complexities, nuances, and conflicting demands of their new senior positions. Day in, day out, they are asked to wear different hats, satisfy competing constituencies, and manage delicate relationships. Tossed into the fray, some people quickly demonstrate that they have been promoted past their level of optimal performance. It is not a matter of needing more time, experience, or coaching; they just do not have what it takes.

*Tryouts.* If all your executive team slots were filled by safe, senior people with long track records, then you as CEO would be failing in your responsibility to develop the next generation of leadership. Long-term succession management requires that you occasionally take some long shots and give the most promising members of the next generation the chance to grow and prove themselves in the big leagues. That means that some people will join the team with the clear understanding that they are not going to walk in on day one as fully functioning members of the team, operating at optimal levels. It also means that some appointments are deliberate gambles: tryouts, by definition, carry with them the probability that some candidates will not make it. When you toss a bunch of youngsters into the grown-ups' pool, most will tread water and stay afloat until someone teaches them the fine points of swimming, but others will thrash around and start sinking out of sight. It is the CEO's job to figure out which ones are drowning and pull them out of the deep end before it is too late.

*Outsiders.* In one company after another you hear the same complaint: "We've got plenty of good managers, but very few who are ready for the top jobs." The accelerating pace of change and the intensified competitive demands being felt in every industry are exacerbating the problem of insufficient bench strength. As a result, more and more organizations are recruiting executive team members from the outside. That is understandable; typically, outsiders bring new skills, knowledge, mind-sets, and ideas about culture. However, outsiders also carry enormous risks, far greater than those associated with internal promotions. For a host of reasons— inadequate information, less-than-candid references, the highly polished interview skills normally exhibited by executives at this level—buyers can never really be sure what they are getting. It usually takes from twelve to eighteen months on the job to accurately assess a senior-level hire. By that time, according to our tracking of hires at several large corporations, it is likely that no more than 25 to 30 percent will have lived up to the company's initial expectations; 30 percent will fall short but be good enough to retain in some capacity, and roughly 40 percent should be shown the door.

*Dinosaurs.* These are executives who are perfectly adequate until things change—and they cannot change with them. In every situation we have seen involving large-scale organizational change, there are executive team members who are smart, capable, competent people but who, for one reason or another, just cannot make it in the changed environment. Some violently disagree with the direction of the change. Some find it impossible to manage in the new environment. Some wrestle unsuccessfully with new structures and processes. And some whose performance was acceptable in the past simply lack the higher gear required to meet the new more demanding requirements. For whatever reason, organizational change inevitably results in executive team change.

It is crucial for CEOs to understand these powerful forces that contribute to the high rate of executive team turnover. When it comes to staffing executive teams, there is no zero-defect model. By virtue of team design and task content, it is inevitable that some people just will not work out. Moreover, this is a situation in which attempts at error-free staffing are tantamount to staffing in error; safe choices will not produce standouts.

It is also important to remember that executive team members are rarely innocent victims shanghaied into performing at the corporate heights. Most of the time, they eagerly seek out these jobs, and ought to be mindful of the risks involved in scampering up to the high wire. Time and again, people become prisoners of their own ambition and oversell themselves. It might be hard to believe, but there really are people who have the courage and candor to say, "I'm really not ready for that job." To be sure, they are few and far between, but they ought to remind us that we each share in the responsibility for our own career development.

So CEOs need to differentiate in their own minds between mismatches caused by circumstances and failures caused by their own mistakes. As we discuss shortly, it is tremendously important for CEOs to confront and deal with their personal feelings about these instances of failure, and that is impossible if every failure, no matter what its cause, becomes a source of debilitating guilt.

## Recognition: Understanding the Warning Signs

The truth is that few senior executives perform their jobs flawlessly. Considering the inherent complexity of these jobs, it is foolish to think that every executive will perform each of the distinct roles with equal grace and skill. Ideally, each member was recruited to the team because of the special ingredients he would add to the mix; presumably, each person's strengths will lie in different areas.

The first hard decision for the CEO is differentiating between normal weaknesses and fatal flaws. At some point the CEO becomes plagued by the recurring question, Is this guy going to work out, or should I start thinking about a replacement? Obviously, there are not any pat answers—but there are warning signs that should alert the CEO that it is time to move the problem to a red-hot front burner. These signs include

- *Performance.* Start with the basics. Are the jobs of the executives in question getting done? Are their units achieving their goals? Assuming CEOs have been clear with these executives about their responsibilities, are they meeting them? Are they demonstrating the managerial skills and technical expertise required by their jobs?
- *Internal consistency.* One measure of performance is to look at how successfully executives are achieving goals imposed by others. A second measure is internal consistency: are these executives meeting the goals they set for themselves? It is one thing to argue that imposed goals are unrealistic; it is quite another to fall short of what you came up with yourself.
- *Shifting the blame.* This is one of the clearest warning signs. You can generally assume you have a serious problem on your hands when executives start blaming all their shortcomings on external forces beyond their control—the sagging economy, wily competitors, fickle customers, undependable suppliers, uncooperative colleagues, surly employees.
- *Denial.* This is a major, major problem. If executives keep insisting they are going to make their numbers when all the objective indicators are to the contrary, you know you have something to worry about. The same goes for a refusal to acknowledge the obvious existence of problems in relationships—with the CEO, with peers, with subordinates.
- *Signals from peers.* The members of the executive team generally know when one of their peers is fouling up. Yet in most organizations the prevailing culture discourages them from openly criticizing a colleague. A CEO who suspects there is a problem should start watching for subtle messages in the form of body language, behavior, and language. Even when people do not intend to send signals, they do.

Those warning signs can help. At the end of the day, however, it comes down to a judgment call by the CEO. Like lots of major decisions—and more than most—this one comes from the gut. By this point in their careers, CEOs have probably developed some strong instincts about people, and it is important to pay attention to those internal warning signs. Constantly waking up at 3 A.M. worrying about a particular executive is usually a good sign that something is definitely wrong. Here is another: try doing a dry run on a scene in which you are explaining to an executive why he is being removed from the team. Sit down and write out the specific reasons you would give. The resulting insight can be powerful. "When I look at this list," said one CEO, "I can't believe I've been ignoring this for so long." Other CEOs role-playing the scene have stopped suddenly, surprised by how "right" the scene feels. That is a pretty good indication that it is time to surface the problems and get serious about dealing with them.

It is rare at this stage for CEOs to make a final decision that problem executives are beyond help and that salvage efforts will be futile. More often, these warning signals point to situations that are headed downhill but have not yet reached bottom. Yet the truth is that CEOs who sit and wait for conclusive information before starting to act have waited too long. Given the amount of time generally invested in trying to coach an executive back to success and, if that proves unsuccessful, finding a replacement, a CEO who procrastinates until the situation is irreversible has probably squandered six months to a year of valuable time.

## Diagnosis and Coaching

All of these warning signs—the observable performance and behavior and the CEO's personal apprehension—are merely indicators of symptoms. Before the CEO can rationally decide on the next step, it is essential to diagnose the problem and search for the real causes in order to determine where the problem lies and whether there is any reasonable way to fix it.

Moreover, assuming that the CEO's strong preference is to provide the problem executive with coaching and remediation that will help the executive succeed—rather than summarily dumping that person—then diagnosis is the starting point. One way to attack the problem is to start by assembling all the available information—both empirical and anecdotal—that describes the executive's performance and behavior in these seven diagnostic areas (see Figure 6.2):

1. The executive's relationships with his own team of direct reports
2. The executive's effectiveness within the organization he leads
3. The executive's relationships with peers on the executive team
4. The executive's relationship with his immediate boss (the CEO or possibly the COO)
5. The executive's performance of the strategic and technical elements of the job
6. The executive's performance of external responsibilities toward customers, suppliers, the investment community, governmental agencies, and so on
7. The executive's personal issues, such as career goals, ambition, self-confidence, and family relationships

The goal at this point is to look for patterns of problems. Sometimes the diagnosis turns up patterned inconsistencies—for example, the executive's relationships with subordinates are uniformly horrendous, but relationships with peers and bosses present no apparent problems. All such patterns are important indicators of particular problems and point the way to areas where coaching might be productive.

If the diagnosis is done well, the results will bring the CEO to the first major fork in the road. Sometimes the choice is clear: the executive's fundamental problems may simply be uncoachable.

You can coach technique. You can coach certain behavioral patterns—how people deal with subordinates, for example, or how they operate within teams. You can coach technical expertise to a certain extent, and you can use coaching to bring someone up to speed on basic knowledge. At the end of the day, however, you cannot coach character, integrity, or basic intellectual capacity. You cannot coach a fundamental change in personality. And you certainly cannot coach someone out of pathology.

So at this point the CEO faces two critical questions. First, the fork in the road: does the diagnosis indicate that the executive's

**Figure 6.2. Executive Coaching Framework.**

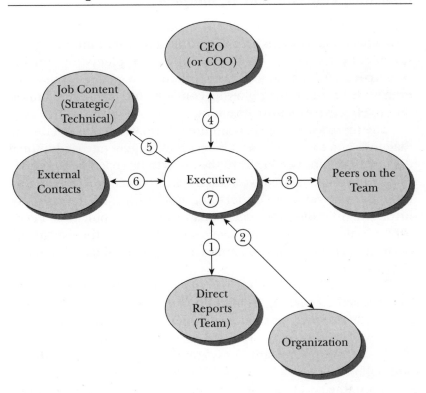

problems lie in coachable areas? Second, what results can be expected from coaching, and over what period of time? In other words, what is the maximum return that can be expected on the investment of time, effort, and lost opportunities? In the final analysis, given the best of coaching, how good can this person ultimately be—and is that result worth the time and effort it may take to get there?

Those are very, very tough questions. Unless the situation is a total disaster or the problems involve issues of integrity or intelligence that are clearly beyond coaching, the inclination at this point—as it probably should be in most cases—is that the organization and the CEO personally are so heavily invested in the executive's success that some period of coaching seems reasonable.

## Coaching: Concepts and Techniques

It is not our intent here to present a comprehensive guide to executive coaching. There is a considerable amount of literature that specifically addresses such coaching and plenty of outside resources available to any CEO who chooses to go that route. However, we have found the following concepts and techniques important to effective executive coaching.

The first idea is to go beyond the information collected during diagnosis and to collect—and if necessary to generate—additional data that pertain specifically to the areas to be coached. Generally that requires the active involvement of the executive who is being coached, who needs to understand how critical his constructive involvement in the process will be to its ultimate outcome. Peers, subordinates, and others with special insights into the executive's performance and behavior should also be debriefed as the coaching proceeds.

The second idea is to specifically identify who will be responsible for active coaching. It might be the CEO, another executive, an outside resource, or some combination of all three. Whoever is involved should be in a position where he can observe the executive in actual working situations and provide real-time feedback and skill practice.

Third, the coaching has to include benchmarks and deadlines. At critical steps along the way specific indicators must demonstrate how much progress is being made and how quickly. If the exercise is to be of any use, these indicators cannot be moving targets; they must define reasonable expectations of improvement. Coaching is like any other business process—it must include ways to measure progress and improvement.

Finally, it is important for the CEO to involve the board in the situation. There are several reasons. First, it is in the interest of the CEO to acknowledge to the board that he is aware of a serious problem and is taking steps to deal with it. Second, in some situations this group can be a helpful sounding board, and certain members might be in a position to provide some coaching. Finally, by making a commitment to the board that the situation will be resolved one way or another by a certain date, the CEO is forced to address the issue head on. We have worked with CEOs who had put off dealing with executive team problems for years but later said they wished they had given themselves an artificial deadline by committing to one in discussions with their boards.

## The Moment of Truth: Making the Tough Decision

The good news is that coaching sometimes works. There are plenty of success stories, which is one reason why coaching remains such an attractive and humane alternative to forcing executives to walk the plank at the first sign of trouble. The bad news is that coaching sometimes fails; with each passing month there is abundant evidence that progress is either elusive or so minimal as to erase any hopes of getting the executive up to the required speed by the established deadline.

Yet even in those situations many CEOs will look for reasons to procrastinate—to lower the bar and ignore the deadlines. Some will go to practically any lengths to avoid pulling the trigger. We have identified several reasons why so many smart, capable chief executives will go to such incredible lengths to avoid removing one of their direct reports:

*Narcissism.* CEOs, as a class of human being, possess an unusually high need to be loved, admired, and respected by everyone within their sphere of influence. That is an important component of their personality and a big part of what drove them to become a CEO in the first place. For these people, face-to-face firings are particularly tough; they are well aware that when you sit across a desk from someone and hand out a pink slip, the person is unlikely to respond with love, admiration, and respect. Not surprisingly, these situations are particularly difficult for CEOs who have been promoted from within the organization. In all likelihood the senior people they are replacing were, just a short time ago, their own peers and colleagues. There is no getting around it; these are painful, sometimes devastating situations. That is why CEOs recruited from the outside are much more likely to conduct wholesale housecleaning of the executive team if that is what the situation calls for.

*The big fall.* The CEO is well aware that he is dealing with highly successful people. This may be the first major failure they have ever experienced in their adult lives. The shock of that first failure, compounded by the stakes involved—money, security, professional reputation, career expectations—all suggest that this will be a crushing blow to the executive, making the CEO even more reluctant to lower the boom. There is no way to ignore the consequences for the individual, but it is equally important to keep in mind, once again, that these are not innocent bystanders. The vast majority of executives at this level actively sought higher and higher jobs, knowing that with each successive promotion both the benefits and risks increase proportionately.

*The failed rescue.* Many CEOs entertain savior fantasies, overblown and unrealistic notions of their own ability to turn people around and fix hopeless situations. They truly believe that skillful managers should be able to help their people get better. Perhaps if they had given the person better guidance, stronger direction, and more effecting coaching, none of this would have happened. As they lie awake at night, anguishing over the decision, they are troubled by the thought, "If I can't make this work, then maybe I'm really not as good as I think I am." The truth is that any manager can do only so much. Executives are the product of years of personal and professional experiences that shape their personality, behavior, skills, and management style. For CEOs to think they can personally reverse years of training and experience in a relatively short time is not only unreasonable but, in the words of one CEO, "the height of arrogance."

*The burden of guilt.* Beyond the coaching issue, CEOs sometimes feel immense guilt about the situation in general, blaming themselves for poor judgment in selecting the person in the first place. Somehow they should have been sufficiently prescient to know the person would not work out. Now, because of their poor judgment, the executive has given up a good job and secure future with his old company, uprooted his family, turned his life upside down—and all for nothing. That scenario ignores several important considerations. First, the executive acted as a free agent, knowing in advance that any move to a new job or a new company invariable involves a certain degree of risk. Second, it implies that every appointment to the executive team should be a sure bet—and as we described earlier, the very nature of the team compels the CEO to take risks.

*The rusty sword.* One of the benefits of being the CEO is that you can delegate some of the more distasteful chores to other people. That includes firings. After a while CEOs simply get out of practice; the longer they go without actually dealing with these situations face to face, the harder it becomes to contemplate doing it. The unavoidable fact is that some executive responsibilities cannot be delegated, and dealing with dysfunction within the executive team is one of them.

*Kremlin watching.* Forced departures from the executive team— even when cloaked in ambiguous, even misleading announcements—are highly visible and closely followed, both inside the organization and among concerned external constituencies. A single departure is a major event; two departures within a relatively short time is a trend, prompting people to speculate freely about instability and discord at the top of the organization. Before long, however, people realize that the world has not turned upside down: no one is being shot in the parking lot at dawn, they still have the same job and the same boss they had last week, and things get back to normal. Not only do people realize that the appearance of instability was not as serious as it seemed, but as the CEO puts in place a carefully chosen series of replacements, accompanied by deliberately managed communications, he sends clear and powerful messages, internally and externally, about how the organization is changing and about the style of behavior and level of performance that will be demanded of senior executives.

*The essential link.* CEOs are often concerned about the impact of senior-level dismissals or reassignments on outside constituencies. Executive team members sometimes cultivate close ties with outside groups, such as customers, community leaders, the press, or the financial community; they come to be viewed as essential links to the outside world. Fear of a backlash has prevented more than one CEO from replacing a problematic subordinate who was the darling of the stock analysts. It is not unusual to hear things like, "I know we should get rid of Tom, but the analysts would go crazy; he is worth more than two dollars a share." To be sure, these are justifiable concerns. Yet, somehow, large organizations always seem to weather the departure of these important figures when they finally occur, and the ramifications never turn out to be quite as severe as everyone had feared; the anticipation is almost always worse than the aftermath. The CEO has to keep in mind that the outside constituencies see only a small part of the organization and the executive's role in it and are poorly positioned to weigh the executive's overall value to the enterprise. Additionally, the CEO has to separate the reality of the executive's outside influence from the exaggerated impressions some executives work so hard to create.

*The irreplaceable cog.* This is the internal version of the essential link. Over time certain people become enshrouded in corporate myths that cloak them in an aura of near-invincibility. People come to believe the place will grind to a halt without the special talents of these chosen few. Often these are executives who have some particular technical expertise or a unique knowledge of "how things really get done." Again, CEOs are extremely reluctant to replace these people. Yet the truth is that in all but a rare handful of cases, their talent or expertise is never unique or as crucial as it seemed. Indeed, some executives are particularly adept at spreading the notion that they are irreplaceable, but once they are gone, somehow or other the company survives. In fact it often turns out that the sales force or information technology group or production operation runs better once the executive is removed and rational business processes replace a disorganized cult of personality.

*The incomplete file.* The failure of coaching is a condition, not an event. Even though they would make life easier, situations in which definitive empirical data clearly demonstrate that an executive should be sacked are the exception rather than the rule. CEOs who keep hanging back, waiting for more and more information, will almost certainly wait too long. By the time that kind of information surfaces, the executive in question will have caused serious measurable damage to the organization.

*The empty bench.* This is an all-too-common problem: as much as the CEO would like to get rid of someone, there is no obvious replacement in sight. Given the high stakes involved in putting the wrong person in the job, there is a tendency to hang on to the devil you know rather than gambling on the devil you don't. Yet at some point CEOs have to ask how long they, the team, and the organization can continue to tolerate inadequate performance or disruptive behavior. Granted, hiring from the outside is a gamble—but inherent in gambling is the potential for a big win. Drawing to an inside straight is risky—but does it make more sense to keep playing a weak hand that you know is a loser?

We do not mean to underestimate the complexity of the choices facing a CEO when it comes time to make the final decision. Obviously, these are difficult decisions that must be undertaken soberly and with all due deliberation. What we are suggesting, however, is that in the final analysis there are relatively few real limitations on the CEO's capacity to act; by and large, the constraints are intensely personal and self-imposed. Moreover, the consequences of acting are rarely as dire as they seem at first glance; to the contrary, they often pale in comparison with the consequences of failing to act.

A few years ago we worked with the president of a major corporation who had put off firing a disruptive but highly influential member of his team for more than a year and a half. Finally, we asked him to pull out his wallet, write a check for the full amount in his checking account, and make a wager with us that his subordinate would prove to be successful within six months. He told us we were crazy.

"Then why is it," we asked him, "that you're afraid to bet $10,000 of your own money that this guy is going to make it, but you're willing to bet millions and millions of dollars of the shareholders' money on the same thing? What are you seeing that makes you think, after all this time, that things are going to get better? Where are the signs of progress? What gives you that kind of confidence?"

There are always reasons to put off the decision: you need just a little more information, you want to wait for the results of one more quarter, you want to provide a little more time to develop a prospective replacement. Many CEOs have told us in hindsight that they came up with all kinds of rationalizations to put off a decision they knew was inevitable. In the end all they succeeded in doing was hurting both the executive team and the organization and also prolonging the agony of a stressed-out executive who was left twisting in wind, awaiting his fate. In reality no decision is, in effect, a decision to continue accepting an unacceptable situation and a decision to put off the inevitable process of finding a replacement.

## Pulling the Trigger: Actions and Implications

Again, our intent here is not to provide a step-by-step manual on how to perform dismissals. However, certain actions and implications are particularly pertinent to removing people at the executive team level.

The first issue is to decide whether the executive to be replaced should be reassigned or removed. This is one of the issues that makes the executive team unique. In most situations when people are not working out in a particular job but still can contribute to the organization, they can be reassigned to a different boss or to some other unit without subjecting them to public humiliation. When people leave the executive team, there is nowhere to go but down or out.

And the tendency is to assume that executives have to go. The metaphors that crop up during these situations can be fairly brutal, as in "never leave the wounded on the battlefield." Yet there is an undeniable logic to this view; given the personality of the executives involved and the circumstances leading up to their removal from the executive team, the obvious next step may be to have them escorted out the door as quickly as possible. Relegating them to less prestigious positions, where they will seethe and become lightning rods for dissent, makes no sense.

Other cases, however, are much more difficult. Generally, CEOs think they are doing executives a favor by asking them to leave the company, saving them from the humiliation of accepting a lesser job. Yet some people prefer to stay. Many of those who fail at the top are feeling frustrated and perplexed because they are in so far over their heads. Although it might not be their first reaction, they are actually relieved when someone else makes the decision for them and removes them from the job they knew they could not handle. And after they get over the initial shock and disappointment, they are perfectly happy to stay with the organization and do a lower-level job that plays to their strengths. For the CEO the issue in this case is not to make choices for people but to give them sufficient time to clear their heads and think about the options.

A related issue is what we describe as the *paradox of improved performance.* Our firm worked with a corporation where the vice chairman became totally obsessed with succeeding the chairman. Over time he engaged in so much posturing and positioning that he became totally ineffective. Finally, the chairman sat him down, explained that things were not working out, and gave him six months to find another job. At that point his performance soared; he probably enjoyed the most productive six months he had ever experienced with the company. Had the CEO been wrong to fire him? No. As long as he had stayed with that company, he would have driven himself to go after the top job, and his dysfunctional behavior would have continued. As soon as he was freed from that obsession, he stopped playing games and just did his job.

We see that situation repeated time and time again. People who have felt pressured, cornered, topped-out—whatever the source of their stress—instantly do better when relieved of the pressures inherent in their executive team positions. That does not mean CEOs should reconsider their decisions or second-guess themselves; instead, it should be viewed as concrete evidence that these people were in the wrong job under the wrong set of circumstances.

The third issue is the need to carefully manage the communications surrounding the removal of an executive team member. This situation has been complicated in recent years by the fear of litigation that could arise from any communications that are seen as harming someone's reputation and limiting their career opportunities.

Unfortunately, fear of such litigation, compounded by common standards of corporate civility, has resulted in a tradition of dismissal announcements that completely obfuscate the real situation. Rarely is anyone fired; instead, executives leave "to pursue other interests." In the absence of hard information people create their own fantasies—often involving dark conspiracies and shadowy motives—and reach their own conclusions about what really happened. That is a major problem. It would be bad enough if senior management were merely missing the opportunity to send strong messages about corporate standards and expectations. Even worse is that in the absence of any message, people can easily construct bizarre scenarios that carry messages the absolute reverse of what management wants to convey.

In the current litigious environment, management's options are limited. One approach is to design communications that send implicit messages. Not everyone deserves a tearful send-off with the CEO's sincere gratitude for years of faithful service and best wishes for future endeavors. These days, a terse message that someone is leaving—period—makes it clear to everyone that this executive is not sailing away on the victory barge. Second, after obtaining legal advice as to what is permissible, the CEO should explain as much to the executive team. That might seem obvious, but it is amazing how common it is for senior executives to be left without a clue about why one of their colleagues has vanished. In too many organizations it is a topic that is just not open to discussion.

## Avoiding Future Crises

In the aftermath of an executive dismissal there is often a good deal of soul searching. The more reflective CEOs ask themselves questions such as, How did this happen? Where did I go wrong? How did I let things get to this point? Is it possible to avoid this happening again?

Obviously, there are no guarantees of success at any level and certainly not at the top. For all the reasons we have discussed, it is inherently impossible to make fool-proof appointments to the executive team or to think that once the right team is in place that all its members will continue to succeed until they become CEO or reach retirement age. Error-free staffing is not a realistic goal. Instead, the CEO should be looking for ways to avoid letting troublesome situations simmer in the background until they suddenly explode as full-blown crises.

And yet, in one organization after another, the tools and techniques used to monitor performance, identify problems early on, and take steps to rectify them seem for some reason to apply everywhere in the organization—except in the executive team. It is not uncommon for companies to use formal performance appraisals everywhere in the organization—except in the executive team. Somehow, there is an assumption that the CEO is so familiar with the team members and every aspect of their performance that he has no need to use the same assessment techniques that are required of every manager and team leader in the organization. We have worked with companies where the members of the executive team—some of whom have been in their jobs for years—have never received a single formal performance review from the CEO.

The most obvious way to keep serious situations from sneaking up is to make a commitment to continual assessment. There is simply no substitute for it. The CEO has to employ a wide array of techniques—surveys, 360-degree feedback tools, outside consultants, frequent appraisals tied to specific objectives and deadlines—in order to stay on top of the situation. The work of senior executives is simply too important for poor performance to go unnoticed—and unaddressed—for any significant period of time.

## Summary

Despite all the attention the press gives to "killer CEOs" and the "Chain Saw Al" school of management, the truth is that when it comes to their own direct reports, most CEOs procrastinate and take too little action. Do not misunderstand; we are not advocating ritual public executions just for the sake of showing stock analysts how tough you can be. To the contrary, we propose that CEOs have to look at executive team staffing from a deliberate standpoint, one that acknowledges the risks, the high probability of mismatches, the changing demands, and the shifting dynamics that are inherent in these unique teams. Therefore CEOs have to accept as a given that the team's composition ought to keep changing over time. And the consequence of this given is that CEOs should view their own role in identifying and implementing these changes as an integral part of their job, not as an aberration.

Once CEOs understand this inherent instability in the composition of the executive team, they should put into place the assessment processes and support systems that will help them manage a perpetually fluid situation. These tools are necessary and

helpful—but only in the right hands. In the end there is no substitute for managerial courage. The CEO, and only the CEO, is the
one who must assess all the information, weigh the odds, objectively balance the interests of the individual against the demands
of the enterprise, and then act—swiftly, humanely, and decisively.

## Chapter Seven

# The Importance of Trust

*A. Elise Walton*

The executive team can be a make-or-break resource for the chief executive officer. A team that works together effectively and collaboratively amplifies and extends the leadership of the CEO. It communicates messages better and aligns organizational activity for more effective outcomes. It minimizes waste, makes more out of less, and achieves that elusive goal of synergy.

Yet for many of the clients my colleagues and I have worked with, the executive team is a source of frustration and failure. A lack of trust seems to create much of the frustration, which can be sensed in these comments from CEOs and senior executives:

> There is still a severe lack of trust within the company as a whole—this is a very big problem. Whatever you say, people interpret it as though you have a hidden agenda. People are trying to control each other by asking for a lot of data, facts and information, as opposed to trusting each other.

> Trust is a very big issue within the Executive Committee. There is none.

> John has a personal style that conveys that he does not trust you, but I don't think that is really the case. I think he just trusts himself more than anyone else. He has more information than others, he keeps it close to himself, and he uses it to manipulate the outcomes. He never likes to tell you what he is thinking. His style is not a collaborative management style on decision making.

To the great annoyance of their colleagues, team members often work their own agendas, undermine decisions unfavorable to their causes, and work backroom deals. For example, a CEO who wanted to convey a new business model focusing on profitable revenue found his direction undermined when a direct report gave deep product discounts to buy market share. And a corporate strategy executive trying to create a corporate identity found his work undone when an operating unit differentiated its logo and product packaging from the corporate message.

A common problem created by lack of trust occurs when a course of action does not receive full support from those given the task of executing it. The general commands the troops to take the hill, yet they straggle off in different directions.

A low trust environment prevents groups from genuinely working on and solving common problems, but a high trust environment offers an executive team the opportunity to experience genuine communication that can result in aligned action. In a high trust environment people can express thoughts, opinions, and feelings, and they also can hear and value thoughts, opinions, and feelings different from their own. They can make assertions and investigate them as a team without turning being right into a win-lose competition.

This chapter will outline drivers of trust, the issues that emerge from lack of trust, and finally, actions that can be taken to enhance trust and genuine communication.

## Drivers of Trust

There are many drivers of trust, but these three are especially important: competence, character, and mental models.

### Competence

Competence is an important underpinning of trust in an organization because people need to depend on the performance of others. Competence consists of three main components:

- *Knowledge*. This is the intellectual capability to reach the right conclusions and chart a meaningful course of action. Questions concerning knowledge are often raised in cross-functional issues. For instance, product engineers often wonder if sales has sufficient knowledge of the product to sell it effectively.
- *Skill*. This is the influence and savvy necessary to make an idea become a reality. Skill most frequently comes to bear on issues of influence and execution. Maybe a strategy officer has come up with a coherent strategy but lacks the skills to make it come alive in the organization.
- *Experience*. This third component of competence is a combination of knowledge and skill. Experience is a culmination of wisdom that has been earned and demonstrated through work.

## Character

Character, which broadly falls into the areas of intentions, consistency of behavior, and integrity, also is an important driver of trust.

- *Intentions*. Intentions are a major issue because for trust to develop there must be a belief that separate activities are aimed at achieving similar goals. However, a fundamental human tendency to misattribute intentions is at work in organizational life, and it often derails genuine communication and team performance. In the *sinister attribution error*, for instance, people attribute malevolent intentions to authority figures. In the *actor-observer attribution error* people see their own behavior as a response to organizational forces but think behavior in others is driven by personal and character-based motives. Finally, there are self-serving attributions used to enhance one's self-image.
- *Consistency of behavior*. Consistency of behavior enhances or depletes trust because a person may trust another's motives ("he has the good of the corporation in mind") but not trust the person to translate those motives into a durable point of view or a consistent, predictable set of actions. That is, consistency is part of character-based trust because it becomes equated with individual style. People differ in matters such as how much data they need to

make a decision, how comfortable they feel with making a decision, and how willing they are to reopen decisions. What one person sees as an important recognition about the need to change direction, another person sees as failing to stay the course. Given the natural human variance in behavioral consistency, differences in this dimension can lead to a lack of trust.

• *Integrity.* This part of character is particularly relevant to how people use judgment and make choices in organizations. For instance, knowing how and when to share information is a matter of judgment. Some people use poor control, sharing information and confidences when that is inappropriate. Others overcontrol information, using it as power or keeping others uninformed to prevent them from influencing a decision process.

## Mental Models

Mental models, or mind-sets, are driven by an individual's own needs and feelings. It is difficult to develop trust in this area because motives are attributed—inferred and not available for direct observation. Mental models are affected by framing effects, occupational background, roles, relationships, personality and opinion groups, and the current situation.

The *framing effect,* which promotes a restricting or defining of issues according to personal filters, often prevents executive teams from seeing and acting on issues. In working with teams my colleagues and I use the model shown in Figure 7.1. It illustrates that each individual has feelings and needs that are often unobserved. These individual needs are filtered through a mental model (moving up the left-hand column in the figure); applying if-then logic translates these feelings into actions.

For instance, suppose John likes to build friendly relationships with his executive colleagues and believes that one way to do this is by telling jokes (a mental model). He tells a joke in a meeting, and his colleagues reach different interpretations, depending on their own feelings, needs, and mental models. They may think "people who tell jokes are funny people" or "people who tell jokes are trying to get attention"; each thought leads them to make attributions about John's motivations and intent (to be funny, to get

**Figure 7.1. Sources of Misinterpretation.**

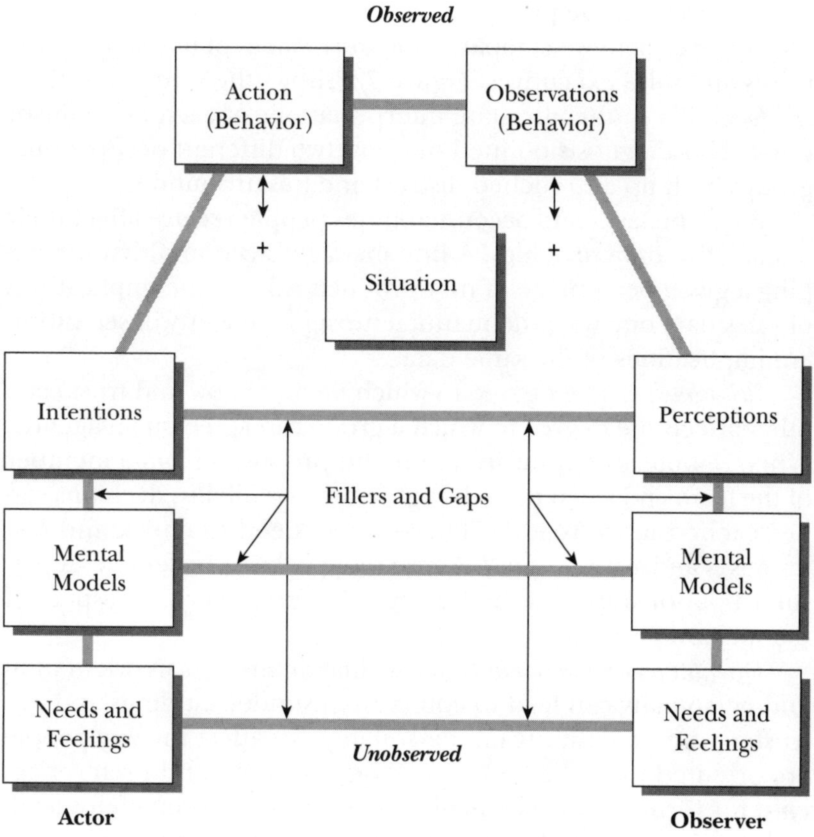

attention). More often than not, these attributions are incorrect or at variance with John's model.

This model indicates that trust is complex. People commonly see many issues and possible actions in a single situation. These perceived differences derive from their various perspectives on the situation, their different mental models. The following filters contribute to the ways people perceive things:

*Occupational.* Occupational background colors perspectives on problems and issues. For instance, CEOs with backgrounds in finance will support cost control actively and focus on managing

Wall Street expectations. Conversely, CEOs with backgrounds in engineering will focus on the new product portfolio and shield themselves from the press.

For one client we compared the work values of marketing executives and sales executives. Figure 7.2 shows the values and their *shadows,* that is, the alternate interpretations of each behavior or value. This diagnosis pointed out how two different occupational groups built up entrenched distrust and misattributions.

*Role.* The tasks and accountabilities people receive affect their perspective on a problem. A line manager accountable for shipping a given percentage of new products will see the implications of sales data one way; the manufacturing manager will see different implications of the same data.

*Relationship.* The degree to which people know and trust each other affects the degree to which a group can agree on an agenda. When people accept information and proposals from a member of the team and when there is high source credibility, decisions can be reached more readily. There is less need to check and test premises and assumptions because the speaker is believable. A person's relationship with the CEO is, of course, a critical aspect of that person's credibility.

*Orientation and personality.* Individual differences in orientation and personality can lead to common misunderstandings and distrust on the executive team. Personality can affect the way people are oriented toward problem solving and work, and preferences exist for formality or informality, orderliness or spontaneity, leadership or consensus. Some team members will be eager to agree quickly on a course of action, and others will think it is more important to build a shared understanding before reaching a decision. Some will be attentive to the needs and emotions of group members, and others will be more directly task focused.

*Opinion group.* A diagnosis often reveals distinct opinion groups within organizations. One company trying to resolve organizational shortcomings found it had three such distinct groups: the line-driven executives, who saw lack of business unit empowerment as the source of problems; the strategists, who saw business unit infighting as the source of problems, and the mediators, who thought people simply needed to try to get along better instead of making structural changes. It was not until these opinion groups were

### Figure 7.2.  Values and Their Shadows.

| Marketing | |
|---|---|
| *Work Values* | *Shadow Interpretations* |
| Need for thoroughness | Slow reaction time |
| Strong profit focus | Low customer focus |
| Value for analysis | Low marketplace understanding |
| Career progress by building portfolio | Focus on "standing out" |
| Strategic focus | Inattentive to current customer needs |
| Medium to long-term focus | Unrealistic current demands |
| Innovation and creativity | Keep trying something new |
| Loyalty to brand profitability | Competitive and cutthroat |
| Transaction oriented | Cold |

| Sales | |
|---|---|
| *Work Values* | *Shadow Interpretations* |
| Sense of urgency | Unforeseen consequences |
| Customer responsiveness | Minimize profit impact |
| Value for experience | Inadequate facts |
| Career progress by time and relationships | Focus on "getting along" |
| Tactical focus | Inattentive to changing trends |
| Short-term focus | Reactive, not proactive |
| Perspiration and dedication | Do more of the same |
| Loyalty to bosses and coworkers | Inbreeding |
| Relationship oriented | Folksy |

teased out that executive team members were able to see why they had experienced so much difficulty forming an agenda and building a coalition around it.

*The situation.* Organizations seek to standardize behavior by controlling situations, incentives, and information in ways that elicit certain responses. In executive life, however, this is not always possible. Although situational factors can help build trust, they are often fluid and lack constancy; therefore relying on situational factors to build trust is tricky at best.

## Issues Created by Lack of Trust

Trust is indeed difficult to achieve and time consuming to develop, but establishing it is worth the effort because it can become a valuable resource and a competitive weapon for an executive team. Consider the costs imposed on an organization because of the following five problems caused by low trust:

*Delayed decision making.* Perhaps the most common cost of low trust is that it delays decision making. Instead of taking action, people feel the need to validate data and check them against alternative sources of information. One executive complained, "Whenever we do a study that suggests a course of action, someone unearths a study done the year earlier that asserts precisely the opposite course of action." The different perspectives may derive from different agendas but also from very different data. A condition known as *data scatter*, which means that different data are available on an issue, leads to data wars. The ongoing battle over which study, which course of action, and which data are right imposes tremendous organizational costs, and the ensuing data wars can take on a theological fervor.

*Excessive preparation.* In a public forum such as a meeting or a review many managers act as though they should be able to answer any and all questions, even those that are ridiculously detailed and irrelevant. This seems to be a common if implicit value in many corporate cultures. In some cases managers have even made up answers simply to avoid appearing ignorant. Saying, "I don't know," or, "I'll have to find out," can be risky when trust is low, because listeners can impugn the speaker's competence and motives.

Because of the fear that premises will be doubted or an argument will be undermined, many decisions are overprepared. Studies and task forces are launched when a direct dialogue could solve a management discussion. Thus the cost of overpreparation soaks up time that could be devoted to straightforward problem solving. Even worse, when managers make up answers on the spot, significant time can be wasted with subsequent efforts undertaken to make those answers stand.

*Undercommunication.* In personally risky environments people avoid clarifying assignments and requests because they do not want to risk someone questioning their grasp of the issues. Often people undertake major efforts only to find out that this work was not what was really wanted. This often occurs when team members believe they have reached an agreement but, not wanting to discover any unpleasant truths, fail to adequately test assumptions and projections. One executive team labeled this *spurious agreement.*

*Implementation dysfunction.* This occurs when people believe that a topic has been covered in specific depth, and they then agree, for example, to "do the right thing" or "put a marketing program in place." This is a formula for implementation dysfunction when each person projects his or her own version of "the right thing" or "a marketing program" into the future. In one case an executive said to a subordinate, "If I'd known what you were going to do, I would have never approved it." He said this despite having approved a fully prepared business plan. It was the lack of translation of the plan into future consequences that was an issue for him, and it led to reversal of direction and demotivation of staff pursuing an important business initiative.

One of the most common dysfunctions is lack of follow-through. Typically, in an initiative undertaken by a team, a project is monitored as it unfolds so the team can see the course of work and react as new information becomes available. However, in order to avoid unpleasant interactions and conflict, some reports are not made until it is too late to make changes. This undermines trust and organizational effectiveness. The desire to avoid conflict—based on low trust and the belief that conflict will be counterproductive—prevents executive teams from doing some of their most important work (see Chapter Eight for a thorough discussion of dysfunctional versus healthy executive team conflict.)

*Underleveraging team capability.* This is another common—and costly—consequence of poor trust. Getting the most out of a group means building on members' different points of view, understanding different positions on issues, and finding a superior, better-informed outcome. This result often occurs during unstructured time, when groups engage in discussions about the fundamental direction and goals of the company, but achieving a whole result that is better than the sum of its parts is unlikely to occur if trust is low.

## Conditions and Tools for Building Trust

Many organizations actively seek to build trust among executive team members. Sometimes increasing trust involves fundamental design changes in team structure—including membership, meeting frequency, and other core design features. Design actions that have a dramatic impact include changing the composition of the team: adding members with different perspectives or eliminating people who harm the level of trust. Another design choice that can improve trust is more clearly specifying people's roles. When people's authority and mission are clearly understood and broadly accepted, they have greater freedom to act, their actions are interpreted in light of their formal authority, and misattribution and distrust are minimized.

Such conditions help teams achieve higher levels of trust. But because CEOs are often forced to stick with the teams they have, some improvements also have to come from within individuals.

Specific activities that can help build the foundation of trust include coaching and giving feedback and developing effective group norms.

### Personal Coaching and Individual Feedback

Making people aware of how their behaviors are perceived is a good first step toward building trust. In the best cases feedback gives individuals a kind of "aha" response—enabling them to see how others interpret their behavior.

Awareness can be built by making people conscious of their tendencies to make attributional errors. This is often best done in one-on-one coaching where a coach investigates the executive's assumptions about his or her own behavior and others' behaviors. Three areas of investigation are particularly crucial to this process.

First, it is often simple to identify uninformed conclusions about why a colleague did something by directly seeking information instead of making assumptions. For instance, one executive assumed an unreturned phone call was an intentionally malicious act when in fact the colleague was traveling and had not received the message.

Second, coaches can help executives recognize and understand the filters, models, and assumptions that they unconsciously apply to activities. In a company experiencing declining earnings the chief financial officer put purchasing restrictions in place. When secretaries pooled their own money to buy office supplies, a colleague criticized the CFO for praising this action, which the colleague found humiliating. Yet upon further discussion the colleague recognized that there was some value in the secretaries' spirit and commitment.

Finally, executives need to understand how they inadvertently send signals. For instance, a CEO may think out loud, and staff will misinterpret those thoughts as a firm decision or an assignment. Jamie Houghton of Corning learned this lesson and made it clear when he was, as he put it, wearing his cowboy hat ("I'm talking as a member of the team") or his bowler hat ("This is a decision and direction to be noted and followed").

Conversational style has a great deal to do with what signals people think they are sending. For instance, one person may think that saying, "I'll think about it," is a clear message that he or she disagrees with a proposal, whereas another might interpret the response more literally. Tone, intensity, and other nonverbal behaviors send signals too. One executive renowned for reading mail in a meeting was unaware that his behavior signaled disinterest in the topics being discussed, not to mention rudeness to other team members.

Coaches can be particularly helpful here because powerful and important executives often do not receive needed feedback. People around those in power are often unwilling to provide negative or corrective feedback, but an independent coach can confront executives with how their own preferences and idiosyncrasies cause undesirable consequences.

## Effective Group Norms

Achieving a better understanding of the concepts of trust and the problems that occur when trust is low is without value unless it is translated into meaningful behavior.

Many teams find it extremely helpful to articulate and monitor a common code of conduct. This can start with a rule as specific as "return phone calls within twenty-four hours." It can also include a statement of team values and requirements for sharing information. The code can come to be accepted as a norm for behavior and form a basis for situational trust.

Another important step to build trust and the potential for genuine communication is to improve a team's conversational capability. When team members clearly understand each other's commitments and intentions, there is less room for misunderstanding and greater room for trust.

Most executives have learned through experience that conversation is a competitive sport. The ability to persuade, debate, refute, and intimidate, if not terrorize, is often an important skill that is rewarded in organizations. Such conversational skills, often deeply embedded in executives by the time they join an executive team, can be antithetical to group members' ability to reason together. For instance, a common counter to a disagreeable proposal is to take it to an extreme, but arguing from extremes hampers a core task of the executive team: making good judgments.

Other conversational techniques that hamper genuine communication and dialogue include jumping to conclusions, personalizing conflict instead of looking at the underlying issues, filibustering, and withdrawing. Teams can address and overcome these problems by using specific techniques. For example, *chairman's privilege* invokes the chairman's authority to structure discussion around an issue. An individual is appointed to "make the case" and others are allowed only questions of clarification and amplification. This technique forces the group to obtain a deep understanding of a particular idea or proposal.

Creating a *container for dialogue* is another technique that can improve the executive team's conversational capability. In this situation, the group's discussion is structured so that the members contribute ideas to a central container where they are not attributed to specific members. This depersonalizes the comments, making it somewhat easier to be forthright, and it also enhances the perception that the final discussion outcome is a group product, not the achievement of a particular individual.

Discussions can also be facilitated by using a methodical approach to collecting data on agendas, attributions, and proposals for action. Such an approach can put mental models and choices in front of a group and force true *listening*, because executives must hear all perspectives and competing points of view.

Executives can also benefit from understanding the structure of their conversations for action (Winograd, Flores, and Flores, 1993; Ford and Ford, 1995). This leads to a need to also understand what the conversation is about.

Each of these and other similar techniques helps build the conversational capability of the group—a capability that contributes to a fundamental grounding of trust.

## Trust and Time

Finally, we need to consider that trust comes about through an iterative process. Trust is at first provisional; it must build over time. As positive experiences accumulate, people become willing to extend greater trust.

Behavior at senior levels is nonroutine and cannot be predicted by formal processes, rules, protocols, or other traditional management methods. Therefore it is important for executives to understand their peers at a more fundamental level—their approach to problems and their conversational style, for instance. This level of understanding can only be developed over time, in the context of ongoing interactions with peers. It also requires some measure of stability in executive team composition.

Thus stability of team membership needs to be weighed against the value of adding new perspectives to the team and other reasons for changing team membership. Stability can be valuable to team members because it takes away the issue of membership for some defined period of time—it frees members up from chronic concerns of "do I belong" to focus on building relationships and communications. The problem lack of stability causes can best be seen in the lame-duck leader, and just as supporters fall away from the lame-duck leader, team members who know that their team's composition will change soon are generally less willing to invest effort and personal risk in group projects.

## Summary

Trust continues to be a necessary but elusive requirement for the effective operation of both organizations and society (Fukiyama, 1994). Because of the costs that low trust imposes, achieving a high level of trust is an important pursuit for executive teams. Fortunately, there are tools—including better communication—to help team members build an atmosphere of trust.

## Chapter Eight

# Recognizing and Resolving Executive Team Conflict

*Michael V. Collins*

*Roselinde Torres*

Conflict in and of itself is neither good nor bad. It exists as a natural by-product of human interaction. Conflict can, however, be constructive, instructive, or destructive. Furthermore, how the conflict is handled can contribute to clarity, focused energy, and committed action—or to increased distance and polarization among the involved parties.

This chapter focuses on conflict within the executive team. Specifically, it focuses on the intervention decisions that challenge those positioned to assist in affecting the course and outcome of destructive conflict. First, we will offer tools to help determine if intervention is needed to resolve conflict. Then we will describe specific interventions that can successfully resolve destructive differences.

Intervening in destructive executive team conflict begins with gaining a better understanding of the conflict context. A preliminary set of questions (described throughout the chapter) can yield valuable data for making informed decisions about where, when, and how to best intervene. Data gathered regarding the context of the conflict directly inform decisions for determining the structure and process of the intervention. The purpose of intervening is to move the involved and affected parties to a point of clarity, focused energy, and committed action. To accomplish these outcomes, we have found success by following the steps discussed in this chapter.

## Conflict Characteristics

When asked to describe conflict in executive teams, managers often cite events or discussions that are currently on their minds or have made an indelible impact. For example:

> We have a major conflict regarding the implementation of centralized centers of excellence. We will not achieve our projected earnings targets because our business unit managers and staff function managers cannot agree on how to implement the centers and realize the projected savings.

> Though we committed to release ten products this quarter, we are only on schedule for two launches because the vice presidents of research and development and operations have a major turf battle going on.

> Seven months into our merger, we recognized that the members of the executive team were operating based on their predecessor company cultures, which were very different. We had an executive team meeting where we put issues on the table and gave everyone a chance to say what they really thought was going on. It was highly tense and emotional, but we hung in there and really decided things. I think it was the best working session our leadership team has ever had.

> Our CEO is so excited about the new strategy and reorganization that he's charging right ahead. There's not really much room to voice an alternative opinion. Because no one on the team is voicing any disagreement, he thinks everybody is on board.

As these comments illustrate, conflict on the executive team is like conflict on any team. And it is different. How is it similar? When it is destructive, the parties involved actively and passively block each other's goals, show recognizable hostility, and have a usually unacknowledged fear that the conflict will last forever—thus severing any hope of collaborative, harmonious, productive relationships on the team. How is it different? Executive team conflict is unique in that all of the foregoing destructive behavior occurs in an atmosphere of intense power. This team is the highest court of appeal for regional, divisional, and company disagreements. This is the arena in which decisions regarding enterprise strategy, company direction, and resource allocation are made.

As a group, if not as individuals, the team members are the focus of much attention. Every corporate executive has an opinion about what they should be doing better, and many focus their careers on getting to be "one of them," on joining the team led by the chief executive officer. There are team members who know they may be just a step away from succeeding the CEO and others who know they are not contenders but may still gain or lose in the succession aftermath. The stakes are high, and no one wants to commit a career-limiting gaffe.

Interventions into destructive executive team conflict must address the usual issues of substance and emotion in the context of this power-charged high-stakes environment (which was described in detail in Part One). Poker is poker, but poker in the barn is different from poker in the boardroom.

## The Conflict Context

Intervening in destructive executive team conflict begins with gaining a better understanding of the conflict context. Five questions can yield valuable data for making informed decisions about where, when, and how to best intervene:

- How is the conflict presenting itself?
- Who are the major players and the supporting cast?
- What is on the line for each person?
- What (and when) was the episodic event?
- What is the CEO's involvement?

## How Is the Conflict Presenting Itself?

Conflict is experienced at a number of levels. Perhaps the most obvious is the *behavioral level*—the observable ways conflict is acted out by the involved parties. There may be raised voices and systematic belittling and ignoring of the other parties and maybe too of their ideas. On one executive team at least half of every staff meeting was taken up by two company presidents, and often others, criticizing each other's opinions—sometimes with unvarnished meanness, sometimes with biting humor. The noncombatant team members would look at their papers, and the CEO would look out the window until things settled down.

Conflict is also experienced on the *emotional level*. The conflicting parties feel a combination of frustration, anger, hostility, confusion, mistrust, and fear. In the executive team just mentioned, most team members felt uncomfortable during these episodes of conflict. However, as they told us later, they saw this as "just the way things get done around here," felt the state of constant tension was a factor in their success, and were concerned that if they were "too nice" to each other the company would fail.

Not all executive teams in conflict express emotion overtly. Many executives have been conditioned throughout their careers to value reason, logic, and fact. To them, expressions of emotion are signs of being out of control and thus taboo. Value is placed on maintaining one's poker face. As one chief of staff stated following a confrontational meeting with a line colleague, "I was very angry about what he was saying, but I was successful in not letting him see it." Though the emotion may not be outwardly expressed, it is present nonetheless.

Finally, there is conflict on the *perceptual level*. The parties directly involved know they are in conflict when they experience their goals being thwarted by others. As the thwarting proceeds, each party increasingly perceives the other in a negative light, ascribing negative motives to the other, making and acting on assumptions about what the other is thinking and doing.

In one company the chief information officer was at odds with everyone on the executive team. He was known to have on more than one occasion "created information about what one person said to another that had no basis in fact" and was said to have used this "data" to pit various team members against each other. Team members did not trust him and, because of his close relationship with the CEO, believed him to be berating them to the CEO. An inordinate amount of time was spent by team members devising systems to work around him.

Given the multiple levels upon which executive team conflict operates—behavioral, emotional, and perceptual—successful interventions must address each of the levels and must be context specific. Bystanders and the person attempting to intervene in the conflict can directly observe only one level (behavioral) on which the conflict is experienced. It is incumbent therefore to gain access to the other levels (emotional and perceptual) in order to have an impact on the course of the conflict.

## Who Are the Major Players and the Supporting Cast?

Executive team conflict occurs in the context of ongoing relationships among team members. This factor needs to be taken into account in structuring the intervention. In one instance, though everyone on the executive team had a stake in the outcome of a conflict between the corporate comptroller and the company president, it was decided to address the conflict "off-line," followed by reporting the results back to the executive team, because the conflict was well-contained between these two individuals.

In another instance a different intervention decision was made. Here the conflict also focused on a corporate comptroller and a company president but involved several other members of the executive team who had unsuccessfully attempted to resolve the conflict and were themselves feeling caught in the cross-fire. This intervention involved an interlocking sequence of meetings, first with the comptroller and company president alone and with the "helpers" alone. These sessions were followed by a meeting with the comptroller, president, and helpers and finally by a meeting of the entire executive team.

Identifying the major players and the supporting cast helps define the initial boundaries of the intervention. It also helps in the assessment of what needs to be done to level the playing field in cases where the conflicting parties are not equal in power.

## What Is on the Line for Each Person?

Conflict exists in the context of interference with goal achievement by the parties involved. Each party wants something, and each has something to gain and something to lose. Find out *what*. Then find out *why*.

A conflict between a new company president and a vice president/general manager, who was his long-time friend, became bitter and began to affect the executive team. In a series of off-line meetings with a third-party consultant, it was uncovered that on the one hand the general manager had been hoping to be named president. He had been a loyal company employee, whereas his friend (the new president) had left the company for a number of years only to be rewarded with a "triumphant return" to the new position. He felt betrayed by his friend—who had not told him about interviewing for the position—and felt that he was now "too old" to leave the company. He wanted the new president to know that he deserved to be president.

The new president on the other hand felt resentful that his old friend did not understand the position he was in. He had been asked to keep his negotiations confidential. He had been advised that the company would "deal with" his friend before he took on the position. He had declined this "offer of help," thinking he could make things work. He did not see himself as being any tougher with his friend than he was with others on his team. If anything, the new president saw himself as "bending over backwards to be understanding, sensitive, and patient." It irked him that "insubordination" was the thanks he got.

## What (and When) Was the Episodic Event?

There may not be one outstanding event, but if there is one, you want—and need—to know about it.

Two members of an executive team had a history of intermittent conflict. Though neither vice president liked the other very much, they were able to suppress most of their rancor and work effectively together when the need arose. That worked until one of them, having had too much to drink at a company social gathering, told a candidate for a position with the other vice president that she was not being selected and gave her a reason in "rather raw and unflattering terms." Never mind that this was not the time, place, or person to communicate the decision. And never mind that the decision was to have remained confidential for another week. The decision communicated was wrong; the woman was to be offered the position. Needless to say, a number of issues raised by this episodic event had to be addressed—along with the resulting conflict between the vice presidents.

Intervention decisions for addressing a nagging long-term conflict are made differently from those for addressing a crisis. Teams go through identifiable stages. In one of them conflict is necessary, normal, and appropriate for moving on to the next stage of development. Just as in adolescence, there are some things you can do to make the passage easier. Ultimately, however, patience and perspective are the keys to survival.

## What Is the CEO's Involvement?

To address conflict on the executive team is to address issues of power. No one on the team has more formal power than the CEO. When there is conflict on the executive team, the CEO has minimally a stake in the outcome and most likely a role in the resolution (see Chapter Nine for a more explicit discussion of the CEO's role in executive team conflict). If the CEO is directly involved in the conflict, there are implications not only for what is at risk for the involved parties but also for the intervention decisions to level the playing field.

Because of the conflict one executive team had with the company president, the team decided on its own to take the rather drastic step of having meetings without him. This action was sanctioned by the president, who was seen as being "a smart man but a maximally ineffective manager and even worse as a leader." These meetings quickly broke down, however, as conflicts that were originally inherent between members were made clearer by the president's absence.

The initial intervention agreed to by the team with the assistance of outside consultants was an action research approach. It consisted of data collection from all members of the executive team plus selected others; feedback to the president and the team; and a series of action planning, coaching, and follow-up meetings.

## Intervention Decisions

Data gathered regarding the context of a conflict directly inform decisions that determine the structure and process of the intervention. The purpose of intervening is to move the involved and affected parties to a point of clarity, focused energy, and committed action. To accomplish these outcomes, we have found success using the following steps.

- Create the crucible.
- Do the work.
- Test the results.
- Identify the learnings.
- Communicate to the relevant parties.

## Create the Crucible

The first set of decisions involves defining the crucible—the container—the necessary boundary conditions for the intervention. Specifically, explicit decisions need to be made and communicated about intervention focal points, intervention roles, and rules of engagement.

Two executive team members in a health care organization were in conflict. The behavioral evidence of the conflict excluded open arguments in executive team meetings but included avoidance of meeting with each other outside the executive team on items requiring their collaboration. Each also engaged in "constant complaining" to the CEO about the behavior of the other. The CEO directed the two to resolve their issues, using the assistance of a third party.

Conflict context assessment data led to the decision to consider the conflicting pair plus the CEO the focal points for the intervention. The role of the third party was to assist the pair and the CEO in surfacing and resolving the issues. The CEO's role was to resolve the substantive issues the pair could not resolve on their own after initial work with the third party. The rules of engagement specified, in part, that the conflicting parties would not discuss each other with the CEO during the time they were working with the third party, that the CEO would not entertain such conversations, and that at the conclusion of the work with the pair, all parties would meet to talk about the agreements reached, the substantive issues requiring the CEO's resolution, and the support needed from the CEO in moving forward. All of these agreements were discussed in a meeting involving the conflicting pair, the CEO, and the third party before the structured intervention took place.

## Do the Work

One concrete outcome of the process we are describing is a behavioral contract between or among the parties. The contract is a working agreement specifying what each party is going to do. The contract serves as a reminder to the parties of their agreements and is an important tool in focusing follow-up interventions to sustain the changes initiated during the most intense phase of the primary intervention. The path to this behavioral contract involves doing the work of surfacing the issues (the substantive matters, the negative perceptions, the feelings), providing perspective on the process at hand, productively engaging the parties in issue resolution, and building in preventive maintenance procedures. Using the categories just mentioned, Figure 8.1 lists the techniques we have found useful in our work with executive teams.

People making decisions about the appropriateness of the tools and techniques categorized in Figure 8.1 for any given conflict situation should be aware of and take advantage of the following leverage points.

- Tension
- Time
- Timing
- The teachable moment

*Tension.* Anxiety can help make things happen, or it can block them. The ideal state is one in which all parties are seriously engaged in the pursuit of resolution. Some rules of thumb: raise the level of tension if the parties are not seriously engaged. Marathon sessions, deadlines, rewards, and sanctions may be imposed to increase the tension so that the parties will seriously focus their attention. Lower the tension level if the parties are too tense to talk to each other. The data collection methods in Figure 8.1 in which individual data go from conflicting parties to the third

Figure 8.1. Tools for Addressing Executive Team Conflict.

| Intervention Intention | Tools |
|---|---|
| *Surfacing issues* | *Action research methodology*<br>• Individual interviews<br>• Questionnaires/surveys<br><br>*Individual exercises*<br>• Conflict history<br>• Things you do/things I do<br>• Conflict management style instruments<br><br>*Feedback exercises*<br>• Stop/start/continue<br>• More/less/stay the same |
| *Broadening perspective* | Win-win decisions (Filley, 1975)<br><br>The wise decision (Fisher and Ury, 1981)<br><br>Thomas-Kilmann conflict modes (Thomas and Kilmann, 1974)<br><br>Stages of team development (Tuckman, 1965) |

party before the other parties see the product (for example, individual interviews, questionnaires) will serve this purpose.

*Time.* The amount of time the parties spend in conflict resolution sessions, the pacing of the sessions, and the space between sessions all affect the critical variable of intensity. In general the intensity is highest in the beginning phases of intervention, when the tension is highest, and tapers off as the intervention reaches the later stages.

*Timing.* Readiness is the primary issue here. Intervening early in executive team conflict has the advantage of preventing the build-up of emotional baggage, but unfortunately, sometimes the parties are not ready to address the issues until they experience mutual pain and embarrassment. For the intervention to be successful all parties must feel they have "some skin in the game."

**Figure 8.1.** *Continued*

| Intervention Intention | Tools |
|---|---|
| *Productive engagement* | *Meeting management methods*<br>• Prework<br>• Ground rules<br>• Discussion structures (for example, responsibility charting)<br>• Homework<br><br>*Problem-solving approaches*<br>• Separating people from the problem<br>• Joint goal setting<br>• Option identification and evaluation<br><br>*Communication techniques*<br>• "I" messages<br>• Active listening<br>• Paraphrasing<br><br>*Behavioral contracting*<br>• Behavioral negotiation<br>• Experimental period<br>• Follow-up |
| *Preventive maintenance* | Explicit attention to team task/maintenance behavior<br><br>Application of planned renegotiation model (Sherwood and Glidewell, 1973)<br><br>Developing a "culture of authenticity" (Block, 1987) |

*The teachable moment.* It is axiomatic that people are resistant to change. We share the view that people are resistant only to change they do not perceive to be in their best interest. If the intervention process is going well, there is a moment when each party becomes aware of and owns how his or her typical modes of thinking and behaving are contributing to the anger and frustration that fuel the conflict. If the intervention process is going well, there is a moment when each party discovers the real possibility that all parties might find a resolution to what has been causing each of them so much pain. At these times people are vulnerable and open to learning. These are the teachable moments. And they are person specific.

## Test the Results

Inevitably, the clarity reached while doing the work and the promises made fail to last if the intervention is conducted as a one-shot event. Supporting the changes with a time for testing is an important part of the process. Modifying a training design strategy Ron Lippitt used to refer to as *practice/repractice,* we have found success using *the rule of two.* This is our term for a two-meeting follow-up sequence illustrated in this example of addressing the conflict within an executive team in the pharmaceuticals industry.

The intensive phase of working out the conflict between a regional manager and a key corporate staff person resulted in a set of behavioral agreements. The pair agreed upon a "good faith experiment" in which they would live by the agreements for a period of one month, at which point they would meet with the consultant for a follow-up session to assess the results of the experiment. At the first follow-up meeting the behavioral contract was reviewed, and the pair jointly engaged in the identification and discussion of "what worked; what didn't work; what we need to do differently regarding our experiment."

The discussion resulted in a slightly modified contract, and a new testing period of two months duration was agreed upon. The second follow-up meeting began with a brief "check-in" covering the highlights of the two-month experiment from each party's point of view. The consultant then talked about the planned renegotiation model (Sherwood and Glidewell, 1973) and guided a discussion of its application to the work the parties had been doing. Each member of the pair then identified and discussed "how you have contributed to my success the past two months" and "pinches/crunches I have experienced with you in the past two months." The pair were then invited to set their own check-up timetable for meetings without the consultant.

## Identify the Learnings

In combination with the previous test-the-results step, identifying the learning is an important ingredient because it focuses the parties on the instructive aspects of their encounter, it reinforces the fact that the parties have control over their circumstances, and it is an opportunity to debunk any myth that the consultant brought about the resolution through some combination of smoke and mirrors.

## Communicate the Results to the Relevant Parties

As stated earlier, executive team conflict occurs in the context of ongoing relationships among the team members. They have implicit and explicit expectations of each other. Therefore any intervention, whether with the whole team or with a subset, will have an effect on these relationships and, by extension, on what members might expect of each other. To maintain the team's effectiveness, then, it is important to report the results of off-line conflict resolution when the conflict has been publicly known on the team. This report represents an opportunity to appeal to the best in team members by enlisting their support in the service of maintaining an atmosphere of productive openness.

Two senior executives in a consumer products organization had a public and emotional debate about ways to access customer data. They met off-line, agreed on an approach, and coauthored a brief describing their decision, which they shared with their colleagues. Communicating the results with a request for support is also one form of inoculation against those who would collude to keep the conflict going.

## Summary

This chapter addressed the decisions faced by those positioned to intervene in senior team conflict. We see conflict as neither good nor bad, but as constructive, instructive, or destructive. When people see the instructive value in destructive conflict, they have the potential to develop a constructive outcome. When people who intervene understand the conflict context—and use the levers of tension, time, timing, and the teachable moment when deciding on the appropriate focal points, boundary conditions, processes, and follow-up mechanisms—clarity, focused energy, and committed action can result.

## Chapter Nine

# The CEO's Role in Conflict Resolution

*Charles S. Raben*

*Janet L. Spencer*

There is a certain irony to be found in the growing attention being showered on chief executive officers. That attention, and the near-celebrity status it sometimes brings, typically focuses upon the CEO's most public roles—the CEO as corporate icon, the CEO as charismatic leader, the CEO as master strategist, the CEO as turn-around artist.

And yet the same shock waves of change that have turned so many CEOs into such public figures have simultaneously created an unprecedented demand for CEOs to become more effective leaders in ways most people never see. The press, the public, and the financial community rush to judge the CEO's grand maneuvers in the public arena. But much of the real drama is played out backstage, where the CEO's ability to deftly lead an executive team can prove to be the crucial difference between the organization's ultimate success or failure.

In today's complex organization no CEO can single-handedly bring about significant long-lasting change. The job of shaping the strategy, structure, performance, and culture of an enterprise requires the wholehearted commitment and unified action of the executive team, acting as the collective extension of the CEO's leadership. Consequently, the CEO's effectiveness as a leader of change is inextricably tied to his effectiveness as a leader of the executive team. Our experience clearly tells us that the ability to successfully lead executive teams lies to a great extent in the CEO's capacity to recognize, confront, and constructively manage the range of conflict that is inherent within these unique groups of powerful individuals.

This chapter will identify the sources of team conflict, describe the roles the CEO can play in resolving that conflict, and finally, suggest the competencies required for a CEO to be effective in negotiating conflict resolution.

## Sources of Executive Team Conflict

Given the frequency and intensity of organizational change, it is no wonder that opportunities for conflict abound in the executive team. To begin with, the formulation of new strategies is a process rife with opportunities for conflict. Ideally, the process of developing a new strategy is a collaborative activity involving the full engagement of the executive team. If this group of experienced, knowledgeable, and strong-willed individuals is open and honest about its perceptions of the changing environment and what kind of organization the enterprise should become, some disagreement is inevitable.

Frequently, new strategies dictate a need for radically new organizational designs. And the very shape of today's emerging forms of organizational architecture lays the groundwork for conflict at the top of the enterprise. Old architectures based on functional structures are giving way to new designs formed around customer-driven processes. The resulting horizontal designs offer the potential of greater responsiveness to the marketplace but also demand an unprecedented degree of cooperation and collaboration. As lines of responsibility become blurred, opportunities for conflict expand.

Similarly, implementation of a new strategy and organizational design raises a host of difficult issues at the operational level, each providing the potential for additional conflict. The more complex the organization, the more crucial the need for internal congruence, or fit, among the strategy, the formal structures and processes, the work to be performed, the people within the organization, and the informal operating environment (Nadler and Tushman, 1987; Tushman and Nadler, in press). The proper alignment requires an endless series of delicate balancing acts—each involving a range of hard choices and trade-offs.

Strategy development, organizational design, and strategic implementation all demand successful teamwork at the top of the organization. In reality, however, cohesive team performance rarely comes easily. In most organizations conflict remains a constant threat to effective collaboration in the executive offices.

In addition to the nature of the work to be performed, the composition of the team itself represents opportunity for conflict. Previous chapters review in depth the dynamics inherent in putting ambitious individuals with strong achievement needs, diverse perspectives, and highly polished political acumen into an environment where every move is scrutinized and the question of succession is paramount.

Considering the numerous possibilities for dissension, disagreement, and dysfunctional competition, it should not be surprising that conflict within the executive team presents one of the most critical threats to the effective management of organizational performance today.

## Variables in Conflict Resolution

Clearly, executive team conflict comes in all shapes and sizes. Yet many CEOs grow comfortable over time with one or two techniques for handling it—a kind of one-size-fits-all approach to conflict resolution. We would argue that the distinctive differences that characterize various forms of executive team conflict require the CEO to select markedly differing approaches to handling each situation.

The first issue for the CEO is deciding which approach is most appropriate in any given situation. That choice will be shaped by a wide range of variables:

- How severe is the conflict? How closely is it linked to the strategic success of the enterprise? How much longer can the conflict be allowed to continue?
- What is the history of the conflict? How long has it existed, who has been involved, how public has it become?

- Is the conflict primarily related to a particular person—and that person's personality, management style, value system, skill set, and so forth?
- What is the length of the CEO's tenure? Are there behavior patterns that are holdovers from a previous regime, and how long have they been allowed to continue?
- What are the company's accepted norms for resolving conflict?
- How much publicity, both in the organization and among the general public, is the CEO willing to accept in resolving the problem?
- To what extent is the conflict part of an ongoing issue rather than a specific event?
- Can the conflict be resolved in a way that becomes a developmental experience for the team? Can it be used as an opportunity for helping team members learn how to deal with conflict and resolve it on their own?

And a final element must be considered: What, if any, are the constructive elements of the conflict? What trade-offs would be involved in allowing it to go on? Without question there are potentially healthy aspects to conflict: it can be a source of energy, it can stimulate productive debate, it can reinforce an open exchange of information, and it can free team members from the grip of groupthink.

## Seven Options for CEO Conflict Resolution Roles

Depending on the unique characteristics of each conflict, the CEO must carefully select the most suitable role to play in order to achieve the most appropriate solution. It is inevitable that each CEO, based on his own personality and experience, will favor a predominant style for dealing with conflict. The challenge to the CEO in the role of executive team leader is to go beyond the tried-and-true techniques and draw upon an expanded array of alternatives. We believe there are at least seven distinct options for resolving executive team conflict—options that CEOs should apply in the proper situations. In essence each option requires the CEO to play one of the following roles as team leader.

## The Optimist

*The optimist* operates on the assumption that the executive team consists of mature, experienced people who are capable of recognizing and resolving their own conflicts without the CEO's intervention. This role is particularly characteristic of CEOs who enjoy a long well-established relationship with the executive team and is so common that we sometimes refer to it as the default position for many CEOs in dealing with conflict.

The CEO's thinking typically goes like this: "These are my people. I chose them. I trust them. They owe their jobs and their loyalty to me. At the end of the day, I know I can count on them to do the right thing to support both me and the company."

Unfortunately, this view is sometimes nothing more than a rationalization for avoiding conflict by not dealing with it. The fact is that although the executive team's members may sincerely want to do what is right for the company and the CEO, the source of conflict may be too deeply rooted to simply melt away.

Having said that, it is also clear that the optimist role is so common because it is also so appropriate in many situations. For example, we referred earlier to conflict arising from differences in operating style among team members in terms of the way they manage their own units. CEOs might not get involved simply because, unless they hear differently, they can assume their direct reports are managing effectively. Once made aware of the brewing conflict, however, the CEO might well still adopt a hands-off approach as a deliberate move to encourage diverse management styles within the organization.

## The Terminator

Another common role is that of *the terminator.* This is the role sometimes adopted by CEOs who choose to resolve a conflict by taking decisive action to remove its immediate source. Sometimes that means removing one or more of the key players in the conflict. In other situations it involves structural changes.

This approach tends to be used when one or more factors are present. First, the CEO might be convinced that the conflict is so destructive that there is just no time to patiently work through it.

Second, the CEO might simply be fed up and have run out of patience with a recurring conflict that just will not seem to go away with more delicate handling. Third, the conflict might be inherent in the current cast of characters or structural environment, and no resolution is possible without fundamentally changing one or more of the elements involved in the conflict. Finally, the terminator role could play strongly to the CEO's predominant management style if it is a directive, authoritarian approach characterized by personal intervention and swift action.

The judicious use of this approach requires a keen sensitivity to the nature of conflict. Although the terminator role is sometimes essential and unavoidable, it can also be extreme, unnecessary, and counterproductive in terms of helping the team learn how to work through and resolve its own conflicts. The terminator role should be viewed not as a matter of course but as a final recourse.

The key issue for a CEO inclined to assume the terminator role is to be sure to first distinguish the symptoms from the cause. Removing key players will not solve the real problem if the source of their antagonism is rooted in inherent conflicts in their respective assignments. If two units are pursuing strategic objectives that are plainly at odds with one another, replacing the unit heads will not solve the problem; more often than not the same conflict will ultimately play itself out with a different set of characters.

## The Delegator

A third role frequently employed by CEOs is *the delegator.* This role often appears when the CEO becomes aware of a problem, communicates clear expectations that it must be resolved, and then instructs either those involved or a third party—outside consultants or, more frequently, the human resource director—to handle it.

This approach allows the CEO to set a stake in the ground, that is, to clearly convey the expectation that the conflict must be resolved. It also requires that the CEO determine that the conflict has been resolved without knowing the details of *how* it was resolved. Therefore to some extent it limits the CEO's full understanding of the nuances that lie at the heart of the conflict.

The delegator role is quite common in situations in which one of the CEO's direct reports is doing a poor job of leading his own team. Learning that this unit head is for example too authoritarian and is stifling the talent of his or her own direct reports, the CEO assigns the HR director to work closely with the executive team member in question and gives these two individuals joint responsibility for solving the problem.

This approach can be effective if it sends the message that the CEO is using an adult model of conflict resolution—in other words, "I know you are capable of working this out, you don't need me to do it for you." And the final outcome can be a good one if the parties involved do in fact get to the root of the problem and produce a substantial and lasting improvement.

However, there are some serious potential pitfalls. Too often, the delegator role is used by CEOs who simply want to avoid personal involvement in important but highly unpleasant conflict situations. Although allowing direct reports to work out their problems, it also distances the CEO from personally observing how executive team members actually deal with conflict resolution. Again, all the CEO sees is the final result, without knowing how the key players worked through a difficult situation. Furthermore there is a danger that the conflict resolution is being delegated to the wrong person (as in "it's a people problem, so HR should handle it.") Finally, if the CEO uses this approach too often and continually hands off the unpleasant jobs to others, it inevitably fosters the perception that the CEO is ducking the tough chores.

## The Tie-Breaker

Essentially, the CEO as *tie-breaker* resolves conflict by assigning the involved direct reports to present alternative solutions to the problem, with the CEO casting the deciding vote. Consider this example:

A relatively new CEO is confronted with a conflict involving two direct reports, one with a functional role and the other with line responsibility. They disagree over staffing policies that resulted from recent organizational changes. These policies leave some room for interpretation regarding who has responsibility for these tasks at senior levels. In other words, do the new policies mean that the responsibility for these tasks will be centralized or decentralized?

Upon being approached by the two executives, the CEO tells them: "I want you both to prepare your cases and then come back and give me two alternatives. If in the process the two of you can't reach some agreement, then I'll choose one alternative or the other."

This approach offers some distinct benefits. First, it allows the CEO to become actively involved in resolving an issue while remaining distanced from the actual conflict. Second, it effectively minimizes the CEO's investment of time in matters that are less than crucial. Third, it forces the players to thoroughly think through their positions as they prepare their cases for presentation to the CEO. That process sometimes has the happy consequence that the antagonists hit upon some common ground that enables them to resolve their problem without taking it back to the CEO.

The downside of this approach is that it casts the CEO in the role of "the heavy" who often must ultimately select a winner. The implications of that choice may extend far beyond the issue at hand, reshaping the CEO's relationship with each of the players. The "loser" may feel a deep-seated resentment that surfaces in other situations. The "winner" might be seen as the CEO's favorite in terms disproportionate to the relatively minor victory in question. This approach is most effective when the CEO encourages direct reports to work through the problem together and employs the tie-breaker vote only as a last resort.

## The Coach

In situations where direct reports are in conflict with another executive team member or where they are clearly having trouble meeting performance requirements because of conflict in their organization, the most appropriate approach may be for the CEO to take on the role of *the coach*. This role tends to occur in critical situations where the CEO decides the problem is simply too important—to the direct report, the team, and the organization—to delegate to someone else.

For many CEOs coaching is a difficult role. It requires that the CEO be able to communicate concerns to the direct report in an unambiguous, straightforward manner. It takes considerable skill to deliver the kind of message that is often required to convey the seriousness of the situation without leaving the person feeling that he or she has come under personal attack. It then becomes incumbent upon the CEO to work closely with the direct report on resolving the conflict. If objectives are not met in a reasonable period of time, then it is the CEO's responsibility to either reassign or remove the individual.

If successful, this approach strengthens the relationship between the CEO and the direct report and improves the performance of a key player. There are also plenty of ways, however, in which this approach can fail. The direct report may refuse to acknowledge how his or her own behavior may be contributing to the conflict. The direct report may strongly disagree with the CEO's diagnosis of what has to change. Once the coaching has begun, the direct report might refuse or in some other way fail to implement the CEO's suggestions. CEOs also need to be aware that the positive relationships they develop with the individuals they are coaching can easily sow the seeds of new conflict and dissension among envious direct reports who believe their colleague is benefiting from favoritism. If the CEO has been successful in keeping the nature of the relationship totally confidential, other direct reports can easily mistake coaching for grooming.

## The Synthesizer

An even more complex role for the CEO to play is *the synthesizer.* At the same time it can also be one of the most productive, both in terms of resolving specific conflicts and in building the team's ability to deal with conflict on an ongoing basis.

For example, a recent structural change within an organization has created considerable ambiguity and confusion about roles and responsibilities within the executive team. The team members who head two of the respective units have failed to work out their differences; now, they are playing out their conflict in the way they manage their units. The result is a serious lack of alignment within the organization, which is disrupting cross-unit processes and hurting overall performance.

The stakes of the conflict are high, and the problem cannot be allowed to continue much longer. Yet the situation is too complex for the CEO to simply play a tie-breaker role. Instead, the CEO has to bring the parties together and act as a mediator, placing the onus on the direct reports to deal with each other through negotiation, cooperation, and conciliation. Moreover, the CEO is far from a disinterested party to the proceedings; as the architect of the structural changes that sparked the conflict in the first place, the CEO's input is essential. The process, ideally, becomes one of working out solutions, rather than arguing a case and waiting for a ruling from on high. For this working out to happen, the CEO must resist the inevitable urge to dictate a solution until it becomes clear that the parties have no chance of reaching agreement within a suitable length of time.

## The Conductor

Without question, the most difficult—and in the long run the most valuable—role for the CEO to play is *the conductor*. This role requires the full engagement of the CEO in orchestrating an environment that enables the team to surface and deal with conflict openly and directly. The CEO acts as a facilitator, directly intervening to help build team members' collective ability to recognize, confront, and resolve the range of conflicts that exist.

Consider the executive team's process for developing and selecting new strategic objectives. If the process is characterized, as it should be, by openness and intellectual honesty, then it is almost inevitable that sharply opposing ideas will emerge. Conflict in this situation offers inherent danger. Clearly, this is not the sort of conflict that the CEO can delegate to someone else. Nor is it a situation where the CEO should be issuing unilateral rulings. The goal is for the team to work through the conflict—to surface it, examine it, give full expression to all views, honestly consider all options, and then make the appropriate decisions.

The cost of unsurfaced conflict can be enormous. Without question, the best strategic decisions emerge from a vigorous, candid consideration of the widest possible range of plausible alternatives. That simply will not happen if the team's working environment discourages the expression of minority views.

Additionally, executive team members who are compelled to accept a strategic decision that was made without any consideration of their own views will inevitably harbor a sense of resentment. Not surprisingly, they are unlikely to support the new strategy with wholehearted fervor. In some cases, either consciously or not, they may take formal actions and engage in informal behaviors that actually subvert the new strategy.

The airing of all possible alternatives—and the full discussion of them by members of the team—creates a collective memory of how and why particular strategic decisions were made. With the passage of time, as team members encounter difficult situations in which they must decide how to apply the strategy, that collective memory acts as a guide, reminding individuals of the underlying reasons for the strategy and why it was selected over competing alternatives.

Finally, the process of open debate in itself holds inherent value for the executive team. The fact that the process was encouraged and guided by the CEO builds a shared understanding that conflict in certain situations is not only acceptable but valuable and that surfacing and resolving conflict is an important skill that each team member should master.

Clearly, the conductor role requires CEOs to see themselves as team builders, people who can genuinely help resolve complex and sensitive conflicts among others and between themselves and others. It is a role that requires sophisticated facilitation skills. It demands that the CEO create an environment in which team members are assured of continued support when they raise issues involving conflict and in which team members know they will be expected to work together to resolve conflict. It means that the CEO must actively assist the team in establishing norms for acceptable behavior in dealing with conflict.

As we said at the outset, the conductor is a difficult role for any CEO to play. It requires enormous personal commitment, a thick skin, sensitivity toward others, and the resolve to invest a tremendous amount of time in the process. The conductor role, if it is to be effective, cannot be limited to a single event. It requires constant nurturing, continual monitoring, and the creation of special

mechanisms to assess whether conflict is in fact being handled constructively by executive team members, both within the team and
at lower levels in the organizations they manage.

Of all the roles, that of the conductor offers the potential for
both the highest risk and greatest reward. There is a reason people tend to avoid open conflict: in its raw unmanaged form it can
be truly ugly and ultimately destructive. The customs and conven-
tions of business etiquette have evolved over time for the express
purpose of shielding individuals from potentially embarrassing situations. Open conflict brushes aside those social barriers and lays
bare a battleground where there are clear winners and losers, with
enormous consequences for both.

Figure 9.1 summarizes the seven options and their advantages
and disadvantages.

## The Required Competencies

When handled well by a skillful CEO, these roles (in particular, the
conductor) can help build a creative and productive executive
team, one with the confidence and ability to embrace and resolve
its own conflicts. Having said that, we must also say that the skills
required of the CEO are considerable.

Under any circumstances some of the roles we have just presented require fairly sophisticated team-leading skills. And as was
probably apparent, as the list progressed the roles became increasingly complex.

The competencies—skills, knowledge, and abilities—required
of effective team leaders are often absent from and sometimes
clearly at odds with the managerial repertoire of many CEOs. Many
of the skills and personality traits that led to CEOs' success—strategic thinking, the ability to lead quick turnarounds, the talent for
communicating a compelling message to large audiences, mastery
of finance or some technology at the core of the business—have
little to do with the skills of a team leader. Indeed, the patience,
empathy, and ability to deal comfortably with personal conflict may
be totally alien to many CEOs' backgrounds and temperament.

Chapter Three describes a set of desirable CEO characteristics
and traits, including but not limited to the ability to energize,
impart emotional strength and perspective, keep a sense of humor,
and empathize. Beyond that list we would suggest that the role of

team leader requires CEOs to develop an additional set of competencies: some that may come easily and naturally, others that may require substantial effort. In the end each is important.

The first required competency can be described as *peripheral organizational vision.* This describes the CEO's ability to think like a chess player, focusing on a particular point of attack while maintaining a clear overall vision of the entire board. It demands a full grasp of the dynamic relationships that exist at any given time among each of the elements of the organization, and in terms of conflict resolution it means thinking through in advance how each alternative solution will affect peripheral players and issues.

The second competency is skill at *diagnosis,* the ability to quickly and accurately assess a complex situation. This involves sifting through the surface clutter to determine the root causes of the problem at hand, identifying both the core players and the related stakeholders who are likely to be affected by the outcome of the conflict. A crucial aspect of this competency is the ability to step back and objectively examine all sides to an issue before settling upon an appropriate course of action.

A related competency is *situational outlook.* This requires the CEO to understand each conflict as a unique combination of problems and players and to apply an appropriate resolution rather than a generic response based largely on past experience. In particular it demands an appreciation that a solution that has worked in the past might not achieve the same results if applied to the individuals involved in a different conflict.

Clearly, the CEO must develop competency in the area of *facilitation and coaching.* This requires a strong set of interpersonal skills far removed from the corporate icon role so often associated with the position of CEO. These skills include the ability to interpret what people are really saying—rather than what they appear to be saying in what they deliberately convey—and to identify and synthesize related issues. They also include helping people separate their emotional concerns from the true content of their messages so they can deal with the genuine issues and find common ground for conciliation and negotiation.

That kind of effective coaching and facilitation, of course, demands a willingness and ability to become actively and personally involved in the conflict resolution process. This can be an enormously difficult role for CEOs who have habitually attempted to

**Figure 9.1. CEO Options: Advantages and Disadvantages.**

| CEO Role | CEO Response to Conflict | Advantages | Disadvantages |
|---|---|---|---|
| *Optimist* | "I know I can count on my direct reports to work out the conflict—to do the right thing to support both me and the company." | Promotes individual responsibility and the adult model. Allows for differing management styles. | May be a form of avoiding conflict and abdicating responsibility. Can allow difficult conflict to fester. |
| *Terminator* | "I will resolve the conflict myself by removing the source—either the person or the situation." | Direct fundamental intervention will change the conflict. Role may play to CEO's strength. | Can be extreme measure. Does not allow others the opportunity to resolve the conflict. |
| *Delegator* | "I want this addressed, and am leaving it up to you to resolve the conflict." | Sends CEO's clear expectation about resolution. Promotes adult model. | Can be used to avoid personal involvement. Resolution may be delegated to the wrong parties. |

| Role | Message | Benefits | Requirements/Drawbacks |
|---|---|---|---|
| *Coach* | "I am concerned about your performance and want to work with you to help." | Can strengthen relationship. Can improve performance of key player. | Requires high degree of mutual respect and interpersonal finesse. May be perceived as favoritism by others. |
| *Tie-breaker* | "I want you to prepare your case(s), and I will make the final decision if you can't resolve the problem in the process." | Allows CEO to remain involved while keeping some distance. Can minimize CEO's time in less than critical matters. Forces players to think through positions. | Casts CEO in role of "the heavy." Decision choice can adversely affect relationship with direct reports. Diminishes direct reports' responsibility for resolving issue. |
| *Synthesizer* | "I will be involved in resolving this conflict as a mediator—I want you to negotiate and cooperate to find an answer." | Process is one of collectively working out solutions. CEO gains thorough understanding of issues. | CEO must resist urge to dictate solution unless no agreement is possible. |
| *Conductor* | "I will orchestrate the team's ability to surface and deal with conflict and will remain a full participant in resolution of problems." | Cost of unsurfaced conflict is minimized. Team involvement builds commitment. | Requires sophisticated facilitation skills. Requires "comfort" with conflict. Takes time. |

remain above the fray by delegating conflict resolution to others. This competence requires an unusual tolerance for ambiguity and an enormous capacity to remain cool under pressure—to refrain from personal attacks, to confront and deal with anger and aggression without losing perspective and retaliating.

To be truly effective, the CEO must open up and express emotions. Direct reports cannot be expected to drop their defenses and bare their souls if they believe they are the only ones who are vulnerable. Because this role demands absolute candor, it requires considerable self-confidence on the part of the CEO; it is likely that difficult typically unspoken issues will land squarely on the table.

In order to be a successful coach and facilitator a CEO must be motivated by a genuine desire to help others become more adept at resolving conflicts. CEOs whose overarching concern is resolving the conflict at hand and getting everyone back to business as usual will lack the patience and commitment to see the process through to a successful conclusion. CEOs are, by nature, impatient and action oriented: they see a problem; they want it solved. The coach and facilitator role, in the long run, holds the potential for enormous benefits to the executive team and the organization as a whole—but often requires the CEO to develop new skills and adopt a new perspective.

*Mediation* is a closely related competency. However, it demands special emphasis on the characteristic of self-restraint. It requires the CEO to become deeply involved in the process and to be committed to helping the participants work through their problem. In addition it involves the capacity to remain dispassionate and to help guide the discourse without becoming an active participant in it.

Finally, and perhaps most crucially, CEOs cannot hope to effectively resolve conflict without the skill of *clarity and candor*. It is absolutely vital to be able to deliver clear, unambiguous messages in pressured situations. What makes clarity and candor difficult is that one of the most common internal drivers of CEO success is an inordinate desire to be revered, admired, and in some cases even beloved by nearly everyone who falls within the CEO's personal sphere of influence. That is not necessarily unhealthy—it is part of what compels CEOs to aspire to these all-consuming jobs. But that characteristic makes it unusually difficult for them to deliver bad news to individuals with whom they work on a regular basis and is a major reason why CEOs so often delegate unpleasant personnel chores to the HR director.

In conflict situations what people need to hear is what the CEO is thinking. It is essential that CEOs first be clear in their own minds on their precise position and then communicate that perspective in specific terms that leave no room for misinterpretation.

## Summary

In summary, then, we suggest that conflict is a fact of organizational life within executive teams. The sources of conflict always present within these unique collections of senior managers are magnified by the turbulence and uncertainty that inevitably accompany major organizational change. And because the pressure for change is accelerating in almost every industry and business sector, the ability to effectively resolve conflict within the executive team will assume even greater importance in the years ahead.

## Chapter Ten

# The Role of Feedback in Executive Team Effectiveness

*J. Carlos Rivero*

Experienced leaders understand that along with staffing, rewards, and organizational structure, measurement is one of the most powerful tools at their disposal. When used correctly, measurement can prove indispensable in enhancing both individual and group performance. Measurement reinforces priorities, heightens awareness of the need to change, and provides insights into how to change. It gives people a tangible way to assess progress over time and to compare performance among groups.

Yet one of the ironies of organizational life is that the same people who are most experienced at using measurement to enhance performance and drive change in others are also the least likely to apply the same scrutiny to themselves. The same executives who consider measurement and data so essential at lower levels of the organization somehow miss the importance of using the same tools to strengthen the performance of the individuals who literally hold the organization's fate in their hands.

In this chapter I explore how data and feedback can enhance the effectiveness of the executive team. The years of work my colleagues and I have carried out with enterprise-level leadership—powerful results-oriented individuals who are more accustomed to evaluating others than to being evaluated—have led us to develop measurement tools and feedback processes specifically aimed at developing the team at the top. These tools are based on a conceptual model of team effectiveness—one that takes into account the unique dynamics of the executive team.

## The Elements of Executive Team Effectiveness

The quality of team performance at the executive level is critical— not just because of the obvious impact of the team's decisions on organizational performance but also because of the leadership team's role as a model of appropriate behavior. Both heroics and villainy, and all the more customary behaviors in the executive suite, will be played out in countless variations throughout the organization.

Yet if the executive team's behavior is most critical, that team is also one of the most difficult contexts for achieving the full potential of a collective membership. The unique dynamics created by succession issues, visibility, political intensity, and time pressures inherently diminish the capacity of the talented individual members to realize their full potential as a team.

Chapter Two presented a model for thinking about the ingredients of executive team effectiveness: design, core processes, and performance (summarized in Figure 10.1). These various elements are linked. Team composition, for instance, as reflected in the mix of skills and experience of team members, has a great impact on core processes such as how information is shared and decisions are made. That is, how the team is shaped affects how it operates. Another key link is between core processes and performance. At the executive level, performance is directly influenced by the quality, effectiveness, and appropriate management of the team's work, relationships, and external boundaries.

There are two critical dimensions of team performance: *production of results* and *maintenance of effectiveness.* Production of results reflects the team's ability to effectively meet the demands of its role. This includes the top team's capacity to produce consistent positive financial results and maintain organizational performance in the face of strategic and environmental challenges. Production of results also includes the quality of decision making, the ability to implement decisions, the outcomes of teamwork in terms of

**Figure 10.1. Elements of Executive Team Effectiveness.**

| Element | Description |
|---|---|
| *Team design* | |
| *Composition* | Mix of skills and experiences, values perspectives, and other characteristics |
| *Structure* | Includes the size of the team, the boundaries (who's in and out, the specific formal roles, the nature of team and individual roles) |
| *Succession* | Team members' perceptions and expectations of how their performance and behavior affects their succession prospects |
| *Core processes* | |
| *Work management* | How the team organizes and manages itself to perform work |
| *Relationship management* | How the team manages the nature and quality of relationships among its members |
| *External boundary management* | How the team deals with elements outside the team and beyond the organization |
| *Team performance* | |
| *Production of results* | The team's ability to consistently meet the performance demands on it |
| *Maintenance of effectiveness* | The team's ability to meet members' needs and for members to work together over time. |

problems solved and work completed, and finally, the quality of institutional leadership.

Maintenance of effectiveness includes the team's ability to satisfy its members' needs, work together over time, and adapt to new demands, situations, or challenges. Obviously, the two dimensions are closely linked; maintenance of effectiveness is essential to the consistent production of results. Consequently, the team's effectiveness *as a team* directly influences the organization's performance as a business.

When the emphasis is on building a high-performing executive team, the model is helpful in diagnosing the threats to the team's effectiveness and also the team's opportunities and in focusing discussion on these elements. The model can be a road map for discovering and navigating the leverage points of executive team effectiveness. When assessed against the various components of the model, teams begin to reveal their sources of greatest strength and areas of dysfunction.

There are numerous tools and techniques for maximizing the different elements of team effectiveness and shoring up weaknesses. New teams may be launched with considerable fanfare, formal charters, and statements of performance expectations. Team composition can be enhanced by selection systems that minimize bias and clarify relevant criteria. Decision-making procedures can be aided by computerized decision support systems. Rules of the road can be defined to govern how individuals interact with one another. And this list goes on.

## Using Data and Feedback to Achieve and Maintain Effectiveness

Data and feedback play an important role in determining where focused attention and effectiveness interventions can have the greatest value for an existing team. An initial assessment of the team against the dimensions of the effectiveness model provides the diagnosis from which eventual prescriptions will stem. Additionally, a continuing stream of information is required to monitor improvements and identify new areas that require attention. All complex group interactions are awash in data concerning interpersonal dynamics and team processes; the difficulty is converting these data into meaningful insight.

The primary concern of the executive team is making decisions and producing results, not working the "soft" issues of team process. In the absence of good information on how the members are working as a team, internal and external pressures tend to eclipse the team's attention to its own effectiveness and grind its processes to the point of dysfunction. A systematic approach to gathering team effectiveness data can be a powerful defense against this inevitable drift toward entropy. Data-based feedback enables the team to be self-corrective, preventing errors and engaging in continuous improvement.

In a benign environment with willing participants, there are unlimited opportunities for gathering data and sharing feedback. Each time the team meets, for instance, it can close with a *process review,* or discussion of what went well and what did not. However, most executive teams have little time or tolerance for wallowing in group processes and interpersonal dynamics. The great need of executive teams for meaningful data on how they are doing coupled with these teams' proclivity to shun such self-study has led us to develop feedback tools specialized for this audience.

These tools are designed to be straightforward and time effective; they are jargon free and brief. They emphasize actionable behaviors, both in their content and in their deployment when feedback is shared. Feedback plans are developed with an understanding of what is unique about the executive team and are sensitive to power issues and the potential for explosive conflict. Importantly, data interpretation and the search for meaningful insights are done collaboratively with the team members—either as a group or as individuals. The complexity of the executive team's charter, uniqueness of its strategic challenges, and strength of the personalities and interactions involved defy a cookie-cutter approach to assessing effectiveness or designing team development plans.

Given that perspective on the use of data, the following sections describe two of these tools and discuss how they are used in enhancing executive effectiveness.

## The Executive Team Effectiveness Questionnaire

The Executive Team Effectiveness Questionnaire my colleagues and I use is designed to capture data pertinent to the elements of the team effectiveness model. The instrument requires team members to reflect on all aspects of the team's functioning at a level of specificity that lends itself to actionable insight. For instance, respondents evaluate their team's context and design in terms of issues such as clarity of charter, appropriateness of size, and availability of resources. Additionally, team members reflect on core processes such as the team's decision-making process, relationships between team members, and the distribution of work. Importantly, each member also provides data on the team leader: does that leader establish clear goals and priorities, encourage open dissent, make clear decisions, keep team members informed?

Typically, the instrument provides space for respondents to express in their own words a call to action to their teammates and leader by identifying what the team should start doing, stop doing, and continue doing.

When the responses of all the team's members are aggregated, the quantitative data provide a comprehensive snapshot of the executive team. The precision inherent in numerical ratings makes it possible to present the data in straightforward ways that send powerful messages. For example, given the behavioral specificity of items, juxtaposing the most positive ratings with the most negative ratings sends a stark message of what is working and what is not. A thematic analysis of written comments can be used to supplement the numerical ratings, providing rich detail.

The confidentiality maintained throughout the process allows the gathering of data on issues that might otherwise be undiscussable. Survey data surface those sensitive issues the team might habitually avoid; they free the group to confront subjects implicitly viewed as off limits. Skillful facilitation of the feedback discussion can then create a safe zone for moving toward problem resolution.

For instance, troublesome issues such as the size of the team are often obvious yet difficult to resolve. Many executives reveal in interviews that they belong to too many unwieldy teams, yet few can imagine a nonconfrontational manner of broaching such a politically sensitive subject as asking team members to withdraw. Even though a more streamlined team would improve the effectiveness of the group as a whole, the prestige of executive team membership and the accompanying face time with the CEO, may override individuals' concerns regarding the value of people's personal contribution and team effectiveness. As simple as this problem may seem, team members often will avoid dealing with it unless there is some formal feedback process that puts the question on the table anonymously.

More complex than this "simple" example of team size is the taboo on discussion of CEO succession. At senior levels this issue is ever-present and rarely discussed. As discussed in earlier chapters, the divisive political behavior that can result when the question of who's next in line is left unresolved can paralyze team performance. Again, open discussion of this issue is unlikely to occur in the absence of tools or processes that provide team members with an opportunity to surface their concerns.

In addition to providing team members with a mechanism for raising team operation issues, the Executive Team Effectiveness Questionnaire simultaneously serves as a source of upward feedback for the CEO. Under the best of circumstances, upward feedback is difficult; when directed to the CEO, it is often distorted by layers of executives' self-preserving comments and diluted to the point of uselessness. The questionnaire gives team members an anonymous opportunity to offer feedback on leader behaviors such as establishing clear goals and priorities, being decisive, and ensuring frank and open exchange of ideas. Having been reinforced, praised, and affirmed through most of their careers, many CEOs overestimate the extent to which they embody these qualities; upward feedback provides a much needed reality check at the top.

The impact of the data gathered by this tool ultimately depends on the quality of the feedback process. The data can be fed back in any number of ways. At one extreme, data on team effectiveness can be designed into the standing agenda of the team and become an integral part of how a team does its work. Alternatively, the issues surfaced by the data can be addressed at an off-site meeting called specifically for that purpose. In all cases, the data should serve as a catalyst for exploration and the search for understanding, with the emphasis on delving beneath the surface story contained in the numbers. Insight leads to impact when the feedback discussions are translated into specific action plans and interventions for enhancing the team's inner workings. Progress against these action plans can become a new source of team evaluation, creating a sustainable information loop and allowing the team to self-correct.

Just as it is critical to assess the team's collective effectiveness, it is equally important to provide feedback to the individual members. The tool just described is targeted at team feedback; the discussion to follow describes a tool designed to help individuals improve their own effectiveness as executive team members.

## The Managing Lateral Relations Questionnaire

The Managing Lateral Relations Questionnaire (MLRQ) is an instrument that assesses how individuals function in lateral work relationships. A lateral work relationship is one that exists between peers "across the table." Data from these relationships shed light on one of the most problematic dimensions of the executive team—horizontal, often cross-business leader relationships.

In hierarchical relationships senior executives can simply impose their will to resolve conflict. Power becomes the arbiter of disputes. Peer relationships are more complex, lacking a clear decision hierarchy and structured lines of influence. Appealing to a higher authority is an option, but it typically occurs at considerable cost to the disputants' reputation. In short, managing lateral relationships is at least as challenging as managing hierarchical relationships and requires a distinct set of skills. The career path to the executive suite demands effectiveness in managing both directions of the hierarchy. Upon reaching the executive suite, the importance of lateral relationship skills increases dramatically.

Through our research and client experience, my colleagues and I have identified a core set of dimensions of lateral relationship skills (see Figure 10.2). The MLRQ is a tool that translates each of these dimensions into a specific behavior that can then be measured.

In practice, team members are evaluated as individuals on each of these behaviors by their peers and other relevant stakeholders. The questionnaire elicits perceptions of how the individual behaves in terms of observable concrete practices. That behavioral emphasis is important for several reasons. Data based on behaviors, as opposed to impressions, are more informative, credible, reliable, and ultimately have more impact. The instrument asks people, "To what extent do you observe the individual doing the following things?" The rating is then based on frequency of action, rather than on a subjective evaluation of the action. Use of this instrument also begins to establish a true team norm of feedback. Feedback is equated with improvement and willingness to use a fact-based management approach in the team.

**Figure 10.2. Relationship Practices.**

| Dimension | Description of Behavior |
|---|---|
| *Innovating* | The responsiveness of the individual to new ideas for problem solving and conflict resolution |
| *Advocating* | The extent to which the individual can clearly express and support his or her own views |
| *Including* | The extent to which the individual listens to include others in discussions. |
| *Trusting* | The extent of the individual's openness and honesty in personal interactions |
| *Collaborating* | The extent of the individual's teamwork and problem solving |
| *Supporting* | The willingness of the individual to provide assistance to others |

A defining feature of the MLRQ is that it is a multisource instrument; it combines people's self-ratings with observations of them by others. In the simplest case these others are the other team members. However, it is also common practice to include the CEO as a rater as well as representatives of other relevant groups such as customers, suppliers, and subordinates.

One output of this process is a display of the individual's self-rating contrasted to an aggregate of all the others' ratings of that individual. Thus the individual can, at a glance, focus on those areas where peers disagree with his or her self-image. Another visual element of the data display is a graphic that describes the range of colleagues' responses, showing whether a perception is commonly held by others.

Such multisource feedback is a powerful driver of individual change and development for several reasons. First, multisource feedback has high credibility. Although an individual may disregard any single person's perceptions, it is difficult to be so cavalier when faced with the consensus of others' opinions.

Also multisource feedback dramatically contrasts the gap between self-perception and others' perception, helping to over-come deeply entrenched patterns of denial. Finally, because the data from all the raters on the team can be aggregated, multi-source data have the effect of creating a level playing field, where everyone's opinion is equally weighted. This attenuates the dis-proportionate impact of powerful team members and gives voice to those less powerful members whose opinions are at risk of being dismissed.

In contrast with the team-based instrument described earlier, where the data are fed back to the team as a whole, MLRQ data are geared toward the individual. The data can be used in a number of ways to help individuals assess their strengths and limitations in working with others. In this context the emphasis is on overcom-ing individual resistance to negative feedback, clarifying inconsis-tencies in self-versus-others' appraisals, and in developing specific action plans for addressing weaknesses. Additionally, MLRQ data can be aggregated to convey information about the team as a whole.

Few executives receive honest unbiased feedback about their critical skills. Not only is such feedback rare but when it does occur it is often discounted because it is perceived as politically moti-vated. Yet the team's ability to function efficiently is directly tied to the interpersonal competencies of each member. For that reason the MLRQ and its associated feedback processes are powerful tools for enhancing team effectiveness.

## The Role of the CEO

As in so many other aspects of organizational life, the CEO plays a decisive role here in promoting the use of data and feedback at the organization's senior levels. The challenges facing the CEO are to motivate the implementation of data and feedback processes and to model their effective use.

The CEO has both implicit and explicit levers for responding to these challenges. As a motivator the CEO must explicitly convey belief in the importance of feedback as a tool for individual and team development. This includes making the time for data gath-ering and feedback activities, often in the face of more urgent demands, as well as providing the resources for team members to follow up with developmental opportunities. Another explicit motivator is to unambiguously recognize and affirm those who demonstrate the ability to learn from feedback. The most powerful motivator, however, is walking the talk. By being a full and enthusiastic participant in individual and team feedback processes, the CEO implicitly acknowledges their importance.

In addition to motivating the implementation of data and feedback systems, the CEO must model the behaviors critical to the success of the process, such as nondefensiveness and openness to change. As a role model, the CEO has a powerful influence on team members' assumptions, beliefs, and expectations. The code of conduct that governs executive team members is inferred, in large part, from the behavior of the CEO. When the CEO personally is unwilling to accept open and honest feedback, it is unrealistic to expect others to behave any differently.

## Summary

Measurement can contribute to executive team effectiveness. Appropriately gathered data and well-designed feedback can become invaluable for steadily improving both individual and group performance. They can refocus the team on its primary tasks, show team members why behaviors and practices ought to change, and give them information about what and how to change.

The Executive Team Effectiveness Questionnaire and the Managing Lateral Relations Questionnaire are two instruments based on a conceptual model of team effectiveness that can provide meaningful data for executives within the special dynamics of the executive team. Feedback based on these quantified data can lead executives to explore specific team behaviors and their own individual behaviors in useful depth and then to shape the action plans and practical interventions that will lead to routinely better team results.

None of this can happen without the ongoing and committed support of the CEO for using data and feedback at the firm's senior levels. The CEO's essential role is to motivate the team to implement strong data and feedback processes and to model the effective use of the results.

# Leading the Organization
## The Work of Executive Teams

The first two parts of *Executive Teams* have examined what executive teams are, how they are structured and organized, and how they function. It is now time to review how the team can lead the organization in building a solid platform for success. There are a number of value-added roles that only the executive team can perform: Part Three explores four of the most important roles, elaborating on how the executive team model applies to each.

Chapter Eleven addresses the objectives of governance and how the executive team can best meet these objectives and perform its governance duties. It describes the core organizing principles of executive team work—identifying, processing, and acting upon the most vital information to the company—and the team task of defining the company's identity and allocating resources.

Chapter Twelve frames a collaborative process that executive teams have successfully used to formulate organizational strategy—arguably the most significant executive team role. This process structures and supports constructive debate among team members, providing a logic flow for thinking about strategic alternatives and a set of techniques for getting collaboration in the production of a robust strategy.

Chapter Thirteen reviews the importance of extending executive team capability by establishing strategic change teams. These groups of senior executives are tasked with addressing mission-critical enterprisewide issues such as organizational design, transition management, and so forth. This chapter discusses the composition of these teams and how they can best be used to implement strategic change.

Chapter Fourteen, the last chapter in the book, outlines the executive team's critical role in changing the operating environment, or culture, of a company and implementing a new culture. Step by step, it provides guidelines for what the team must do to recognize a change is needed, to act as the chief architect for that change, and to lead its implementation.

## Chapter Eleven

# The Process of Governance

*A. Elise Walton*

The core work of the executive team is governance. *To govern* generally means to guide, to direct, to regulate, to administer policy, and to exercise authority (Merriam-Webster's, 1994). Legally and historically, the task of the chief executive officer and the executive team has been to govern the corporation on behalf of the shareholders, or investors. Much of the current literature on governance examines the relationships and responsibilities of the board of directors and senior management. Particularly in recent years, as boards have become more active, the governance task of boards of directors has been more specifically outlined.

This book takes *governance* broadly to mean the authorities, roles, structures, processes, and relationships that run the corporation. It includes the board of directors, board subcommittees, legal relationships with external parties, major executive committees, organizational structure, and executive subcommittees. The main arena for governance action, however, is the CEO and the executive team.

This book also differentiates governance from *management.* Governance and management share features, such as monitoring and oversight, yet governing is fundamentally different. Governing is broader, encompassing policy setting, direction setting, and corporate investment decisions. It deals with ambiguous problems and trade-offs, more so than management. Whereas management may be amenable to certain routines, governance is clearly and consistently nonroutine. Finally, management can be exhibited throughout the organization, but again, governance is the core work of the executive team.

Governance almost always implies balancing unlike types of trade-offs and demands. For instance, managers may have a target and a sum of independent activities intended to get them to that target. Managers may be advocates for their divisions, for their product lines, and for their customers. Executive team members often find themselves in a quandary when they realize that their task is no longer advocacy but arbitrating among the different and dissimilar claims made on the corporation (more investment, more dividend, new strategies, and so on).

This chapter first examines the primary objectives of governance. It then describes how to design and run governance processes so these particular objectives can be obtained.

## Governance Objectives

There are seven primary objectives of governance that the executive team and other top leaders must accomplish.

1. Determining and monitoring corporate identity and mission
2. Effectively managing trade-offs between constituencies
3. Making and executing speedy, reasonable decisions
4. Setting internal policies, processes, and rules
5. Managing external relationships and dependencies
6. Managing interunit relationships
7. Ensuring current and future executive capability

An understanding of each of these important objectives is necessary to designing and implementing effective governance processes.

## 1. Determining and Monitoring Corporate Identity and Mission

The primary objective of determining and monitoring corporate identity and mission must answer the fundamental questions of why the company exists, what it stands for, and what its aspirations are. A related subobjective is to set and enable strategic goals. The degree to which governance is involved in business strategy depends on company structure. Executive teams in conglomerates rarely do more than monitor the strategies of their subsidiaries, but teams in integrated companies find strategy making and monitoring to be a critical governance function.

In any case the minimum objective is for the executive team to define the corporate identity: Why does the corporation exist? Whom does it serve? How does it justify its existence? These are valuable questions to ask and answer, particularly as they pertain to how the corporate center and governance actions add value for shareholders (Buchanan and Sands, 1994). It is this added-value formulation that provides a context for making trade-offs between constituencies, allocation decisions, and so on.

## 2.   Effectively Managing Trade-Offs Between Constituencies

Because most corporations have as their charter the provision of return to shareholders and the delivery of safe, valuable offerings to customers, many governance issues revolve around the simple but ongoing set of trade-offs an executive team must make between a focus on customer offerings and the need to provide shareholders with a reasonable return. For corporations, governance includes complying with the legal and fiduciary obligations of the corporation in those areas where responsibility must reside at the corporate level.

These tensions between constituencies are played out at many levels in the organization. Balancing future-oriented investments (with longer-term payback but potentially more risk and poorer current performance) and short-term performance often creates conflict. Conceptually, the tension is resolved in the term *profitable growth*, but in day-to-day matters there are always choices about sufficient funding for new products, demand generation, and so on and about other soft costs that make for future product and market success.

At the executive level the tension manifests itself in making decisions about efforts to fund and to cut. Depending on the type of organization, these may be straightforward financially oriented portfolio decisions, or they may involve trade-offs between product programs and cost targets. In a full operating company, management must work out costs and trade-offs among product design, manufacturing, distribution, and sales.

These decisions are affected by the stockholders' preferences. Some stockholders are more interested in value appreciation and growth than consistent earnings. Corporations such as Netscape offer stockholders growth potential but low current earnings. In these cases management must achieve and sustain corporate growth rather than deliver predictable dividends. Other companies, such as AT&T, appeal to investors seeking predictable income. Managers in these companies need to manage to ensure quarterly dividends. Some companies retain strong family representation on the board of directors and find that these stockholders have complex concerns relating to family-owned stock valuation, dividend income, and voting rights.

Customers interests are also a concern for governance. Companies that derive a significant portion of income from identifiable customers (superstore chains, major industrial buyers, and so on) find that these customers exert significant influence on major corporate decisions. Major technological investments may be affected by consideration of customer needs (Grove, 1996). Honoring a major customer contract that was underbid can cost millions of dollars. To renege on the contract may help the shareholders but hurt customer and public relations.

Governance must also attend to the interests of employees and communities. Plant closings may benefit shareholders but hurt employees. In some settings plant closings may be too costly to benefit shareholders. In 1996, Texaco found itself facing a major boycott due to alleged discriminatory practices. This imposed costs on shareholders, customers, and many others. Deciding upon a course of action was a governance issue.

To make appropriate trade-offs between constituents' interests, governance activity must do three things: process information and create knowledge, allocate decision rights, and allocate resources. In the step of processing information and creating knowledge, the executive team must identify the demands of constituencies and understand the mechanisms necessary for meeting their demands and expectations. In allocating decision rights executive teams must determine who can make what decisions about investments, direction, and other key governance issues. Based on this information and these decision rights, the team then allocates resources. These resource decisions lay the track for the company's future success or failure. Major decisions such as funding new products or cutting a dividend are outcomes of governance that drive corporate future in a particular direction. Management time and attention, corporate endorsements of community projects, and other intangible resources also must be allocated in making trade-offs.

## 3.   Making and Executing Speedy, Reasonable Decisions

Many factors have contributed to time compression in industry, but the net effect is that markets favor organizations that act with speed. Overall, technology has outpaced human ability to ingest and manage information and act on it. The information explosion means that more and more facts are available, and for some the pursuit of information has become a substitute for judgment.

## 4.   Setting Internal Policies, Processes, and Rules

Often internal policies, processes, and rules concern corporate identity or trade-offs that must be made. Governance usually involves creating policy pertaining to use of the corporate name and logo, human resource practices, foreign country practices, and many other important organizational activities. A corollary of this objective is that policies and rules create the context for performance; in creating policy and rules, governance communicates what is valued and what is unacceptable. When consequences are associated with the policies, the policies and rules will drive behavior in the organization.

## 5.   Managing External Relationships and Dependencies

Managing external relationships and dependencies is often done at a corporate level, where these relationships are significant industrial, commercial, governmental, or community associations. As has been noted in the past, organizational roles that gain internal power reflect the organization's key dependencies. For example, a drug company is extremely dependent on FDA approval for new product development and introduction. Often a corporate-level relationship and sizable operational activity develop to move proposed products through the FDA approval process. As a result, this external relationship becomes part of the corporate governance agenda.

## 6.   Managing Interunit Relationships

In corporations with some common or pooled resource or some interdependency along the value chain, interunit conflict emerges. How and when this conflict is raised to a senior level and how it is handled are vital governance issues. (As discussed in more detail in Chapter Nine, existing conflict resolution processes may reflect CEO preference and style rather than a formal governance process.)

## 7.   Ensuring Current and Future Executive Capability

A vital mission of governance is to ensure the perpetuity of the corporation. This in turn depends on management's ability to have superior leadership, or as one CEO has put it, "to win the human capital war." Therefore the task of leadership is to ensure that the right people are being developed so that sufficient experienced talent will exist to run the company in the future.

## Governance Design

Designing and running the right governance process is essential for the health and sustainability of an organization. Governance is a mix of organizational structure, executive staff capabilities, decision rights, and meeting processes. Bringing all of these together into an effective and engaging working process is often a difficult task.

The first step in governance is establishing a clear corporate identity and underlying economic model of the organization. This can be done by answering a few critical questions: What are investors' expectations? What are the organizational goals? What are the economic dynamics in the business? Why will the organization win in the marketplace? What degree of integration is required among organizational activities?

The economic model is affected by many things. Where offerings are interdependent, governance typically pursues integration and synergy, and the economic model is that of an operating company. When offerings are unrelated, as in a fully diversified holding company, the economic model is similar to that of a portfolio manager. Often the model reflects underlying economic and operational reality and also executive preference.

In most organizations, business and industry are important to the economic model. Conditions that influence how the executive team will govern the organization include marketplace buying factors and the process technology for making the product or delivering the service. Also to be considered are break-even production volumes, new product introduction cycle times, distribution costs, buying patterns, and any other factors that affect the value of integrating interdependent activities.

All organizations must accomplish a set of tasks along the value chain (design, market, develop, manufacture, distribute, sell, lease, dispose of, and so on). Figure 11.1 indicates the key organizational activities that must happen to create value for the shareholder and the customer. How they are organized depends on the economics of the products, industry, and business.

These organizational activities can be viewed from three perspectives or groupings: buyer (customer/geography), offering

**Figure 11.1.  Organizational Activities.**

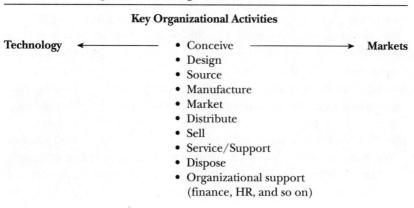

**Key Organizational Activities**

Technology ←———————— 
- Conceive ————————→ Markets
- Design
- Source
- Manufacture
- Market
- Distribute
- Sell
- Service/Support
- Dispose
- Organizational support
  (finance, HR, and so on)

(product/service), and activity/function (research and development, manufacturing, sales, and so on). These primary perspectives are often correlated with the "pure" types of organizational
structure: a *regional organization,* a *business unit organization,* or a
*functional organization.*

These pure types are rarely seen in large organizations. Since
the concept of the strategic business unit was introduced, the idea
of grouping by product has become very popular. Many of the Fortune 500s have structured into product lines or business units. Yet
because these companies each evolved from a single product line,
they still have a high degree of operational interdependence
between products—even when those products are sold into very
different markets.

This legacy means that the product units are typically interdependent. They may share technology platforms, customers, manufacturing facilities, and so on. The challenge for this type of
organization is to leverage scale where appropriate—with the associated costs of integration and interdependence. This typically
means that functional activities remain integrated under one manager. Manufacturing, sales, and research often are pooled
resources shared among different business units.

Consider Drug Company X as an example of a functional company that was forced to change. As health care became more costly
and increasingly a subject of public debate, this company realized
that its medications would have to be both cost effective and med-
ically effective. It needed to sell its products not only against competing medications and generic imitations but also against
alternative treatment protocols. This meant that Drug Company X
needed expertise in the progression and development of the dis-
eases its medications treated. For this reason it structured into diagnosis related groups (DRGs), similar to business units but lacking
the end-to-end authority and accountability assigned to traditional
business units. Numerous resources were pooled, including manufacturing, drug development, and approval labs, the hospital sales
force, and the practitioner sales force. This organizational arrangement maximized both functional expertise and cost consolidation,
while maintaining a focus on profit and loss and on the customer.

Many companies today employ an *interdependent business unit*
structure. It is similar to a matrix structure but differs in that busi-

ness units are the company's primary strategic building blocks. The business units emulate stand-alone businesses, focusing on profit and loss and market success. They contract for resources internally and externally to do the required work along the value chain. This means that internal functions are suppliers to business units. The business unit forecasts and commitments create the corporate outlook. The interdependent business unit structure allocates primary decision rights to the business unit managers.

Interdependent business unit structures create governance problems and opportunities for the executive team. The team processes information from multiple viewpoints—a business unit perspective and a functional perspective. This means there is information overlap—business unit managers must understand the manufacturing program, the sales forecasts, and the technology plans. These multiple sources of information make for better data but more conflict.

Following the establishment of a clear corporate identity and underlying economic model, the next step in governance design is to translate that identity into tangible operational practices. This translation effectively allocates decision rights—through structure, process, roles, and accountability. This design step begins with defining the role of the *center*, or the corporate group, including the executive team and the CEO. The center's role can be defined by three primary decisions: the degree of centralization, the degree of formalization, and the degree of involvement.

## The Degree of Centralization

The degree of centralization is affected by the identity and underlying economic model of the firm. The interdependence between a company's products, services, and offerings also affects this governance choice, as does management preference. The same company may have been run in a highly centralized fashion by a CEO who liked to delve into the detail and in a decentralized way by a CEO who preferred to address the strategic issues and leave operational detail to the vice presidents.

Centralization can be represented as a range of choice, from federalist models where authority and information are dispersed to models where decisions are made by a powerful center. The corporate center is involved in a range of activities, including directing or defining work, controlling and overseeing work, supporting units, and finally, executing on behalf of units. The degree of depth in each area determines the degree of centralization. Does the center define and monitor financial targets only? Does it define core business processes? Does it support units in the execution of business and operational processes?

Typically, integrated businesses or businesses with high breakeven economic models that require substantial investments require more centralization. Companies that have a public identity to protect may be more centralized. Companies with few natural linkages between units, companies that are geographically dispersed, and companies that value innovation more than cross-unit transparency are less centralized.

Executive team members in highly centralized companies typically spend more time together to gain a common understanding of issues and actions. They also need to be in touch with operations and will discuss business and operating matters when together. In a highly decentralized situation, authority rests with the unit executives. Also, the configuration of the senior team is different, the quantity of time members spend together is less, and they discuss operating issues.

## The Degree of Formalization

The role of the center is also defined by the degree of formalization. Both ABB and GE allow subsidiaries a great deal of decision authority, but ABB has a more informal management system than GE. For many years ITT was a model for formalized processes and simultaneously a model for conglomerate management. Discipline was tight, reviews were structured, and pro forma information was expected.

Formalization has most recently been driven via consistent organizational processes, often through reengineering efforts. Not surprisingly, as many companies grew in the 1960s and 1970s, processes multiplied. Yet these processes often lacked the coherence and sense of direction that would have made them a competitive advantage to the parent company. The lack of formalization, and the additional attraction of consistency and transparency in processes, made it easy to find opportunities for internal improvement.

For instance, one company structured as a large set of loosely linked businesses found that its product development cycle time (time-to-market) took far too long across all its businesses. It commissioned a major consulting study to develop a process tailored to its unique configuration of customers, offerings, and technologies that would decrease time-to-market and create a formal, consistent set of review "gates." This is not a unique event. Most companies have undergone some corporate-driven reengineering of processes, the most common of which are time-to-market, logistics (supply chain and distribution), and market-to-collection (sales and order administration).

These processes formalize management into common corporate processes and create a common language for reviewing and monitoring operations. Although the center usually views these efforts as "support," operating units often view them as interference, overhead, or bureaucracy. Yet when the processes are designed and implemented effectively, they validate themselves by improved yield, better product, and tangible results, which turns critics into supporters.

Formalization may be an asset or a liability to executive teams. Standardized information is an asset because executive team members can navigate pro formas more rapidly than they can learn format along with content. Yet formalization can also be a liability. When information and data are shared in routine ways, the event can become a ritual rather than an added value. Members tune out, do their mail, or amuse themselves by interrogating others during these information-sharing sessions.

## The Degree of Involvement

Finally, as corporate governance becomes a more and more complex task, executives are increasingly looking to other sources of expertise and authority for input to the process. Perhaps the most common area where involvement has increased is the board of directors. Traditionally, the board of directors has been involved or informed on major organizational issues, such as investments, executive appointments, restructuring, and acquisitions. These days the board is far more engaged in such activities as oversight of ongoing business issues, monitoring, and providing consulting assistance on organizational problems (Werther, Kerr, and Wright, 1995).

For example, one company took its board for a three-day off-site meeting at which board members worked on organizational issues, much as an executive team would have done. The proposals and suggestions from this meeting were used to drive annual efforts and targets. Another company, on the brink of bankruptcy, enrolled the board in creating and monitoring the "get well" plan for recovery. Involving the board accesses resources and experience not available internally and gains board members' commitment and understanding on any given course of action.

Involvement of the board, although clearly beneficial in some ways, also creates challenges for the executive team. Most directly, board members gain influence on the composition and roles of the executive team. Boards are often involved in succession planning and identifying top talent. More generally, board involvement means that the executive team must constantly ingest board members' external viewpoints. Although the executive team can benefit from these viewpoints, they often create conflict and additional work as the team incorporates this new information into its thinking.

Governance involvement may also encompass interest groups drawn from the community, employees, or major customers. An analysis of how senior executives spend their time indicates that substantial intervals are spent with customers, governmental bodies (particularly those that influence the core business), and employee or union representatives.

Governance design, then, consists of gaining clarity around the corporate identity and the underlying economic model. This involves high-level choices about vital information that must be attended to and the allocation of decision rights. Governance design must then translate high-level principles into operational practices, including structure, process, authority, and so on. These operational practices should reflect the underlying constitution of the firm and also can be arrayed along dimensions of centralization, formalization, and involvement. The choices about centralization, formalization, and involvement have consequences for how the executive team works.

## Governance Processes

Governance processes are mechanisms and forums for identifying and resolving conflicts that occur within the executive team. Governance processes also include those embedded sets of rules and procedures that prescribe behavior. Much like juridical law, these processes are usually built up over time, in line with guiding principles outlined in the governance design.

Most companies have a formal set of committees and meetings that includes the following:

- *Policy committee.* This committee usually consists of the most senior executives and those whose position provides a good purview of the long-term health of the company: the CEO, president/COO, chief financial officer, chief strategy officer, chief technical officer, and those who manage key external dependencies (for example, those involved with labor and the like). When devoted solely to policy, this committee meets once or twice a month.
- *Strategy committee.* This group sets and defines long-term strategies for the corporation, often in conjunction with the policy committee. This activity is particularly important when the company comprises interdependent business units.
- *Operations committee.* This committee performs the monitoring function in more centralized companies. It usually meets more frequently than other committees, weekly for instance, and includes senior-level operating managers.
- *Process committee.* This group is usually set up to manage core formalized processes, to perform linking functions, or to consolidate core expertise and competencies. Process committees bring diverse yet related perspectives together for joint problem solving. For example, the Forward Looking Work forum in one company brings technologists and marketing roles together to talk about how product designs will fit into different selling environments. In another company, the Technology Funding Board reviews and approves joint (inter–business unit) development efforts.
- *Communication meetings.* These annual or semiannual meetings are held by top leaders to communicate messages face to face

and to sense reactions and concerns of a broad group of leaders.

- *Plan reviews* (by business line or region). Top executives hold these monthly or quarterly sessions to review financial performance of the operations, to determine whether the projections and plans are being achieved and whether operating performance is in line with expectations, and to take corrective action where appropriate. These reviews keep management in touch with the state of the business and are usually more frequent when results are at risk or poor.

These committees and meetings represent ways executives can manage the interdependencies of their separate units. At one company a matrix for cross-matching key governance tasks and senior executives was laid out to help the executive team define the committees and meetings and arrange natural groupings of executives to fill these assignments.

## Operational Governance

*Operational governance* refers to the major tasks of managing the businesses that make up a corporation. Operational governance is a subset of corporate governance and may be tightly linked to it in the more centralized organizations. As integration requirements increase, operations are more interdependent, and the executive team faces greater operational governance requirements.

In the end the actual work done in organizations has to do with balancing and managing the trade-offs that must be made to create a complex set of outputs. Solutions are like so many simultaneous equations: production must be managed to create the lowest-cost high-quality output; marketing and sales must forecast what will be bought and when; product development must foresee emerging demands and offerings. Each sector of the organization would like to solve demands on it in what it perceives to be the most straightforward way.

Multiple perspectives—product and functional interests, or product and customer interests—are combined at the top, increasing executive team conflict in deciding how to solve demands. The manufacturing manager wants the forecast from sales, the business unit managers want to tweak the sales forecast to reflect their goals, and so on. Frequently, one hears, "Why can't they just agree?" This reaction often results from the frustrations of tending to the different needs represented on the executive team and the naïve expectation that a single approach will be the right answer. Each of the perspectives represented implies and constrains choices for governance.

As these perspectives compete, there are *contested zones* where decision authority is unclear. For instance, product managers balk at the pricing actions taken by customer organizations, viewing discounts and rebates as "giveaways" and symptoms of poor marketing and selling. Sales or customer organizations complain about product managers' unreasonable, out-of-touch pricing expectations. These differences can play out into expensive studies aimed at proving who is right and who is wrong. Usually, either side can mount an equally persuasive study. But the studies fuel, and are fueled by, unclear roles, and the competing authorities spend more time arguing about the decision than making it.

To resolve these conflicts (or, better yet, proactively avoid many of them), it is necessary to define the authorities and relationships among the elements of the business. For instance, functions that serve as support—finance, law, human resources, and others—are typically *network* organizations. They have dual accountability—to a corporate network and to a product, functional, or customer organization. Typically, the most thorny role is that of the interdependent business unit manager. This manager's common complaint is, "How can I be held accountable for things not directly under my control?" To the extent that a business unit accepts functional agendas, it is hard for it to achieve business goals.

Management must create a context for resolving conflicts by returning to the objectives of governance—ability to make swift decisions, identify clear accountability, make effective resource allocation decisions, and execute operational decisions in line with policy. Decisions can be made more speedily where there is clear authority and accountability, which can also be described as role clarity. Often it is processes that clarify roles.

The multiple mechanisms for negotiation and control fall into these categories:

- *Direct.* Manager has direct, hierarchical control over assets, resources, and people. Resources can be hired or fired, bought or sold by manager. Orders go directly through a chain of command.
- *Contracted.* Manager controls or influences assets, resources, or people indirectly via market-like mechanism. Divisible resources (for example, sales reps' time) are contracted for or bought by manager. Contracted costs are usually those that occur when a cost center provides a service to an internal buyer.
- *Negotiated.* Manager controls cost of goods by paying a transfer price for materials or goods. This occurs when there is a direct pass through of goods from one unit to another and both units are measured on profit-and-loss statements.
- *Allocated.* Indivisible resource costs are assigned to manager.

Typically, the business unit manager will have all types of cost on the unit's P&L statement. The manager can clearly be held accountable for direct costs, and if roles are such that the manager has authority in the contracting relationships, also for contracted costs. Allocated costs cannot be part of the business unit scorecard.

The biggest conflicts revolve around contracted and negotiated costs. The recurring question of who decides is played out frequently. Some of this simply reflects the negotiations of managers who want to get a clearly achievable target and therefore try to find cost reductions wherever possible. Some of it is the unfortunate reality that the business unit can make more money at the conference table than in the marketplace.

Moreover social dynamics also come into play on executive teams. Members of the executive team, as individuals, usually consider themselves peers and therefore dislike or avoid the concepts of customer-supplier relations or even superior-subordinate relations in determining targets and goals. A statement like, "Why should I listen to him? He doesn't have half my experience," reflects a social (or experience-based) concern and a dismissal of the role requirements present at the table.

Thus it is very useful for the team to clarify a series of processes that spell out roles of who does what with whom. Most companies have a planning process that requires that outlooks be generated and agreed upon. The planning process is an important mechanism for specifying authorities: who sets strategies, who sets targets, who supports the goals of whom, and so on. Typically, in the interdependent business unit model the business unit sets targets and goals and contracts with internal suppliers for the resources and the consequent costs required to meet those targets. Numerous other processes can also clarify roles and speed decisions. The most common ones are product development (or time-to-market), supply chain management, internal venturing, and demand generation.

## Measurement, Control, and Consequences

Finally, organizations need mechanisms for control—for understanding whether the governance process is achieving its desired ends and for taking action when performance is off course. Organizations and processes have metrics and targets that must be achieved, and an organization in control is one in which the targets are met and performance is within some acceptable variance from what was forecast.

It has often been said that the ability to govern rests on the ability to generate consequences, good and bad, for performance. Therefore inspection and monitoring of performance are necessary features of governance processes. There are three basic ways in which organizations attempt to measure and control.

First and foremost, corporations create visibility of market consequences. This is the oft-cited line-of-sight to the customer. The more directly managers experience the market reaction to products, sales, and marketing programs and customer satisfaction, the more the business can react appropriately to market and customer changes. The need to create this line-of-sight is one of the most powerful drivers behind the creation of business units. By making business managers aware of the market consequences of their actions, market awareness and reaction time improves.

Second, organizations can establish control through concrete internally generated rewards and sanctions. These can be as episodic as a president's award for special achievements or as consistent as sales compensation bonuses based on revenue generation. The creation of reward systems is a substantial topic in its own right, but rewards and sanctions form a powerful set of motivators and consequences.

Third, corporations can create control via values by establishing clear definitions of what constitutes ethical and unethical business practice and by making dismissal a consequence of violations. Definitions of values, however, are more thorny. Corporations have increasingly come to make formal statements of their corporate values. But where these stated values are not also expressed as performance expectations, they lose much ability to influence behavior. Executives and managers frequently test the stated values against their own sets of inferred unstated values.

## Summary

As I have outlined here, governance is a complex issue. It incorporates a high-level set of objectives and design choices that an executive team can make to realize those objectives. Governance design rests on an organization's established identity as well as its underlying economic model. The form governance takes depends greatly on this model: holding company, operating company, and so on. An increasingly common model is that of the interdependent business units, which combine the profit-and-loss focus associated with independent business units and the functional excellence associated with functional organizations.

Critical areas for governance design revolve around the role of the organizational center: the degree of centralized decisions, the degree of formalized processes, and the degree of involvement among the board, the center, and the units. Governance design also encompasses the processes that are used to manage the company. They include several types of committees and operational processes that the executive team frequently uses.

## Chapter Twelve

# Developing Strategy

*Janet L. Spencer*
*Daniel Plunkett*
*David Bliss*
*Lilian M. King*

In the cyclical tides of management trends, strategy is back on the rise. According to a recent *Business Week* article (Byrne, 1996), business strategy is now the single most important issue confronting today's executives and is likely to remain so for well into the next century. Strategic planning, which many perceive to be the most important executive function in corporate America, is riding the crest of management popularity and is creating an impact perhaps greater than it did during the original strategy era in the 1960s. More than ever before, business school and consultant gurus are generating models, terms, tools, and techniques generally intended to clarify the murky waters executives must navigate in planning how to compete in an increasingly fluid and turbulent business environment. Recently, the popular and business presses have been flooded with strategy material ranging from how to think about strategy development (Coyne and Subramaniam, 1996; Grove, 1996; Prahalad and Hamel, 1989; Hamel, 1996; Slywotsky, 1996) to how to develop and implement strategy (Collins and Montgomery, 1995; Galpin, 1997; McGrath and MacMillan, 1995; Stalk, Evans, and Schulman, 1992). Professors, consultants, and executives are all contributing to the wealth of concepts and theories suggesting when, why, and how to recreate an organization's strategy. The fact that the grand strategist himself (Porter, 1996) recently addressed that elusive question "what is strategy?" attests to the resurgence of this critical topic.

In the wake of all this emphasis on strategy, we have witnessed an interesting phenomenon occur with our CEO clients. Although the increased focus on this topic has, without question, produced a sea of innovative concepts, theories, and processes, the net result of the proliferation in strategy material is that many CEOs are over-whelmed with—even drowning in—questions regarding how best to proceed. "All the abstraction makes for interesting reading," they say, "but how should I *do* it? Should I identify and build on my organization's core competencies? Or should I try to ascertain where the value is migrating in my industry—or outside my indus-try—and develop plans to address that? Should I engage in processes that are founded on gaming theory . . . or scenario plan-ning . . . or discovery-driven planning? Most important, how should I involve others in my organization—my executive team and oth-ers who will be responsible for implementing the strategy?" The reality is that strategy waters, though undoubtedly tricky and often even treacherous, can in fact be navigated by the CEO and the executive team—if they have a structured and logical process for collectively addressing the complexities inherent in developing plans to compete.

This chapter is not intended to be a full how-to guide to strat-egy development. Instead, it offers a perspective on the role of the executive team in strategy development, a general overview of the principles to keep in mind when developing strategy, and a set of steps to follow in creating a plan for the organization's future. We begin with a brief overview of the strategic choice process—a method for strategy development—its underlying philosophies, and the benefits an executive team can derive from approaching strategy development using this method. Following this initial grounding, we briefly review a set of important considerations that must be addressed before embarking on strategy formulation—considerations that may mean the difference between a successful strategy initiative and one that falls short of delivering a robust plan for the company's future. Finally, the remainder of the chapter reviews each major phase of the strategic choice process, highlighting main concepts and some important dynamics inherent at various points in the process.

## Understanding Strategic Choice

Grappling with complex and ambiguous questions regarding how to best position the organization in the midst of changing markets, technologies, customer requirements, and so on can be both invigorating and frustrating for the executive team. Without a well-defined plan for making progress on vital decisions, the prospect of determining a strategic direction for the organization can be overwhelming. Our experience has led us to the conclusion that such a plan must allow the executive team to engage in full discussion and debate of options available to the organization. Historically, strategy development efforts have been confined to a handful of senior executives with heavy influence from outside experts, but the costs associated with approaching strategy development in this way are significant:

- Less commitment is generated through engagement of key individuals in the process, and this may seriously hinder implementation; because plans developed are not fully informed by the expertise residing in-house, the strategy itself may not be actionable in the sense of being realistic and viable.
- Each senior executive who will be responsible for implementing the strategy holds a position on strategic options that reflects deeply held assumptions regarding how the company functions, what is happening in the world, and his or her own value sets and role within the company. Unless these positions are openly acknowledged and debated, the day-to-day decisions made by these executives will reflect individual interpretations of what the strategy is and how it should be operationalized. This is likely to lead to conflicting, even competing efforts throughout the organization.
- Often decisions regarding the scope and direction of strategic efforts are one-off, or one-shot; plans for R&D, distribution, marketing, and so on are developed in the absence of an enterprisewide integrated view of how key decisions affect one

another. This can result in disconnects among business units, wasted time and effort, and significant opportunity costs.

*Strategic choice,* the approach to strategy development described in this chapter, is based on a collaborative process that structures interaction, constructive debate, and choice within the executive team. The process steps form a logic flow for thinking about strategic alternatives and a method for getting the team to work together productively (see Figure 12.1). In 1992, chapter coauthor David Bliss described an approach that is both a way of thinking about the critical assumptions that influence strategy development and a process for effectively engaging the executive team in the task. The model depicted in Figure 12.1 represents enhancements to that original approach, based on further application and refinement with numerous clients.

In essence the process in its current form engages the executive team in three sequential stages of discussions:

1.   The first stage lays an important foundation consisting of a shared view of

- Market and industry dynamics
- Current company strengths and weaknesses
- Determinants of future success

This stage requires that underlying assumptions regarding each of these issues be openly discussed and that the executive team develop a collective perspective with which all can agree.

2.   Once the foundation of a shared view has been developed, the executive team progresses to stage two, which involves arraying the company's capabilities (current and future) with potential market opportunities (also current and future). Analysis of the resulting picture leads the executive team to identify the *sweet spots,* the select few strategic directions team members believe are worth exploring in detail. They then work to flesh out these potential directions by developing a complete business case for each, reviewing the merits and potential risks of each.

3.   In the last stage, having debated and discussed a number of viable alternatives, the executive team makes its final strategic

**Figure 12.1. The Strategic Choice Process.**

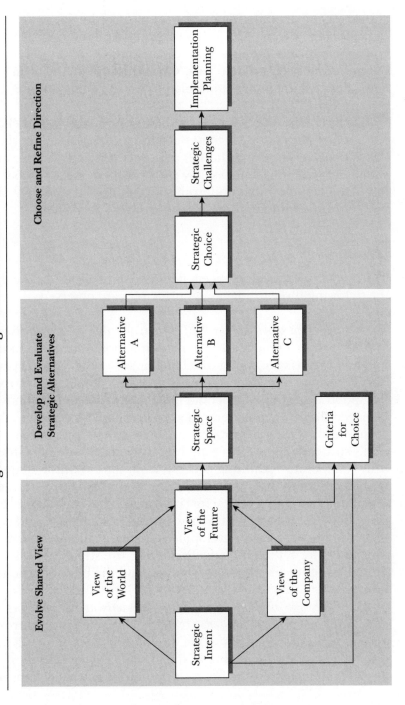

choice for the organization using a set of agreed-upon success criteria to screen each option for merits and risks. It then subjects the choice to rigorous testing—from team members, others within the organization, and outside review. Once this is done the team creates a detailed implementation plan to use in rolling out the chosen strategy.

Each of these stages is discussed more fully later in this chapter, but first it is important to understand the principles on which this approach is based. Although the process itself is flexible and should be somewhat situationally tailored, there are a number of fundamental tenets that underpin strategic choice, and they cannot be altered without undermining its intent and value.

## Principles

The process of strategic choice is designed to explicitly ensure that the following three fundamental principles are observed.

1. *The right people are involved.* The true value in this approach to strategy development is in the planning, not in the plan. Industries and markets are constantly changing; as a result specific plans start becoming outdated as soon as they are committed to paper. It is the strategic thinking behind the plan, carried in the minds of managers and executives and reflected in their daily decisions, that unifies and focuses the application of resources to the organization's strategic intent. Bringing executive team members into a truly collaborative planning process, from start to finish, helps to build a common understanding of the organization's strategic intent and develops those factors critical to achieving success. It is the process of struggling with the complexity, ambiguity, and conflict inherent in strategy development that is, in and of itself, most valuable. The act of collectively shaping the strategy leads to a shared mind-set among those who will lead the business into the future.

2. *Varying—and often competing—underlying assumptions are identified and openly addressed.* Strategic choice elicits, up front, assumptions and beliefs about the way in which the business is and should be run. Each member of the executive team maintains an implicit model of how the business operates and what actions will

lead to success. These models are derived from the member's individual background, education, position within the company, and past successes and failures in his or her own career. Positions on strategic options and decisions are the reflection of these deeper, personally held assumptions about the company and the world in which it operates. Strategic choice helps make these implicit individual models explicit—a vital step that allows the team to identify areas of disconnect and create a shared model for formulating alternatives and making choices.

3.   *The strategy chosen is holistically developed.* Strategic choice rigorously forces the team to develop, examine, and then choose among integrated strategic alternatives. Each alternative represents a set of linked decisions (including decisions about functions, business units, resources, and so on) that together make up an entire strategy. In other words each alternative contains a set of intricately related resource allocation decisions regarding cash, capital, facilities, people, technology, organization, and the like. Strategic choice ensures the development and thorough consideration of a range of alternatives that taken together define the boundaries of the strategic envelope within which the company can operate. It is through discussion and debate of these fully defined alternatives that the team can make a fully informed and complete choice regarding its future direction.

When these principles are adhered to and the general steps involved in strategic choice are followed, significant advantages are gained.

## Advantages

The strategic choice process is designed to result in a robust, complete strategic plan. That is the tangible outcome generated through the work of the executive team. However, a number of additional benefits are to be gained by approaching strategy development this way:

- Strategic choice positions the company for long-term success as the executive team develops both a strategy and a process for renewing that strategy in the future.

- Strategic choice enhances collective understanding of industry complexities and improves senior management's ability to identify and appropriately target marketplace opportunities.
- Strategic choice ensures that the people who manage the resources and who will ultimately be responsible for implementing the strategy develop a common understanding that will guide their operational actions.
- Strategic choice builds the executive team's capability to detect and therefore preempt competitive threats.
- Strategic choice promotes the organization's capacity to anticipate and successfully meet future customer requirements.

In order for these advantages to be realized and for a robust strategy to emerge, significant time and effort must be invested in the process of discussing, debating, and deciding which path the organization should follow. However, before convening the team to embark on this effort, the CEO should carefully consider a number of issues ranging from deciding who should participate to the clarification of key roles to defining the desired end state. Addressing these issues up front will help position the effort and should reduce ambiguity (and therefore the possibility of wasted time and effort) later on in the process.

## Initial Considerations

Development of a successful strategy depends, in large part, on successful up-front planning, which means that several issues should be clarified and communicated at the outset for all involved. It should be recognized that strategy formulation is a journey, and as such, neither the process nor the end point are completely predictable. To reduce the level of ambiguity and to answer the questions often explicitly raised or implicitly held by those involved, the CEO should address these six considerations:

- Clarify who is running the show.
- Make the time.
- Carefully select strategy team members.
- Clarify roles.
- Define the end point.
- Start with what exists today.

The following descriptions of these considerations offer directional guidance to CEOs as they think about positioning the strategy planning effort with those involved.

## Clarify Who Is Running the Show

Developing strategy is not a delegatable task. Responsibility for both the process and the strategy that is ultimately developed rests with the CEO. Even though it is likely that other players outside the executive team will be involved (as described later), it is very important that all concerned recognize that the CEO is in charge. Strategy development is neither a staff function nor a process that can be directed by outside "experts." Formulating the organization's plans for future competitive success will undoubtedly take CEO and executive team time and attention away from other important issues, yet there is no more important initiative for this group of leaders to embark on.

## Make the Time

It will take several months of attention to complete this process, including a total of several weeks' worth of actual work by the executive team—this is in-the-room, strategy-focused work with nothing else on the agenda. In addition to that total number of team working days, team members will have to spend time between meetings engaged in number of activities, including collecting market data for their portion of the business for input early in the process and reviewing outcomes of each stage with their direct reports and others to get reactions and input for the next stage of work.

It is also important to recognize that the time spent on the strategic choice process is qualitatively different than the time the members of the executive team spend on other activities—there is a great deal of pressure on this group to make the right choices for the company's future, which can cause significant tension among the players. A number of very tricky group dynamics are likely to emerge depending on where the team is in the process (many are reviewed in the section on applying strategic choice)—these need to be carefully managed in order to move the dialogue along constructively and with as much efficiency as is possible.

## Carefully Select Strategy Team Members

Although we are using the term executive team in this chapter, at times a separate strategy team may do much of the work described here. Ideally, the executive team and the strategy team will be the same, because one of the goals of strategic choice is to involve those responsible for implementation in the development of the strategic plan. There are times, however, when it may make sense to convene a strategy team that represents a subset of the executive team—when, for example, the team is simply too large or it has overrepresentation from certain businesses or functions. In this case it may help to consider creating a core strategy team that has extended team members who become involved only at critical points in the process.

There may also be times when it makes sense to involve members who do not sit on the executive team—key business leaders, for example, who report to an organizational span-breaker but whose input is required due to the different nature of their businesses.

Ultimately, the team must reflect the full range of knowledge and experience in existing and emerging businesses and also in enabling business processes. In addition the team will be most successful if it constitutes a critical mass of people who have demonstrated an ability to work collaboratively, manage conflict, and appreciate alternative viewpoints. Accordingly, members chosen specifically to sit on the strategy team should each have the following selection requirements:

- A superior performance record and the respect of their peers
- Hands-on experience in one or more strategic businesses or enabling processes
- Demonstrated teamwork capabilities
- Demonstrated openness to new and different ideas and perspectives
- Motivation and availability to work under the constraints of a challenging process over a period of several months

This wish-list of qualities obviously needs to be balanced with the existing makeup of the current executive population, but the fact that strategy team composition is a substantive contributing factor to success in strategy development cannot be stressed enough.

## Clarify Roles

A number of distinct roles must be filled during this process. Here are a few of the more important roles to consider:

*Team leader.* The leader (the CEO) will often play the role of full participant during this process. However, the team leader also has the responsibility to

- Maintain an enterprise focus in the room, keeping attention concentrated on the future and discussion on track (not allowing other agenda items to reach the table and confuse the process).
- Set the tone for discussion by openly sharing opinions, eliciting input and discussion from each team member, and encouraging challenge and debate.
- Make the final strategic choice if the group cannot come to consensus.
- Structure sessions before they begin (setting the agenda, determining in-room roles for facilitation, note taking, and so on) and making assignments for between-meeting work.

*Individual team members.* Members are expected to represent their business or function—at the same time they are asked to view all issues presented and discussed from an enterprise or systemwide perspective through each stage of the process. They are also required to take on and complete critical between-meeting assignments.

*Internal strategy person/group.* This group takes responsibility for the bulk of marketplace data collection and validation. It also needs to play a major role in ensuring the production of quality strategic alternatives—determining how well each alternative fits the chosen criteria for a strategic plan.

*Internal coordinator.* This role may be filled by a chief of staff, head of HR, head of marketing, or head of strategy. In essence the role is to coordinate with the team leader at each stage of the process. Often the coordinator's staff become responsible for the majority of logistic support.

*Strategy subteam or core planning team.* This is usually a small highly focused team established to support the executive team throughout the strategic choice process. This team can serve various roles ranging from actually working each phase of the strategic choice process ahead of the executive team then "teeing up" issues to be addressed, to serving primarily as a source to validate the outputs of the executive team. However its role is ultimately defined, this team can provide valuable arms-and-legs support to the executive team.

*Consultants.* The strategic choice process can be greatly enhanced by outside third-party facilitation. At different points in the process third-party individuals may play the role of

- Process expert
- In-the-room facilitator
- Coordinator of external resources
- Direct support for the team leader in and between sessions

## Define the End Point

The work culminates in two documents: a strategic plan and a strategy presentation. The strategic plan contains considerable detail regarding all aspects of the strategy as well as an overview of critical implementation steps and will be intended for use by the executive team and selected internal constituents. The presentation gives the 50,000-foot overview of the strategy and is intended for public consumption (all employees and possibly external constituents such as the board). Strategy development is finished when both documents have been completed and tested by the team and by selected others.

## Start with What Exists Today

It is important for the team to consider at the outset virtually all recent information relevant to how the organization has pursued, positioned, or discussed its strategy:

- Any current or recent work on developing strategy should be carefully reviewed for potential input into the strategic choice process. Even strategy development attempts that lost steam or were incomplete will undoubtedly yield valuable data that may simply need to be updated or validated.

• Position papers or speeches by the CEO or executive team members that have referred to the organization's strategy or have begun to position the organization for the future should be considered. These papers and speeches may reflect not only the current thinking of at least some team members but also implicit public commitments to an organizational direction.

• Any information that can be drawn from the media's treatment of the organization can be useful. Also any statements made to the media regarding the strategic intent of the organization are critical input. All of this material should be collected, synthesized, and distributed to the executive team by the strategy subteam or core planning team.

Once these initial considerations have been addressed and all are in agreement on the basic parameters of the process (including the logic flow of strategic choice, who will participate, how and when, and so on), it is time to begin the series of discussions that will generate important decisions for the company's future.

## Applying the Strategic Choice Process

The remainder of this chapter addresses each step in the strategic choice process—its objectives, the general approach it involves, and some of the potential group dynamics that may play out. Again, our intention here is not to provide a cookbook approach to strategy development but to offer enough information that the reader can envision what this process actually entails and therefore be better equipped to determine the potential for employing the strategic choice process in his or her own organization.

### Evolve a Shared View

The overall objective of this first stage is to establish, through discussion and group analysis of data, a common understanding of marketplace dynamics, the company's current position, and aspirations for the future.

### Strategic Intent

The first step in this initial stage is a focus on developing the organization's *strategic intent*. As defined by C. K. Prahalad and G. Hamel (1989), an organization's strategic intent is stated by its set of tangible corporate goals. These goals define a point of view about the competitive position the company hopes to build. They are aspirations, yet realistic in the sense that they clarify boundaries for how the company intends to compete. Developing strategic intent is an important step in the strategic choice process because executive team members need some initial grounding in how they collectively envision the business they are in. This step provides them with a basis for collecting and analyzing the appropriate market data and for understanding the organization's internal dynamics as they relate to that marketplace. It should be noted that as the team progresses in its thinking further on in the process, the strategic intent may well be altered or even changed completely—however, planting an initial stake in the ground on this issue is critical for allowing the team to move forward.

As the team defines the company's strategic intent, its objectives are to answer the questions, What business we are in? and, What kind of company do we want to be? Its purpose is to develop a *high-concept* statement that represents a collective view of "what we do, who we do it for, and how, generally, we get it done—today." This purpose requires the team to have a series of discussions that work and polish the high-concept statement. Attempting to distill the essence of the organization and its current position in the marketplace into a few sentences can be a trying exercise; however, gaining agreement on the nuances of words and phrases is critical to the vitality of the strategic intent.

A couple of risks are inherent at this point in the process. The first is that if all beliefs and opinions are not fully disclosed, hidden agendas may play out later on. Passive compliance with the strategic intent chosen may signal less than full commitment, which can later result in resistance to the company's new direction. It is important, in this step and throughout strategic choice, for true resistance to be dealt with openly and fairly. Unless this happens, individuals can go underground where they subtly sabotage the work being done. Alternatively, they may continue to vocalize their dissent and be overtly disruptive in the team.

The second potential risk lies with how CEOs play out their role. It is critical in this first step of the strategic choice process that they carefully balance sharing their personal perspective with soliciting the perspectives of others. If this is not done well, they can either sway the outcome or give in to the group consensus without fully buying into the strategic intent. Their behavior at this point will undoubtedly set the tone for later discussions, so attention to what they state as their position and how they state it is very important.

### View of the World

There are several important objectives for the second step in strategic choice: team discussions geared toward developing a collective *view of the world*. This view includes an understanding of

- Industry and general environmental trends and how these will affect the company
- Marketplace characteristics and dynamics and the identity of current and future customers
- Current and future competitors' overall strengths and weaknesses and how the company differentiates itself from them today

Data are needed from both external experts and internal sources to inform these discussions and provide independent perspectives on all aspects of the marketplace, to help the team expand its thinking, and to inject provocative opinions on industry issues. These sources can be widely varying in the data they use to form their perspectives, in their actual opinions, and in their style of interacting with the executive team. It is critical for the team to gain exposure to as many of these perspectives as it feasibly can: industry analysts, futurists, university professors, executives from other companies or industries, consultants, and sources for general competitive analysis studies. Customer perspectives should be incorporated in the data that are reviewed; if these perspectives are not sufficiently addressed through market research, the team should consider sponsoring some sort of activity to collect additional data (interviews, focus groups, surveys, and the like).

The work of the team at this juncture is to contemplate the data and the implications they present, making sure to address each of the questions in Figure 12.2. These questions should not be considered an exhaustive list, but they cover a fair amount of ground and can help the team begin structuring the information it is assimilating.

There are a number of dynamics that may be at play as the team wrestles with developing a shared view of the world. For example, it is likely that team members will feel both energized and overwhelmed. The more they learn, the more they may begin to wonder, How can we possibly develop a strategy that will meet the market demands? Individuals may experience some degree of anxiety either from being overwhelmed or from seeing a picture of market trends that does not, at face value, bode well for the company.

In addition some or all of the team members are likely to feel anxious about the amount and quality of data being collected: Are these the right data? Are we missing something? Are we going to draw erroneous or misinformed conclusions if we don't have the right information now? There is a balancing act that must be carefully managed between gathering *enough* data and being comfortable *enough* with the picture that emerges from the group discussions to move on. A significant challenge at this point is helping the team feel comfortable with being *roughly right*—in other words, no matter how much data the team has, that information is by definition dated and incomplete, and at some point team members need to say, "This is enough for us to go on." Having said that, it is also true that insufficient or misleading data at this point can represent an enormous risk to the success of the process and ultimately the strategy itself.

There are other risks inherent in this step, one of which is that the team may be overly influenced by one or two sources of information and then fail to give adequate consideration to the full scope of opinions. Also the team may not able to manage conflicting data, where two sources are virtually diametrically opposed in their views of trends of the future. Both of these dynamics must be watched for and managed should they become apparent to the team leader.

## Figure 12.2.  Questions to Address in
## Developing a View of the World.

**Environment**
- What are some of the major shifts occurring in the industry today (for example, changes in buying patterns, consolidation/disaggregation, and so on)?
- What will be the largest areas of opportunity during this period?
- What will the industry look like in the next five to ten years?

**Markets**
- What are the markets that we serve? What are the defining characteristics of these markets?
- What share of each market does the company have?
- What are the markets that we could serve in the future? What are the defining characteristics of these markets?

**Competition**
- Who are our key competitors today (in our ideal markets)?
- What is their overall strength in the industry (strong, moderate, or weak), within each of the services/products we sell?
- How would the marketplace rate us on each of these services?
- How can we best differentiate ourselves from these players?
- Who will our key competitors be in the next three to five years?

**Customers**
- Who are our primary customers today?
- What are the current consumer demographics, and how are they changing? What is influencing these shifts (changes in technology, government regulation, societal demographics, and so forth)?
- How are our customers distributed geographically?
- How are our customers segmented (different customer needs, company offerings, and so forth)?
- What do these customers spend (each) on the products/services related to our business, and how much of that figure do they currently spend with us?
- How do our customers perceive us in terms of product quality, service, prices, customer relationships, and so on?
- Who are the customers that represent the largest opportunities for us (those we should be targeting for the next three to five years) and why?
- What will these customers spend on the services we offer?
- Why will future customers choose to do business with us?
- Roughly, what is the percentage of overlap between these future customers and our current customers?

### *View of the Company*

The objectives in establishing a collective view of the company are for the executive team to analyze, understand, and define the

- Core capabilities of the organization, delineating strengths (things the company does well) from true core capabilities (those strengths that truly distinguish the company from its competitors)
- Weaknesses within the organization, including their order of priority and the root causes behind them

As in establishing a view of the world, data are required to inform the discussions. Some of the sources to go to are

- Recent employee surveys (on culture, climate, values, satisfaction, and so forth), which can provide a broad picture of the organization
- Customer surveys and focus groups, which can provide a very important view of the organization from those who matter most
- Industry surveys and ratings (for example, from J. D. Powers & Associates), which can provide a publicly acknowledged, "objective" view of the organization

Two common dynamics occur in this step. First, when wrestling with core capabilities, it is normal for teams to debate and disagree—they often find it difficult to narrow down the list of strengths into those that represent points of competitive advantage. And it is important to understand that the discussion is as important as the outcome itself and therefore should not be limited or shortchanged. Second, when discussing weaknesses, it is common for team members to feel that they are rehashing old problems and covering ground that's been discussed (without resolution) for years. Wallowing in these issues, they may go beyond the point of describing a problem to venting through telling numerous anecdotes, all of which basically tell the same story. This can cause members to feel frustrated and depressed. They despair of ever being able to resolve the problems. To combat both these dynamics, it sometimes helps if team leaders use an organizing heuristic to assimilate the data as the team works through developing its shared list of both core capabilities and organizational weaknesses. This heuristic can structure the conversation so that all relevant bases are covered and can keep the conversation from becoming too circular. Two examples of heuristics that teams have successfully used at this point in the process are the model of organizational effectiveness (see Chapter Thirteen and Figure 13.1) and the value chain (see Chapter Eleven).

As in most other steps in the strategic choice process, some risk is involved at this point. One risk is that unless enough information is collected to inform the discussions (that is, data collected from sources outside the room), certain problem areas may not be identified. Experience tells us there is often a gap in perceptions—or a disconnect—between the executive team and the rest of the organization, and it is important that the discussion of both strengths and weaknesses be based on a range of data. Another risk is that organizational weaknesses or problem areas may at times involve certain individuals in the room or the functions they represent and that these problem areas are not openly identified and discussed but are masked or even totally avoided in order to avoid contention. Obviously this leaves important information off the table. As with most other risks in this process, it is up to the CEO and his supporters to be vigilant in watching for these dynamics and in assuring openness and constructive candor in the room.

### View of the Future

The primary objective in this last step in stage one is to articulate a clear statement about what the future is likely to hold and how the company will be positioned vis-à-vis key stakeholders and related constituencies such as customers, competitors, and employees. This statement represents the coming together of the shared view of the world and view of the company. It says, in essence, "given the world as we see it and given the company as we believe it exists today, here is how we envision our future."

Thus this step requires making some predictions about what the future may hold and positioning the company in that picture. Because these are predictions, there is no way to tell whether they are right or wrong. This often makes some team members uncomfortable and even skeptical about giving the necessary time and attention to this step. They may push to finish this work early or may avoid participating fully while the team wrestles with it predictions. It is also possible that one or more team members may object strenuously to looking too far down the road (because "it isn't possible" or for fear of diluting the focus on short-term survival or the like). Apart from these dynamics, time spent on developing a view of the future will help prepare the team for stage two, where it will need to identify, develop, and evaluate alternative paths that the company might take. Having an established view of the future ensures that the paths chosen to explore will lead to a end desired point.

## Develop and Evaluate Strategic Alternatives

The main purpose of stage two is to array existing and potential capabilities of the company against existing and potential markets in order to pinpoint attractive strategic alternatives—viable strategies that reflect the opportunities of the future, are actual and aspirational, and can realistically be achieved by the organization. These strategic alternatives represent the many paths the company can potentially take to achieve the team's agreed-upon view of the future. Once they have been identified, they are fleshed out in order to make explicit what the various paths entail. Finally, the team discusses and evaluates the merits of each alternative as it is presented. Before diving into the work of identifying strategic alternatives, however, the team needs to develop a set of criteria that will ultimately enable the team to make the final choice from among the strategic alternatives.

### Criteria for Success

The objective in the first step of this stage is to create a list of the essential elements of a successful strategy. The team must do this before beginning the process of identifying strategic alternatives, as the process itself has the potential to bias the criteria that would be chosen. These criteria must be well grounded in the strategic intent that was developed in the early stages of the team's work, and also must reflect the position the team articulated in its view of the future.

Developing success criteria can often be facilitated by having the team finish the sentence, "A successful strategy will . . ." The team should also be sure to address both external and internal concerns. For example, after discussion centering on finishing the sentence, external criteria might be listed this way: "A successful Company X strategy will enhance our image and increase market recognition, leverage our top 100 targeted clients, increase our global capability," and so forth. A list of internal criteria might say, "A successful strategy will promote clarity of roles and accountability, build a sustainable, repeatable product-development process, facilitate internal sharing of knowledge, methods, and expertise" and so forth. The purpose of this step is to generate not a short list of top criteria but a complete list of all relevant criteria that the team believes will be important to future organizational success. Later in the strategic choice process, strategic alternatives will be compared to these criteria in order to inform the final discussions that produce the ultimate choice of strategy.

### Strategic Space

Discussion of strategic space can be the trickiest part of the strategic choice process and is very dependent on the quality of work done in stage one—on the degree to which the team has accurately and comprehensively developed shared views of the world, the company, and the future. Objectives here are to

- Build on the shared knowledge resulting from stage one, in order to define the boundaries of options available to the organization.
- Search within the boundaries of options and identify true strategic alternatives that the company can explore.
- Select among the alternatives those that could best propel the company toward its strategic intent.

The work of the team in this step typically begins with a discussion of the rationale behind articulating strategic alternatives, which can be stated as follows: too often, strategic decisions within organizations are made as one-off decisions. For example, a decision to move in one direction—say, to make an investment (acquire a company, begin a new product line, and so on)—may obviate another intended direction. These one-off strategic decisions ultimately result in serious costs to the organization in the form of conflicts and of wasted time and effort.

As defined by Bliss (1992) an *integrated strategic alternative* is "a set of related decisions that, taken together, define a coherent strategic direction. It is a linked set of decisions—investments and disinvestments—with a consistent pattern of resource allocation decisions including cash, capital, facilities, people, technology and organization. [It] is both a description of a destination and a path to reach the destination" (p. 243). Such integration cannot be achieved with a series of one-off decisions.

Once the rationale is well understood by the team, its work is to first identify the strategic alternatives. One particularly useful technique to elicit them is to a develop a matrix that illustrates existing and potential capabilities arrayed against existing and potential opportunities—information that surfaced in the view of the world and view of the company discussions. Working with this matrix, the team selects those areas where significant capabilities and opportunities intersect. Discussion of these intersections, or sweet spots, focuses on those that make sense as a potential strategic direction. When three to five distinct alternatives have been identified for further development, the high concept is expressed for each by outlining a definition of the alternative (including offerings to deliver and markets to exploit), the key customer segments and competitors, the points of competitive advantage, the potential market size and growth opportunities, critical success factors and challenges, and the investments that will need to be made.

The work to be done in this step is very conceptual and requires juxtaposing a number of issues. Not all team members have the ability or tolerance for this type of discussion. Those that are less comfortable thinking at this level of abstraction will have difficulty that may be expressed through silence or continued pushing back at choices others are trying to discuss. At times these individuals may push very hard toward choosing only alternatives that build on today's capabilities, in today's markets—those options that are less anxiety provoking because they involve few "big bet" changes. It is also possible that some members may become disengaged and withdrawn, due to feeling uncomfortable, confused, anxious about narrowing the field of opportunity through this discussion, or even complacent. Once again, it may not be possible to avoid these dynamics, but if they begin to play out they will need to be managed carefully so as to get the maximum input of all players.

### Strategic Alternatives

Once the high concepts have been developed for each alternative chosen, the objective of this next step is to define and build a case for each alternative. To do this, the team breaks into subteams (one subteam per alternative), and these teams often include others in the organization whose specific expertise is needed for this detailed phase of work. (Thus use of subteams also achieves the objective of engaging critical persons and constituent groups who have been out of the loop to this point.) The work of each subteam is to answer the questions in Figure 12.3 with enough detail for the executive team to fully understand the essence and implication of each alternative.

Clearly, this is the time when the between-meeting heavy lifting is done. There is a risk that if the executive team and the subteams do not devote enough time to this step, the final choice of strategy could be based on weak cases. There is also a risk that one or more subteams may not be able to obtain the information needed to build its case. In this eventuality the team leader must decide whether to delay the next step in the process if more time is needed or whether to eliminate the case as an alternative if the data cannot be obtained.

At the end of this final step of stage two, the team should be well prepared to go into its last rounds of discussion on options in order to make its final strategic choice.

## Choose and Refine Strategic Direction

Choosing and refining a strategic direction is the final stage of strategic choice that must be completed before the work of the team is announced to the organization and implementation begins. The overall purpose of this final stage is to select a strategic direction from among the alternative cases that have been

## Figure 12.3.  Strategic Alternative Framework.

**Environment**
- What are some of the major shifts occurring in the industry today (for example, changes in buying patterns, consolidation/disaggregation, and so on)?
- What will be the largest areas of opportunity during this period?
- What will the industry look like in the next five to ten years?

**Markets**
- What are the markets that we serve? What are the defining characteristics of these markets?
- What share of each market does the company have?
- What are the markets that we could serve in the future? What are the defining characteristics of these markets?

**Competition**
- Who are our key competitors today (in our ideal markets)?
- What is their overall strength in the industry (strong, moderate, or weak), within each of the services/products we sell?
- How would the marketplace rate us on each of these services?
- How can we best differentiate ourselves from these players?
- Who will our key competitors be in the next three to five years?

**Customers**
- Who are our primary customers today?
- What are the current consumer demographics, and how are they changing? What is influencing these shifts (changes in technology, government regulation, societal demographics, and so forth)?
- How are our customers distributed geographically?
- How are our customers segmented (different customer needs, company offerings, and so forth)?
- What do these customers spend (each) on the products/services related to our business, and how much of that figure do they currently spend with us?
- How do our customers perceive us in terms of product quality, service, prices, customer relationships, and so on?
- Who are the customers that represent the largest opportunities for us (those we should be targeting for the next three to five years) and why?
- What will these customers spend on the services we offer?
- Why will future customers choose to do business with us?
- Roughly, what is the percentage of overlap between these future customers and our current customers?

developed, further develop that choice by defining more implementation details, and subject the final, detailed choice to intense
critical review.

### Strategic Choice

In many ways, making the choice is the culminating point of much
of the work done by the team to date. The sole objective in this first
step of stage three is to compare and contrast the cases that have
been developed for the alternatives and then to make the final
choice about the strategy to adopt.

The work begins with an in-depth review of the alternatives as
they have been developed and a thorough discussion of the merits and risks of each. Applying the success criteria generated earlier to the alternatives as they are presented helps the team
effectively evaluate the most relevant advantages and disadvantages
of each. Our experience in working with teams through this phase
suggests that more often than not a hybrid strategy is developed—
one alternative is used as a foundation, and modifications are
made to it that incorporate advantageous elements from one or
more of the other alternatives.

During this process the team must be encouraged to be critical of the cases and to thoroughly assess inherent value. It is possible that given the composition of certain subteams, team
members may think, "They really know more than I do on this subject, so I don't really need to understand the nuances of this
approach." This is a dangerous mind-set—the entire team is
responsible for making the final strategic choice, and the only way
for it to do this effectively is for all members to be equally
informed. Therefore challenging and questioning in this step is
critical.

Typically, somewhere during the discussion of the value inherent in the different approaches, the focus begins to settle on one
or two options. Thus the process of "choice" may seem slightly artificial in that the final choice typically emerges from the discussion;
nevertheless it is important to bring final, formal closure to the
selection. How the final choice is made varies from team to team.
What is most important is that the process for a final resolution is
made clear in advance of the discussion. The team leader needs to

be absolutely clear prior to the meeting on how he or she will handle the situation if a unanimous choice can't be made, and the leader should share that decision with the group at the outset of the discussion.

High anxiety is not unusual at this point, as it is now time to make real decisions about the future of the company. This anxiety can play itself out in a number of ways depending on the individual, and it is difficult to predict how particular team members will react. Individuals with a high need for closure may feel relieved that the process is finally nearing its end and a choice is being made. They may push for the decision to be made very quickly, thereby cutting off input or rushing others' thought processes. Other team members may become uneasy because choosing a strategic direction means eliminating some options—these individuals may find ultimate decisions unnerving as they have difficulty accepting the risk that choice entails. They may be the last ones to hold out on casting the final vote and may feel a need to dwell on their reservations about the decision on the table. Team leaders need to be very sensitive to underlying emotions (including their own) and must balance conflicting styles to get the most from the group that is possible.

Finally and ideally, the team makes a choice that all parties agree with. In reality some agree with the choice more than others. If any one individual is in violent disagreement with the final choice, it is a risk to the implementation of that choice. It is very important that strong views of this kind be surfaced and dealt with, either in the room or alone with the leader.

### Strategic Challenge

Once the actual choice of alternative has been made, the team often feels (deservedly) that its work is done. Typically, team members have spent several months in discussion and debate, building a shared view of where they would like to take the company and how to best to get there. It is critical, however, that they realize that others in the organization have not yet been down this discovery path and that a significant communication effort now needs to be launched to bring everyone on board. Also it is important for the team to acknowledge the need for a quality assurance check on their work. The first task in this strategic challenge step has three objectives: to anticipate reactions (internal and external) to the strategy chosen, to develop a shared response to these reactions, and to prepare for rolling out the strategy.

To achieve these objectives, the team first needs to contrast the strategy it has chosen with the strategic intent it developed earlier: Will the strategic direction satisfy the intent of the company as outlined, or does it take the company down a different path? If there is a serious discrepancy—if, for example, the strategy chosen will substantively change the nature of the business and will redefine the company as it offers very different products, serves very different markets, and so forth—the team should reconsider the strategic intent of the business. If, however, the strategic intent can be upheld by the strategy chosen, the team should then move into a *self-critique mode.*

The team's next task in this step is to effectively challenge the strategy they have developed and adopted. Team members need to step back from their work and play devil's advocate. Some individuals will have trouble with this, finding it difficult to let go of something they created just as they've begun to really embrace it. The leader must push the group to examine the plan from a number of perspectives: senior management, Wall Street, frontline employees, customers, suppliers, the board, and so on. One very effective technique at this point is to have the team brainstorm questions that others will have—in effect poking holes in their work to date. Once ideas for these questions have been exhausted, the team turns its attention to developing answers to the questions, thereby creating a set of talking points that they can each use when addressing a challenging audience.

The final task in this step is to bring the strategy to key constituents for review and input. The team generates a list of internal and external players, and individuals are assigned to review the strategy with each one, in person. The questions and answers developed by the team should be used in these discussions. It is important that the team members responsible for participating in these discussions remember that the primary objective here is to get the input of these people—both "good" and "bad" input. Each team member should record the responses of the person he or she talks with and bring this information back to the team for review and discussion. Skepticism from others in the organization during this testing phase should be expected and in fact welcomed. Regardless of the elegance of the plan, people will challenge it almost automatically because they weren't involved in creating it and can't possibly understand how or why the team made all the choices it did unless they poke the strategy a bit for themselves. Team members must guard against being defensive during this process and must be careful not to talk down to those from whom they're seeking input. They should not expect others to understand everything they went through over a period of several months—patience will be essential here.

### Implementation Planning

The objectives of implementation planning, the last step in the strategic choice process, are to

- Identify the important activities that need to occur to implement the strategy.
- Detail as much as possible the action steps that need to be taken (short- and long-term) to implement the strategy.
- Define a process for monitoring progress and assessing the impact of implementation.

It is quite likely that the team will run out of energy at this point. The heavy lifting is behind it, and the rest is detail work. It is very important that the team leader recognize this and work to sustain the momentum. Without an implementation plan, the strategy is likely to collect dust on a credenza. Potential elements of the final implementation plan should include short- and long-term action items, process and project owners, specific deliverables, defined performance measures, critical success factors, and potential obstacles to implementation.

It is our experience that designating some sort of transition manager and/or transition team at this point can help ensure the success of strategy implementation. Once the plan has been created, people have a tendency to go back to focusing on day-to-day operations, assuming that implementation issues will be dealt with by other groups. Even when all groups responsibly focus on implementation, it is not uncommon for issues that do not obviously belong to someone to fall through the cracks—and when the chosen strategy represents a significant shift from the present direction, there are often many of these issues without obvious owners. Executive teams are often charged with monitoring implementation, but they are often too large for this purpose and frequently serve better as oversight bodies than as working teams. Designating a small focused group that can keep its eye on all transition issues and do the legwork for the executive team can be critical to successful implementation. Both the transition manager, whose responsibility it is to focus full-time on implementation, and this transition group should be temporary—transition by definition should have a defined beginning and a defined end. (For more on these types of teams, see Chapter Thirteen.)

## Summary

Strategy appears to be back in vogue, and myriad theories, concepts, and frameworks suggest how to deal with it. However, the CEO and executive team, bearing the responsibility for strategy development and implementation, should strive to keep one fundamental truth in mind: Though the topic is complex and the issues are intricate, strategy development can—and should—be done by the executive team. This chapter outlines a process that structures and facilitates executive team strategy formation, building on a set of fundamental principles and a proven logic flow of discussion and debate. This process is designed to ensure that those with the knowledge and responsibility to direct the organization's future make the ultimate strategic choice regarding their company's destiny.

## Chapter Thirteen

# Leading Strategic Change Teams

*Richard F. Ketterer*

*Janet L. Spencer*

Conventional wisdom holds that in today's uncertain business environment strong, charismatic leadership is the key to success. Chief executive officers, in this view, provide the vision and experience that enables their companies to face the perils of the marketplace and achieve outstanding performance. In the 1980s, Lee Iacocca epitomized the charismatic CEO, rescuing Chrysler from the edge of bankruptcy and restoring its reputation and viability as enterprise. In the 1990s, Bill Gates and Andrew Grove, among others, personify a new breed of leaders—CEOs who combine personal charisma and unbridled entrepreneurial spirit, propelling their companies to unassailable industry leadership.

But personal magnetism, however alluring, obscures the fact that strong individual leadership is seldom sufficient for success. Even charismatic leaders need good people around them.

What mechanisms are available to team-oriented CEOs to leverage the knowledge and experiences of people throughout their organizations? What specific strategies can be used and how do they work? An approach employed by more and more CEOs is to establish *strategic change teams* (SCTs) to drive critical business priorities and initiatives. This chapter defines SCTs and their relationship to executive teams. It describes the scope and nature of their work and how to design and implement them. Finally, it shows how to institutionalize strategic change capabilities into the senior management governance process.

## Strategic Change Teams Defined

SCTs address critical issues of mission that are relevant to the organization as a whole. They are chartered on a time-limited basis by executive teams to generate innovative solutions—and viable implementation strategies—for tough issues that strongly affect the organization's future capabilities, performance, and competitive position in the marketplace. The following six features further describe what is unique about SCTs and how they differ from other teams.

- SCTs operate in a challenging environment, in close proximity to CEOs and their executive teams. Previous chapters have explored at length the unique dynamics of the executive team environment.
- SCTs not only operate in a difficult environment, they tackle complex companywide issues. Whereas teams at other levels typically focus on a discrete set of tasks, SCTs address broad institutional issues. Does the enterprise have a clear and compelling vision and strategy? If the strategy is clear, is it being deployed successfully throughout the organization? To what extent are the organization's structure, work processes, operating environment, and competencies aligned with its strategy? The goal of SCTs is to find answers to these questions and to use these answers to resolve fundamental enterprise issues for the good of the company.
- Responsibility for establishing SCTs—and for holding them accountable for results—rests with the CEO and the executive team. Strategic issues are best addressed when top management agrees on the need for change and on the approach to address the problem. Without clear agreement about roles of the executive team and of an SCT, pressures invariably weaken the SCT's capabilities and ultimately its impact. Conversely, a clear senior management mandate and direction vastly increase a SCT's chances of success.

- SCTs not only define what needs to change but also how changes are to be implemented. Unlike traditional "blue ribbon" task forces, SCTs embed change strategies into their work, producing an implementation road map and communication plan. This means thinking about implementation issues not as an add-on but as an integral part of the team's overall charter.
- SCTs by their very existence challenge existing attitudes, assumptions, and solutions. This is true whether the presenting issues involve incremental or radical discontinuous change. In both cases SCTs start with a clean slate, questioning existing premises and ways of working. Because their goal is fundamental change, SCTs draw on some of the organization's most innovative and knowledgeable people, often creating what one of our clients refers to as a "dream team."
- SCTs are temporary. That time constraint puts a premium on team members' ability to get their team started up and running as quickly as possible. This calls for a unique set of leadership and team competencies, including the ability to perform under time pressure and other difficult circumstances.

A chapter on this subject would be remiss if it did not point out some of the risks associated with establishing and deploying these teams. The most obvious is that the executive team may abdicate its responsibility for ensuring that enterprisewide mission-critical problems are resolved in the best interests of the company. There is a fine line between chartering a strategic change team to define a problem and offer optimal solutions and delegating resolution of an issue. The executive team must never confuse the latter with the former: its role is to review suggestions delivered by the SCT and ultimately decide which solution to adopt and implement.

Another challenge inherent in deploying a SCT is to free up the time and attention of some of the best executive talent in the organization for the duration of the assignment. Often the individuals most desired for the SCT are in charge of running the largest and most difficult-to-manage divisions or functions.

Finally, team membership is addressed later as one of the most vital SCT concerns, and it cannot be stressed enough; with the wrong members participating, precious time may be lost and the quality of the ultimate solution may suffer.

## SCTs in Action

Given the roles played by SCTs, it is important to examine the specific nature and scope of the work they undertake. As a starting point, we identify the factors that drive successful performance in complex business organizations. It is important to align elements of the organization around a winning business strategy, as illustrated in the model of organizational effectiveness (Figure 13.1).

This model is based on the premise that an organization is most effective when its strategy is consistent with the larger environment and when important elements of the organization are congruent with the tasks required to implement the strategy. SCTs in this context function as levers CEOs can pull to align elements of the organization to achieve desired results. The following examples illustrate how this can be done.

## Strategy Development

As the pace of change has increased in the last decade, so too has the need to reexamine business strategies more frequently (Porter, 1996). In fact more and more organizations are taking a closer look at both existing strategy and ways to update or in some cases radically overhaul it. Although in the past outside consultants were relied upon to develop corporate strategies, an increasing number of CEOs now turn to inside teams to forge strategies for the future (Hamel and Prahalad, 1994).

Developing a clear strategy is especially important when forming a new company after a divestiture. This was the case with a technology company we worked with. The divestiture resulted in a newly formed independent company that included several major business units from the parent company. It was prompted in large part by rapid marketplace changes and a competitive landscape that made improved speed, efficiency, and innovation necessary. The new company and its top management needed to establish a strategy that responded to these conditions and provided the impetus for the completing the birth of a dynamic new organization.

A strategic change team was sponsored by the executive team and was to interact with the executive team as the strategy was developed. The SCT was composed of senior members of the

**Figure 13.1. Model of Organizational Effectiveness.**

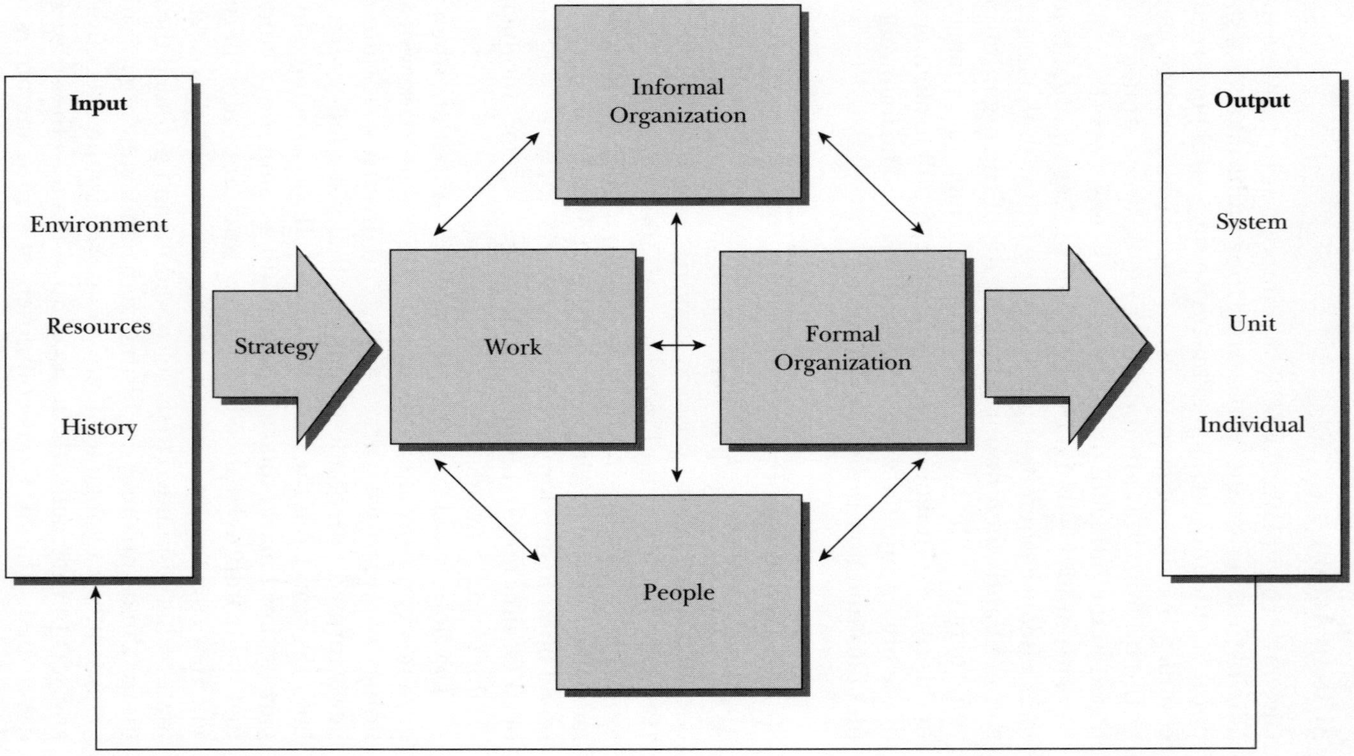

organization, most of whom reported to members of the executive team, from all organizational functions. The SCT worked through each step of the strategy development process one step ahead of the executive team, then offered its conclusions to the executive team for debate, enhancement, and decisions. The executive team and the SCT played off each other throughout the process of strategy development, with each interactive step moving closer and closer to a finely honed strategy. The SCT used numerous information sources including analysts, industry experts, noncompeting benchmark companies, outside consultants, and the company's own marketing organization. The result was a strategy that was well conceived and validated against the requirements of the marketplace and the capabilities of the organization.

Of course it is important to remember that as discussed in detail in Chapter Twelve, ultimately strategy and its deployment are owned by the executive team; however, SCTs can help to frame debates and decisions.

## Organizational Design

Another example of a strategic change team in action comes from a global telecommunications company that had to redefine its fundamental strategy to protect its long-distance business as it broadened into new and emerging businesses such as Internet access and local and wireless services. This fundamental shift in strategy required redesign of the organization's structure, or architecture. To meet this challenge, an SCT was established to align the organizational structure, business model, and core processes to the company's new strategy. Since hands-on knowledge of the business was needed, SCT members were drawn from an interdisciplinary group of managers below the executive team level. The team worked full time for six weeks defining important elements of the organization, including a new organizational structure, roles and accountabilities, staffing criteria, core processes and metrics, and the dimensions of the new operating environment, or culture, required for success in the future. The team's recommendations and implementation plans were presented to the CEO and executive team, then implemented and fine-tuned over a number of months.

## Transition Management

SCTs also have made a difference by helping companies to navigate large-scale change efforts. Such efforts can result from shifts in strategy or from marketplace demands calling for dramatic changes in a company's culture and core processes.

Radical changes in the health care and pharmaceutical industry, for example, led a global pharmaceutical company to restructure its largest division into a team-based organization. An SCT was established to coordinate diverse internal initiatives that collectively defined the transition to the new structure. Specifically, the team's charter was to design the systems and processes that would support the new structure and to develop implementation plans to institutionalize the change. The SCT deployed several subteams to work on detailed strategies for new compensation, communication, performance management, and other systems, monitoring their progress and ensuring consistency among all initiatives. The SCT periodically provided status reports to the executive team and occasionally went to that team for decisions or input on critical issues (for example, just how radically to reshape the compensation system). The SCT was disbanded when the new systems were fully designed and operational.

In another example discontinuities in its marketplace and moves by its leading competitor required a packaged goods company to rethink its strategy and organizational architecture. Seven SCTs led by the executive team were launched to design the business processes, culture, and communication strategies for the new organization. Following this effort, a change management and transition SCT was convened to institutionalize this capability going forward.

As these cases illustrate, strategic change teams can accomplish different phases of change—from strategy development to organizational design to implementation of change initiatives—but they all meet the criterion of addressing fundamental issues of change at the enterprise or systemwide level.

## Boundary Issues

One of the critical roles played by CEOs and executive teams is managing the enterprise's strategic work. This raises the question of the boundaries between the executive team and the SCT structure. Specifically, we need to examine the conditions under which CEOs and executive teams share or delegate work to SCTs, the decision-making authority vested in SCTs, and how SCT members engage the executive team while carrying out this work.

## Sharing and Delegating Work

As the pace of change has increased, so too has the scope and complexity of the CEO's and executive team's strategic work. In response more and more executive teams share or delegate elements of this work to other managers. Of course executive teams can, and frequently do, play a hands-on role with vital strategic issues. The question is, Under what conditions does it make sense for executive teams to share or delegate some of this work to an SCT?

Although every situation is unique, executive teams often share or delegate strategic work for practical reasons. For example, developing a new strategy may require weeks or months of full-time effort—a requirement that forces many executive teams to delegate key aspects of this work to an SCT. Similarly, executive teams may delegate work because it can be more effectively addressed by managers who are closer to the problem or who understand the issue from both a strategic and hands-on operational level.

Conversely, executive team members may be too close to an issue or have vested interests or opinions that preclude an objective view of a problem. In such situations an executive team can sometimes *break frame* by delegating the initial stages of the work to an SCT, freeing the executive team to evaluate alternatives its members might not otherwise have considered. How much strategic work is shared or delegated, of course, varies in each situation. The key is not what work is shared but how clear the expectations and boundaries are between the executive team and the SCT.

## Stakes in the Ground

One helpful step is for the CEO and executive team to put some specific stakes in the ground—nonnegotiable issues or givens that form boundaries or limits. For example, a CEO delivered these stakes in the ground to an SCT chartered to redesign the organization's structure and overall architecture:

- Align product development with the company's infrastructure.
- Significantly decrease layers in the management structure.
- Shift the organization's focus from a national/domestic platform to a global/local platform.

Even with explicit stakes in the ground, SCTs invariably have questions about the nature and scope of their work. For this reason it is essential for the CEO and the executive team to plan an early session with the SCT to review its charter and to raise questions at the outset that clarify the scope and boundaries of the work.

## Decision-Making Authority

Another issue to be clarified is the SCT's decision-making authority. Whether SCT members are not from the executive team or are a mix of executive team members and other managers, the important issue is for all parties involved to understand and acknowledge the decision-making authority vested in the SCT. The CEO and executive team must agree in advance what degree of freedom an SCT has and what authority will remain with the CEO and executive team.

For example, an SCT may be asked to generate and evaluate alternatives (business models, designs, and so forth) and make recommendations to the executive team. However, even in this situation, the SCT may make choices that eliminate certain options and create others. For this reason, SCT members need to know what authority they have to consider alternatives without having to consult senior management each step of the way.

## Engagement Process

Finally, there is a need to clarify how SCT members will interact with the executive team while work is under way. As mentioned earlier, an agreed schedule of briefing meetings can create an appropriate forum to review milestones and clarify critical issues. In addition, informal briefing sessions between SCT members, the CEO, and executive team members can also foster a healthy dialogue between constituencies involved in the process.

Unfortunately, if healthy lines of communication are not established at the outset, senior managers may use off-line, or informal, channels to influence or shape the SCT's work. Many strategic issues raise political concerns, but the resulting off-line efforts to direct the process undermine the SCT's credibility and, if not checked, can ultimately doom the quality and integrity of the overall effort. For example, one executive team member held breakfast meetings with SCT members who reported directly to him, inquiring about the team's progress and offering "suggestions." Such unwarranted behavior can be avoided if the CEO and executive team agree at the outset which communications are acceptable and which are not—and if all parties hold each other accountable for following through on these agreements.

## SCT Design and Start-Up

Designing effective strategic change teams involves four important steps:

1. Establishing the team's charter
2. Selecting team members
3. Agreeing on key work processes
4. Embedding a quality assurance process into the work of the team

### Establishing an SCT Charter

Once a CEO and executive team agree to create an SCT, the next step is to establish the team's charter, that is, communicate in writing the rationale for the team, its core objectives, and its scope of work. This step can help the team avoid the false starts and misunderstandings that can undermine its subsequent effectiveness and impact. The following elements, summarized in Figure 13.2, can serve as a guide for establishing an effective team charter.

## Selecting the Team

Selecting good people to serve on an SCT is one of the most important but often poorly executed steps in the team launch. Although having a clear charter and mandate from the CEO and executive team is critical, an equally important step is getting the right people on the team. This means recruiting members not only with strong individual skills but also with the combined skills and chemistry to match the complexity and challenges of the task.

Consideration must be given to the strengths and capabilities of individual candidates *and* to how these individuals fit within the overall team. The first step is to generate a list of qualified and desirable individuals, considering the extent to which candidates fit the following criteria:

- *Individual skills and experiences.* Should we include Don, because he had experience redesigning an organization in his previous job?
- *Individual characteristics and traits.* Should we add Karen, given her analytic capabilities?
- *Organizational credibility.* Should we require Joe to participate, because he has such credibility in this organization?
- *Individuals' teamwork capabilities.* Should we exclude David, given that he is more likely to be disruptive than constructive?
- *Political considerations.* What kind of message will it send if we do not include Jean?

Once a candidate list has been generated, the next step involves examining the requirements at the team level, using these criteria:

- *Organizational representation.* Do all lines of business and staff functions need to be represented?
- *The mix of relevant skills and experiences.* Should we include more than one team member with overseas experience?
- *Team size.* Do we err on the side of inclusiveness and representation or on the side of smaller-is-faster?
- *Executive team membership.* Do we include all, some, or none of the executive team? If we include even one senior-team member, what will this do to the SCT dynamics? What will it do to the executive team dynamics?

## Figure 13.2.  Guide for Establishing SCT Charter.

| | |
|---|---|
| *Statement of situation* | A brief description of the events, changes in the environment, needs for new strategic direction, and so forth that led to the decision to establish the SCT |
| *Objectives* | The primary outcomes that will result from the SCT's work; at the end of the day what, specifically, will have changed or be different as a result of this work? |
| *Scope of work* | The fundamental work or tasks that the team must accomplish to meet its goals |
| *Roles* | Team members' and leaders' responsibilities and accountabilities (for example, as chair or cochairs, core team members, extended team members, and so forth) |
| *Boundary issues* | How the team interacts with other governance bodies (including the executive team) and with operational, business group, or process teams |
| *Timing and milestones* | Target dates and deliverables by which critical objectives will be achieved |
| *Quality assurance process* | How the SCT, CEO, and executive team will evaluate the SCT's performance |

- *Leadership talent.* Who has led a team of this caliber before? Who might be best able to harness the talent in the room?

The selection process, of course, is unique to the company and team and is influenced by a complex set of factors such as the scope of the work and availability of talent and so forth. Regardless of the circumstances, the following tips may be useful when selecting a SCT:

- Individuals with proven track records of working efficiently and effectively on teams deserve extra consideration.
- Individuals who are perceived as highly credible within the organization also deserve strong consideration, as they will prove invaluable during the implementation stages of change.
- Executive team participation should depend on the nature of the task at hand. For example, it can be very difficult for executive team members to participate objectively in a redesign effort as they have more to "win" or "lose" depending on the outcome. At the same time, their participation in a strategy development effort can provide a perspective that may be lacking further down in the organization.
- Smaller (fewer than ten) is generally better, even at the cost of representation (often the team can bring in representative points of view as needed).
- A strong and capable leader is essential. Ideally, this person will have credibility with all team members and be comfortable directing the work of a high-powered group.

## Establishing Effective Work Processes

In contrast to executive teams, which generally operate as part of a permanent workgroup, SCTs usually function on a time-limited basis and under severe time constraints. The element of time, not surprisingly, places a premium on developing an effective team start-up—one that minimizes risks while building team momentum and team synergy as quickly as possible.

Many SCTs work hard to build an effective team from the team's very first meeting. Although different principles and methods can be used, we have found the most important issue for team members is to develop a shared understanding about the team's underlying mission and how the team will work together to achieve this mission. At a minimum this means clarifying and gaining commitment on the team's charter and goals, key roles and accountabilities, core work processes, rules that will guide team interactions, and finally, quality assurance mechanisms the team can use to evaluate its progress over time. Figure 13.3 summarizes key elements of a team-building framework to facilitate the start-up and effective implementation of new SCTs.

## Establishing a Quality Assurance Process

A critical challenge facing SCTs is achieving quality results on time. Given the risks involved in strategic change work, there is little room for sloppy thinking, missed deadlines, or subpar deliverables. A critical goal is quality work, completed on time, presented in a way that fosters understanding and agreement on key issues. How does an SCT know whether it is achieving its objectives and milestones along the way? What can the team do to increase the chances for success?

One essential step is to build quality assurance mechanisms into the SCT work process. As its starting point, the team has to adhere to basic principles of team effectiveness and decision making. Are discussions being dominated by a few individuals or are diverse voices being heard? When tough decisions have to be made, are the decision criteria—and the decision process itself— clear to everyone involved? If the team's "rules of the road" are made explicit at the outset and continually monitored, the quality of the team's deliverables will be significantly enhanced.

Adhering to effective processes is a necessary but not sufficient basis for success. A strategic change team must also evaluate its results against its charter and design intent. Do the team's recommendations address the fundamental issues that prompted the team to be established in the first place? To what extent are key design criteria met by the SCT's preliminary results? Asking these questions while work is still in progress is invaluable quality assurance, often leading to critical midcourse corrections and quality improvements.

One additional step is to establish a just-in-time engagement process between the SCT, CEO, and executive team. Internal quality checks are important, but they are no substitute for testing ideas with the CEO and executive team prior to issuing final results and recommendations. Preliminary results can be fed back to individual executive team members or the entire team or both at different times. In one situation we know of, SCT members met individually with each executive team member then shared their interim findings with the entire executive team a week later. This technique allowed the SCT to confirm its core findings,

# Figure 13.3. Team-Building Framework.

1. **Context and team charter**
   - What is the role of this team in the larger system?
   - What are the team's performance requirements?
   - What are key relationships with other teams?
   - What are the team's rewards and consequences?

2. **Goals**
   - What is the value-added work of the team?
   - What is the core content of the team's agenda?
   - What are the measures of team success?

3. **Roles**
   - What is expected or required from team members?
   - What are the special roles (for example, leadership)?
   - What do subgroups require of each other?

4. **Procedures**
   - How are meetings structured?
   - How is the team's agenda created and managed?
   - How are decisions made?
   - How is team output managed?

5. **Interactions**
   - What behavior is expected or required of members?
   - Which operating principles will govern behavior?

6. **Team quality assurance**
   - How will the team be initiated or launched?
   - How are work sessions started?
   - How are work session process reviews conducted?
   - How are periodic process reviews conducted?

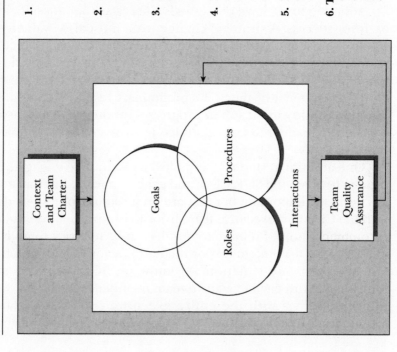

Delta Consulting Group, 1991.

modify other results, and increase the level of senior management understanding and support for the SCT's overall recommendations.

## Institutionalizing Change Capabilities

Strategic change teams by definition are chartered to address specific mission-critical issues; however, the usefulness of SCTs raises the question of how to embed ongoing strategic change capabilities into the organization. Different companies approach this issue in different ways.

As discussed throughout this chapter, more and more organizations are establishing SCTs at an enterprise level to address strategic needs as they arise. This allows executive teams to identify critical strategic issues and then share or delegate key elements of the work of change to the specially created SCTs made up of managers outside the executive team.

Because this approach calls for the use of new people to address each new strategic need, one important issue is how new teams can avoid spending time rediscovering the wheel. To retain valuable experience and learning, organizations using the SCT approach often set up a small dedicated team of change professionals or line managers to assist newly established SCTs. Thus, even though new individuals are used on different teams, hands-on knowledge about how to implement SCTs remains available to the teams. Over time, the repeated use of SCTs leads to the development of a cadre of experienced professionals who know how to start up and deploy fast-cycle strategic change teams.

In addition to building SCT capability among an increasing number of managers below the executive team, a number of organizations are institutionalizing strategic change by making it a part of their formal governance process. For example, due to fundamental changes in the structure of its industry, a two-billion-dollar packaged goods client recently established a standing subteam of its executive team to find ways to make drastically reducing operating costs an ongoing process. To avoid treating this problem as a short-term issue, the team was established as a permanent subgroup. Because its goal is to continually come up with new ways to reduce costs, in a sense it is reinventing its approach and methods each year. Over time the team not only has built up significant expertise in this area but also has embedded cost reduction capabilities as a sustainable core competence throughout the company.

Still other organizations make strategic work a formal and ongoing part of their executive team governance process. Because tactical issues often drive strategic issues, some executive teams focus a section of their meeting agenda on strategic concerns. To ensure greater attention to strategic issues, some teams go even further, convening specially designed off-site sessions (sometimes as many as four a year) to focus senior management attention on critical strategic enterprise issues.

## Summary

As competitive pressures and the pace of change have increased in recent years, a growing number of CEOs and executive teams have recognized the need to address strategic organizational issues on an ongoing basis. To meet this challenge, top managers are spending an increasing amount of their time working on strategic enterprise concerns. However, given the complexity of the issues that arise and the demands placed on executive team members, there are limits to how much hands-on involvement is possible. To fill this void, CEOs and executive teams are turning to specially designed strategic change teams to address critical strategic issues.

In many ways the use of SCTs marks a fundamental shift in approach to internal governance and the management of organizational change. In contrast to the traditional CEO model in which strategic work is carried out by a few top managers, the new model broadens ownership to the CEO and executive team and, by extension, to a cadre of managers outside the executive team. In essence, SCTs create a *shared division of labor,* in which the CEO and executive team retain ownership of key strategic issues while sharing core elements of this work with a broader coalition of managers throughout the organization.

## Chapter Fourteen

# Creating a High-Performance Operating Environment

*Peter K. Thies*

*David B. Wagner*

Part Three of this book so far has described three of the executive team's roles in leading large-scale change: governing the organization, developing strategy and deploying strategic change teams. However, the executive team's leadership of change efforts does not stop there. Why? Because changes in strategy and structure alone do not effect the necessary behavioral change. Many other factors affect people's behavior.

Cases in point: even after strategic and structural changes, it's common to hear employees say things such as

"We have reorganized, but nothing's really changed."

"The real problem is that everyone's accountable but no one's accountable."

"We can't seem to keep good people."

"We need to change the mind-set in this company. We're too bureaucratic—we need to be fast and flexible. We have to change our culture."

## The Concept of Operating Environment

The executive team must create the conditions necessary to fundamentally affect people's behavior so that it supports the strategic and structural change. This work involves changing an important component of any organization: the *informal organization*, also called the *operating environment* or *culture*. In addition to the formal organization—structure, systems, and processes—every organization develops a set of informal arrangements that influence the behavior of its members and describe "how we run the place." We define this operating environment as the way people work together in almost every respect to produce the business of enterprise. It includes leadership behavior, norms, inter- and intra-group relations, communication and influence patterns, informal roles (opinion leader, maverick, and the like), power, and politics. The executive team must create a new operating environment that supports successful implementation of the business strategy.

Just as companies need to develop effective operating plans to implement strategies, they also need high-performance operating environments in which to execute these plans. This means that creating a new operating environment that supports a specific business strategy involves changing

- How people operate individually and collectively in relation to the strategy
- How decisions are made
- Patterns of leadership behavior
- How people deal with each other
- The focus of energy and resources
- How people think about customers, competitors, and employees
- How the organization is perceived by the external environment (industry analysts, financial institutions, regulators and legislators, and so forth)

## The Business Case for Changing the Operating Environment

The inevitable question is why should the executive team of a large complex organization accept the task of creating a new operating environment? The answer: the organization's operating environment is critically linked to its performance.

In the 1995 *Fortune* report of the most admired companies in America, several companies such as Rubbermaid, Coca-Cola, and 3M were observed to top the list of admired companies year after year. The article concluded that the drivers of these companies' success appear to be elements of a high-performance operating environment:

- Employees have a strong sense of identification with their company.
- The cultures are robust yet flexible. The bedrock is a set of core values that are renewed over time.
- The companies have a balanced emphasis on three key stakeholders: customers, employees, and shareholders.

The executive team is uniquely qualified to create a high-performance operating environment for the following reasons:

- It has a breadth of perspective on the company's operations no other team has.
- It has tremendous influence on how resources (time, people, and budgets) are configured within the organization.
- It has great leverage as the most highly visible role model for teams in the new operating environment. (In his seminal book on organizational culture and leadership, Edgar Schein (1992) points out that the single most important factor in culture change is leadership behavior.)

Although uniquely positioned for changing the operating environment, not all executive teams are equally prepared for the task, for two important reasons. First, executive team members have varying levels of comfort with the concept and value of their organization's operating environment. They may be reluctant to devote the necessary time and energy to bring about this kind of change. Second, executive team engagement is a necessary but not sufficient condition for changing the operating environment. In addition to convincing themselves of the need to work on operating environment, executive team members must be very effective at engaging others in the change effort as well. Not all executive teams are skilled in these separate yet related areas.

This chapter conveys our experience working with executive teams on changing the operating environment—what the issues are, and how to deal with them successfully. Specifically, we have divided the chapter into four major sections in which we discuss the operating environment and the executive team's agenda, the executive team's role in changing the operating environment, building executive team capability for culture change, and the executive team's role in implementation as a systems integrator.

## Operating Environment and the Executive Team's Agenda

In this section we explore the conditions or symptoms that lead the CEO and executive team to the conclusion that a change in the operating environment is needed. The impetus to change the organization's operating style often comes from the following presenting issues:

- Performance problems (at organizational and individual levels)
- Changes in strategy
- A merger, acquisition, or spin-off
- Changes in organizational structure
- Changes in work processes and technologies
- Changes in people

Indicators of the need for a change in operating environment frequently emerge from a pattern of organizational performance problems that have plagued management for some time. These indicators can range from organizational-level outcomes (such as costs, profitability, and innovations) to individual-level outcomes (such as excessive voluntary turnover and low morale). It is likely that a number of solutions have already been tried and resulted in unmet expectations. People may be saying things like, "We've restructured twice over the past four years, and yet nothing has really changed. The culture around here hasn't really changed that much."

One example of how organizational-level performance is closely tied to operating environment concerns a pharmaceutical company that was having difficulty optimizing its performance across a large number of divisions. One reason for the company's substandard performance was its inability to keep up with its competitors, who were developing strategic alliances with important national accounts. The executive team was aware that it could dramatically increase both revenues and profit if it could propose and secure large companywide contracts that could meet corporate customers' specific needs. However, before the company could develop agreements with these customers, a small number of its divisions would have to provide price concessions or value-added services in order for other divisions to secure much larger sales contracts. In other words, companywide revenue and profit could be increased substantially but only by decreasing the profit of some divisions.

The business rationale for the divisions to cooperate was clear from the enterprise level. However, a number of aspects of the operating environment stymied corporate's attempts to encourage companywide relationships with national customer accounts. The culture was characterized as financially driven and highly autonomous—any attempts by corporate to coordinate the efforts of the divisions were met with high resistance. In addition, people in the divisions emphasized that they were measured and held accountable for divisional performance, even though a substantial percentage of executive compensation was, in contrast, determined by overall enterprise performance. As a result, attempts to establish companywide contracts and strategic alliances with important customers were futile.

Major changes in an organization, whether associated with changes in strategy, structure, work processes, new technology, or people will precipitate the need for the executive team to alter the operating environment so that it is aligned with and supports the new organization. The discussion of the model of organizational effectiveness (see Chapter Thirteen) stated that a fundamental dynamic is congruence among the organizational elements. Effectiveness is greater where the general pattern aligns with or fits the strategy, and when the four components of work, people, informal organization, and formal organization are more congruent, consistent, or have greater "fit" with each other.

Senior executives need an ongoing measurement system to help them track the organization's capabilities and the leading indicators of performance. Without such a system, information about what in the operating environment is not working and why will rarely make it to the executive team. As part of this ongoing measurement, the executive team should be tracking aspects of the organization's operating environment, to determine how well it is supporting the strategy. When questions such as the following are answered systematically, they shed light on the effectiveness of the organization's operating environment:

- What goals and measures do people believe are important in assessing their behavior and performance? How consistent are these with the strategic objectives and desired outcomes?
- What are the implicit rules and policies that guide people's day-to-day behavior?
- What do people believe leads to recognition and reward?
- What do people see in the behavior of leadership? How consistent are these behaviors with the intended operating environment?
- To what extent do training and development programs reinforce the desired operating environment?
- To what extent do the formal and informal communications reinforce the desired operating environment?

In times of significant change the executive team will need to embark on an in-depth analysis of the organization to determine what is and is not consistent with the strategy. This analysis may include interviews with key managers, focus groups with cross-sections of employees, and surveys of representative samples of employees throughout the company or a census of the entire company. Using that analysis to understand which aspects of the operating environment are consistent or inconsistent with the strategy can be both enlightening and frustrating.

However, once the analysis of the operating environment has been completed, the executive team can begin to draw conclusions about the gap between the current versus the desired operating environment, plan the actions required to realign the operating environment, and play an active role in leading the changes required to create that desired operating environment.

## The Executive Team's Role in Changing the Operating Environment

We have concluded that to create real change in the operating environment there is no substitute for active engagement on the executive team's part. This means that the executive team cannot simply be made aware of or sign off on proposed changes. Instead, its role is that of chief architect of the change process. The single largest influence on the success of operating environment change initiatives is the behavior of top leadership.

But carrying out the chief architect role is no easy task. It requires persistence, courage, and vision on the part of those at the top of the house. Consider the reflections of several CEOs we have worked with:

> Nobody at the beginning thought I'd stick with this initiative for more than a few months. That view changed over time as I continued to talk about virtually nothing else.
>
> —Jamie Houghton, Corning Inc.

> When we started [this change process] I knew it was going to be a very different game. . . . I felt that what we were doing was right. . . . When you step into a new leadership position, you have to give people a wake-up call.
>
> —Jon Madonna, KPMG Peat Marwick

> You have to have conviction to move forward when people you trust are telling you to slow down. You have to start the change process and sustain it when others lose faith. Most of the change management efforts that fail do so because leadership quits.
>
> —Craig Weatherup, PepsiCo

Carrying out the chief architect role requires the executive team's active leadership in three important ways: in defining the new operating environment, in engaging itself along with other top leadership in the process, and in developing a strategy for making the desired changes a reality.

## Defining the New Operating Environment

The first step is for the executive team to create a compelling picture of the desired operating environment. Specifically, given a change in strategic direction or a fundamental change in structure, several important questions need to be answered:

- What aspects of the operating environment need to change? (This confirms the problems the executive team is trying to solve.)
- How are the changes related to strategy? (Executives must be able to explain in crisp, concrete business terms why these changes will make a difference.)
- Why change? (The executive team must provide people with a compelling logic that justifies the change.)

There is an important pitfall for the executive team to avoid as it defines the required operating environment. These definitions can become a laundry list of vague terms that are generalizable to any company and therefore applicable—of practical use—in none. A way out of this dilemma is to declare a short list of dimensions (between five and nine) of the desired operating environment. Then, to make the list applicable to the company, attach behavioral definitions to each dimension, describing what it would look like if the change were actually in play in the organization.

## Engaging Top Leadership

The second task for the executive team is to engage itself and other top leadership, such as the officers in the organization or whatever level is perceived to be senior management, in the change process. The executive team's definition of the required operating environment is essentially worthless unless key leaders are involved in creating it and taking ownership for its content and development. There are several benefits to engaging company leaders in this way:

- It develops key leaders' shared understanding and common language for thinking about and discussing the concept of operating environment and the business case for change.
- It ensures key leaders' understanding that changing the operating environment is work worth doing for both strategic and sound business reasons.
- It increasingly involves the executive team itself in the change process. Communicating, test marketing, or otherwise explaining the team's thinking to others develops ownership, understanding, and commitment to the substance of the required operating environment.

## Developing an Operating Environment Change Strategy

The executive team's third task in its chief architect role is developing a change strategy that defines, in practical terms, the path to a new operating environment. The executive team builds the change strategy by making choices around four critical issues:

1. *Content* of the change. The ways and means of developing a vision of a new operating environment (as described previously)
2. *What* to change. Pulling on several important levers for change (institutional leadership, management practices, organizational structure and design, and individual behavior).
3. *How* to create a new operating environment. Using an integrated set of interventions.
4. *Tactical choices.* Choosing when and where to intervene, including determining the timing, sequencing, and target groups for the integrated set of interventions.

This task is explained in more detail in the implementation section later in this chapter.

## Developing the Executive Team's Capability for Operating Environment Change

One way to begin to engage the executive team as well as the organization is to build the business case for changing the operating environment. Making the rationale for change and linking it directly to the strategy helps executives grapple with change as a team and gives their interventions more credibility throughout the organization.

Executive team members may not truly understand the symbolic nature of their actions or the team's role as keeper of the organization's values. Executive team members may overestimate the impact of presentations and formal statements on culture and underestimate the impact of the "little things" they do. They may not appreciate that they wiggle their fingers and the organization sees them waving their arms. They need to understand that they are leading role models.

A new operating environment—and its emphasis on values, how things are done and how people behave—may be perceived as inconsistent with the modus operandi of some executives. Some executives will be able to shift their behavior to be consistent with the operating environment, but some cannot or will not. This risk eventually extends to individuals throughout the organization.

Senior executives are used as weather vanes by the rest of the organization. The change in operating environment will be perceived seriously only if the expectations and accountability for change are applied to everyone, even the senior executives. If senior executives are immune from the shift in required and expected behavior, people will take the change effort much less seriously. We have found that feedback and coaching to executive team members can be particularly effective in aligning leader behavior with the desired operating environment.

Even subtle changes in management processes or individual behavior of executive team members can send powerful messages to the organization. The CEO of one organization, for example, used to consistently place the financial results first on the operating review agenda. Because the organization was trying to shift to being more market driven and customer focused, he decided to require that customer satisfaction and market opportunity data be placed first on the agenda. This sent a strong signal to the organization about a shift in priorities, from a focus strictly on financial results to a focus on the customer as an important driver of financial performance.

## Implementation: The Executive Team as Systems Integrator

Up to this point we have discussed why it is important for an executive team to concern itself with changing the operating environment, the team's role as chief architect of the change process, and the demands of this role on executive team capability. We now turn to issues of execution—how the executive team can put it all together to effectively change the operating environment.

### Leverage Points for Operating Environment Change

There are basically four levers that the executive team can pull to effectively transform the operating environment:

1. *Institutional leadership.* The success of any large-scale transformation is, in part, dependent on the degree to which the CEO, executive team, and senior leaders

- Articulate the new operating environment and expectations for each individual.
- Model desired behavior.
- Provide recognition for behavior consistent with strategic objectives.
- Impose sanctions for undesirable behavior.
- Perform symbolic acts designed to support the new operating environment.

2. *Management practices.* The day-to-day actions of individual managers—how they interact with each other, their subordinates, and their own management—are important leverage points. Whether the emphasis is on open communications, teamwork, customer service, competitiveness, or commitment to quality, individual managers can teach and sustain the new values and beliefs through their interactions with others. Their job is vital; they are the ones who can directly promote behavior consistent with the

desired operating environment on the part of hundreds, even thousands, of people.

3.   *Organizational context.* Efforts to transform the operating environment will fade unless they are supported by closely related changes in the fundamental structures, systems, and processes that drive organizational behavior, such as the appraisal and reward systems, staffing and selection practices, core work, and business processes.

4.   *Individual behavior.* During a period of change, few things hold the attention of large numbers of people or send clearer signals than the treatment of key employees. People keep close tabs on who is up and who is down, who is in and who is out. Whenever possible, it is important to publicly recognize and reward those who exemplify the attributes called for by the new operating environment and to impose sanctions on influential employees who resist required changes.

As the governing body of the enterprise, the executive team has all of these levers available to them. The next issue is how to pull those levers.

## Specific Interventions

Based on our experience, we have identified a set of twelve interventions that when employed by the executive team in a coordinated, integrated fashion, can produce lasting large-scale change in a company's operating environment. Figure 14.1 lists the interventions and specifies the role the executive team plays in using each technique and the likely outcomes of each.

For the change effort to be effective, it is not enough for the executive team to simply pick and choose randomly from this list of interventions—it requires careful and thoughtful tactical planning on their part. It is very important for the interventions to be coordinated, sequenced appropriately, and aimed at the right target audiences if the interventions are to continually build momentum and create the conditions for achieving the desired behavioral change. It is not immediately obvious which interventions are best, and they will be different for every organization.

**Figure 14.1.  Operating Environment Interventions.**

| Intervention | Senior Team Action | Potential Outcome |
|---|---|---|
| Collaborative culture definition | Leads teams that define dimensions and behaviors required for the new operating environment. | Shared understanding and commitment to create new operating environment. |
| Measurement and gap analysis | Commissions assessment of the gap between the current and desired operating environments. | Shared understanding of priority gaps along with specific action plans to address them. |
| Stakeholder analysis and engagement | Analyzes key internal and external stakeholders to understand their position relative to the change. | Commitment by key stakeholders to the proposed changes. Resistance to change kept to a healthy minimum. |
| Senior management behavior | Participates in leader feedback process implemented with all senior managers. | Senior managers model desired new behaviors. |
| Structural change | Leads redesign of systems, structures, and processes to reinforce new behaviors. | New systems reinforce and institutionalize the new operating environment. |
| Management process redesign | Commissions redesign of management structures, processes, and metrics. | Management processes that support and reinforce the required changes in the operating environment. |
| Recognition and reward | Sponsors redesign of compensation and reward systems. | Desired new behaviors reinforced through focused compensation programs. |
| Formal feedback process | Participates in the development and implementation of management feedback process linked to desired new behaviors. | Desired new behaviors reinforced through ongoing formal feedback process. |

**Figure 14.1.** *Continued*

| Intervention | Senior Team Action | Potential Outcome |
|---|---|---|
| Large-group engagement process | Sponsors events and conferences designed to focus and reinforce desired changes in the operating environment. | Concrete changes in the way people work together to accomplish business objectives. |
| Educational interventions | Oversees development of educational and training programs that facilitate the rapid development of the desired new behaviors. | Acquisition of desired new behaviors by managers and employees throughout the business. |
| Communications | Leads the development of communication strategies integrated into a coherent change management message. | Broad understanding of and buy-in to the need for and direction of change. |
| In-depth individual interventions | Conducts constructive coaching and performance feedback for senior leaders. | Senior managers walk the talk or leave the company. |

## Tactical Choices

The executive team needs to make three primary tactical choices around implementation:

- Determining the right game plan or core approach to the change effort
- Choosing the optimal timing and sequencing of interventions
- Selecting the appropriate methods of participation

## The Game Plan

The approach or strategy the executive team should use to create a new operating environment depends on a number of factors, including the size of the organization, the sense of urgency for change, and the strength of the current operating environment. Figure 14.2 compares four game plan archetypes we've seen over time.

## Timing and Sequencing

An assumption behind our approach is that a change in strategy must come first, because that is itself an important driver of the need for a change in operating environment. Our experience also suggests that major structural changes are best carried out early on in the change process, as they can be an important early reinforcer of new behaviors.

Although by no means universally, we have seen certain sequences and timing of change interventions prove more effective than others. The template in Figure 14.3 illustrates one possible approach. Note that in this model structural changes (if needed) and the development of an operating environment change strategy occur in what is called phase 0, an important preimplementation stream of work. Once phase 0 is complete, the remaining interventions to initiate and sustain operating environment change are introduced in phases 1 and 2.

Phase 1 consists of interventions designed to shake things up and initiate change. This is accomplished through a combination of large-group meetings, mass communications, and the introduction of heightened expectations for senior leadership behavior and accountability. Once these interventions take hold, phase 2 interventions are initiated to support, sustain, and embed the change. They include continued communications, feedback processes, reward system redesign, and actions to reward those who demonstrate the desired behavior and deal with those who cannot or will not support the change.

## Methods of Participation

In considering methods of participation, the executive team must choose how to involve people in the change process and the requirements to make for consistency of approach across business

**Figure 14.2. Approaches to Operating Environment Change.**

| Game Plan | Description | Assessment |
|---|---|---|
| *Top-down* | Obtains alignment and commitment of several layers of leadership, starting with the senior team. | Advantages: direct link with strategy, availability of resources. Disadvantage: Takes longer than other approaches. |
| *Bottom-up* | Incorporates a local flavor by starting at lower levels, then working its way up. | Advantages: face validity with the troops, perceived connection to customer. Disadvantages: can stall midstream if real behavioral change is not seen in top leaders. Difficult to obtain resources over time. Propensity to be treated as a "program" or flavor-of-the-month activity. |
| *Periphery-core* | Essentially a *beta test*. Executive team defines operating environment; those at outer periphery test and modify it. Brought back to executive team for continued iterations. | Advantages: potential for innovation. Can achieve visible results in a relatively short time, with high involvement. Disadvantage: can take a long time. |
| *Combination* | Incorporates elements of each. Might include quick hits, innovative large-meeting designs, and unconventional communication vehicles. | Advantages: potential for innovation. Incorporates parts of top-down and bottom-up approaches. Disadvantage: amount of resources required, complexity of coordination. |

units. First, any new operating environment must be developed with the participation of employees across the organization. The executive team must own the change process, but it must choose ways to get input and ultimately ownership from people in the organization.

Another choice is the degree of "federalism" versus "states rights." Creating an enterprisewide operating environment requires processes for aligning executive leaders across the units to a set of basic principles but also giving them appropriate freedom to act and to tailor the approach to their units. In general, organizational states rights increase the more the units use fundamentally different core technologies and serve different customers in different markets and decrease the more an integrated strategy addresses the convergence of products, technologies, and markets across the units.

## Examples of Putting It All Together

This section on implementation has described conceptually how an executive team can change the company's operating environment by pulling on the levers available to it, using a set of interventions sequenced and timed appropriately. As might be expected, in practice systems integration looks different in each organization based on its unique situation. The following are short descriptions of how three different executive teams took on the systems integrator role and changed the operating environments in their organizations.

### *Telecommunications Firm*

A telecommunications company's CEO sponsored an organizational assessment that engaged forty of the firm's most senior executives. The intent of the assessment was to identify the issues facing the enterprise as it prepared itself to execute a recently announced change in strategic direction. The major themes from the assessment suggested that the implementation issues revolved around "how we run the place" and that the operating environment needed to change for the company to execute its

## Figure 14.3.  Interventions Template.

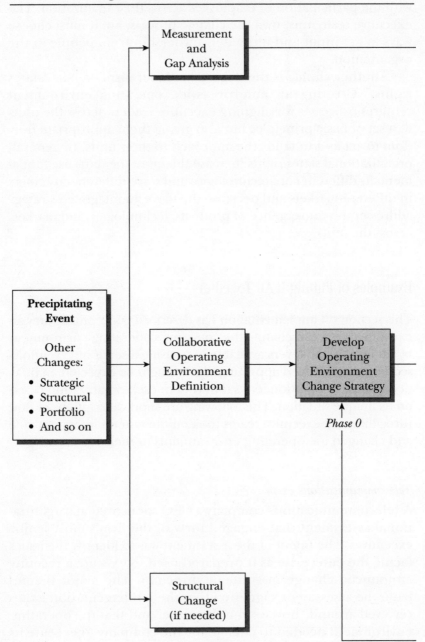

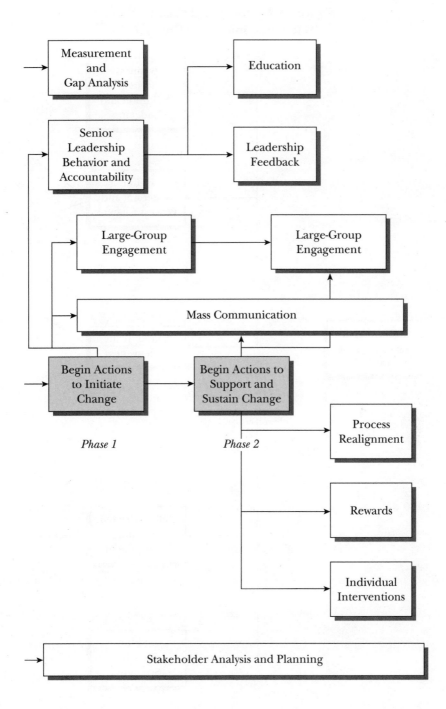

## Figure 14.4. Integrated Change Plan:
## Telecommunications Company

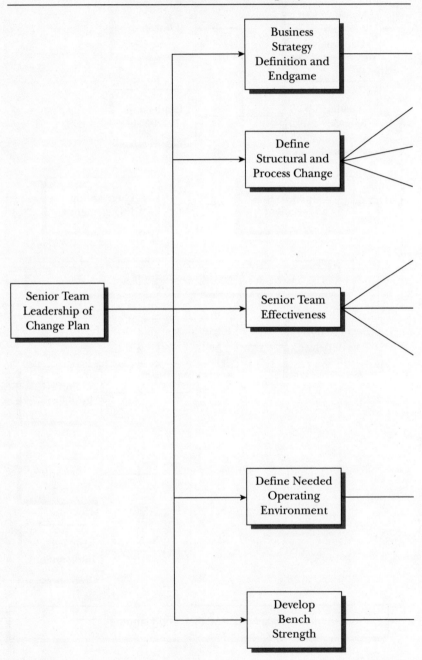

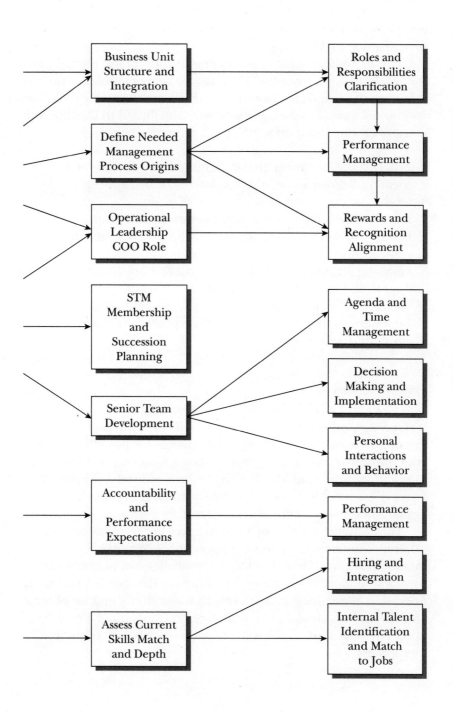

strategic plan. The CEO and executive team worked through the data and agreed on a course of action for changing the operating environment. In doing so they created an integrated change plan (Figure 14.4).

The executive team took ownership for many elements of the integrated change plan. Over the course of eighteen months following the diagnostic assessment, team members actively led or sponsored several initiatives that have contributed to the development of an improved operating environment, including

- Enterprisewide restructuring that improved operational focus and drove accountability down to more appropriate levels
- Improving executive team effectiveness by redefining team membership, work processes, and decision-making procedures
- Focusing annual senior leadership conferences on critical operating environment issues such as people development, accountability, and performance management
- Redesigning the succession planning process and bench strength development process

### *Professional Services Firm*

The CEO and vice chairman of a professional services firm chartered a committee to redefine how the firm manages its most important asset—its employees. The impetus for this effort was the realization that recent changes in strategic direction and the resulting fundamental restructuring of the firm around market groups created the need for a people strategy aligned with business strategy and new organizational arrangements.

The committee was composed of executive team members plus other top-line managers and high-potential executives. Committee members realized that creating a comprehensive people strategy involved making fundamental changes to the firm's culture, or operating environment. With this in mind they put a lot of time and energy into creating and test marketing a vision of a new operating environment, engaging a broad cross-section of people in the process.

In parallel with defining the new operating environment, the committee developed an integrated change plan and chartered three subgroups, each one focused on addressing an aspect of the operating environment critical to the successful execution of the firm's market-driven business strategy and structure. These three subgroups focused on skills, training, and leadership development; recruiting, selection, and orientation; and compensation, career pathing, and performance management. The decision to divide the work in this manner was driven by the data gathered during the committee's work on defining and test marketing its vision of a new operating environment.

The committee members themselves formed the core of these subgroups, and they added resources to each subgroup from inside and outside the firm as appropriate. During the process of subgroup work, the committee decided that a comprehensive skills and competencies framework would drive the initiatives and actions carried out by all subgroups. The result was an integrated change plan for changing the operating environment, as shown in Figure 14.5. The committee addressed issues of timing and sequencing of these initiatives based on the complexity and relative importance of the work in each.

### Consumer Products Company

The members of the executive team of a major business unit redefined their role by creating an "A List" of initiatives they would implement as a team. For each of the eight major initiatives, they developed action plans to drive progress in that area. Not surprisingly, it turned out that many of the actions needed to drive progress in one area had either direct relevance or important implications for the work done in another area. For this and other reasons, they developed an integrated change program as shown in Figure 14.6.

Each executive team member was given responsibility for one or two of the A List items (areas labeled in capital letters in Figure 14.6). This became each executive team member's shared leadership role. The result of this team's work has been a fundamental change in the business unit's operating environment, driven and led from the top by the executive team.

**Figure 14.5.  Integrated Change Plan:
Professional Services Firm.**

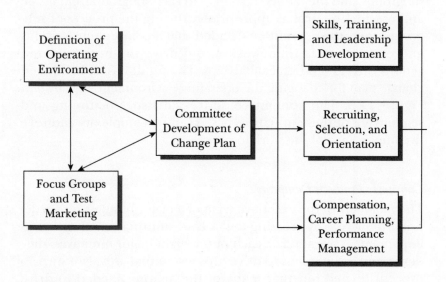

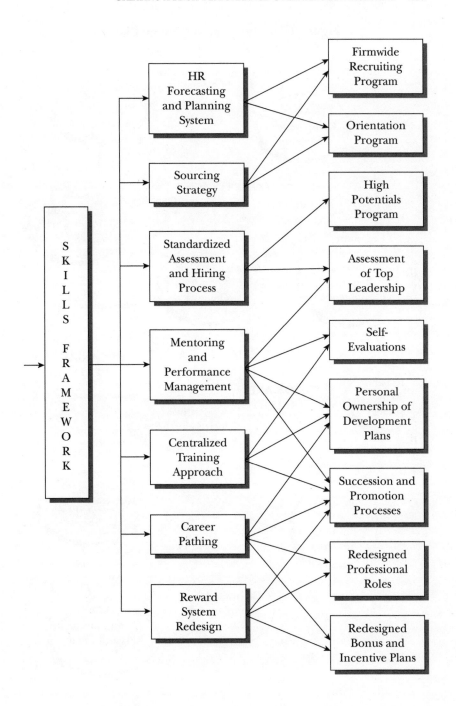

**Figure 14.6. Integrated Change Plan:
Consumer Products Company.**

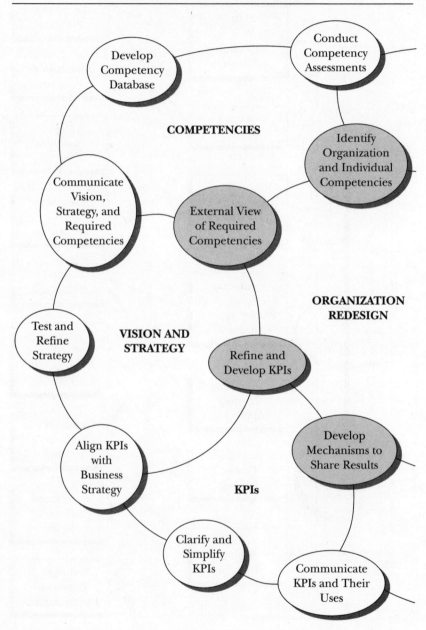

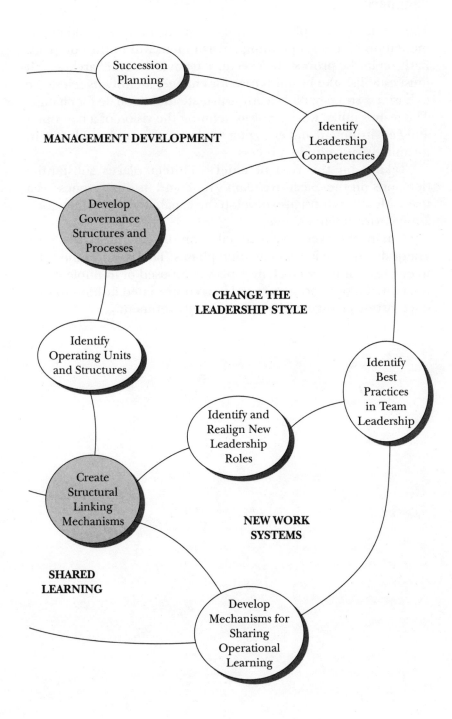

## Summary

The executive team plays a critical role in the definition and implementation of a new operating environment within the company. Early on in the process the executive team is the chief architect. It must establish the business case for change, identify its relevance to business strategy, and clearly articulate the rationale for change. The team's initial work involves defining the vision of a new operating environment and engaging top leadership and employees in meaningful ways in the process.

Taking on the role of chief architect places substantial demands on the executive team's time and its effectiveness as a team. Members must also develop the capability for leading operating environment change.

Finally, the executive team takes on the role of systems integrator during the implementation phases. This requires the team to create an integrated change plan composed of multiple initiatives carried out and sequenced in a coordinated fashion to produce lasting change in the operating environment.

# Conclusion
## The Competitive Advantage of Executive Teams

An executive team that collectively provides strategic, operational, and institutional leadership for an organization is better equipped than just one person to handle the growing pressures exerted today on companies in corporate America. No matter how powerful, experienced, charismatic, or knowledgeable a CEO, no one individual can be expected to bear the weight of running an entire enterprise alone. By using an executive team as an extension of his or her leadership, a CEO can deploy team members' talent as the team collectively processes the important information that its members individually possess in order to make corporate decisions that are better informed and appropriately influenced by the organization's many different facets.

This team approach to running a company will be especially critical in the future as a number of environmental factors, such as the following, dramatically increase the need for a synergistic approach to corporate governance:

- Continuing pressures to demonstrate consistent corporate growth and deliver return to shareholders necessitate that decisions continually be made regarding both new market opportunities and the resulting trade-offs in resource allocations. Given the complexities of most businesses today, one person alone cannot hold all the data required for these decisions in his or her head, much less make the appropriate choices when they involve balancing myriad intricate moving parts.

•   The continuing trend of mergers, acquisitions, and joint ventures is blurring traditional organizational boundaries and increasing the need for partnering capabilities. This in turn creates a compelling need for effective integration and coordination of many organizational units at the enterprise level.

•   Increased competitive pressures and compressed time frames mean that crucial decisions must be made and buy-ins secured across what may be very disparate or relatively unrelated parts of the business. Often these decisions must be made without the luxury of lengthy one-on-one discussions and debates. The executive team, however, can be an effective forum for these critical interactions.

•   As the world rapidly grows smaller through technological advancements, organizations have a growing need to span multiple diverse cultures and geographies and coordinate resources from a distance. This necessitates a greater understanding of the far-reaching implications of leadership decisions. The existence of an executive team allows the responsibility of acquiring an understanding of global dynamics to be extended beyond just one or two people at the top of an organization.

It becomes obvious, then, that understanding and managing an executive team will be critical CEO capabilities. Many points describing how to design, build, manage, and monitor executive teams have been made throughout this book. We close with a few key considerations, those particularly salient to a CEO intent on governing with an executive team.

•   The CEO must learn to effectively manage the team, his or her eyes and ears. The CEO's understanding of the roles played by the team and attention to the care and feeding of this collection of high-powered individuals is crucial to the team's—and the organization's—success. The CEO must also be highly aware of the unique demands—both external and self-imposed—that are placed on the team and are likely to affect its functioning.

•   The team must fully and adequately represent the organization, not just by virtue of team members' respective individual roles but also in the way each member brings his or her knowledge of the business forward and the way each considers critical decisions from an enterprise perspective and demonstrates the vital ability to make decisions that may affect him or her adversely but that are for the greater good of the organization. For this dynamic to occur, and for an executive team to truly work to its potential, the team must obtain a heightened awareness of and appreciation for the healthy aspects of conflict and for trust and must recognize the impact that both conflict and trust have on each person's performance.

- Finally, as team leader the CEO must continually assess executive team performance, collectively and individually, in order to keep the team healthy. It is imperative that the CEO act quickly to resolve conflicts and address poor performance.

If organizational leaders vigilantly attend to the issues outlined in the previous chapters, an executive team can do the work it was created to accomplish. It can become a primary source of strategic competitive strength for the CEO and for the organization as a whole.

# References

## Chapter Two

Beckhard, R. "Optimizing Team Building Efforts." *The Journal of Contemporary Business,* 1972, *1*(3), 23–32.

Bourgeois, L. J., III, and Eisenhardt, K. M. "Strategic Decision Processes in High Velocity Environments: Four Cases in the Microcomputer Industry." *Management Science,* 1988, *34,* 816–835.

Dougherty, D. "New Products in Old Organizations: The Myth of the Better Mousetrap in Search of the Beaten Path." Ph.D. dissertation, Sloan School of Management, Massachusetts Institute of Technology, 1987.

Dutton, J. E., and Duncan, R. B. "The Creation of Momentum for Change Through Strategic Issue Diagnosis." *Strategic Management Journal,* 1987, *8*(3), 279–296.

Dyer, W. G. *Team Building: Issues and Alternatives.* Reading, Mass.: Addison-Wesley, 1977.

Eisenhardt, K. M., and Bourgeois, L. J., III. "The Politics of Strategic Decision Making in Top Teams: A Study in the Microcomputer Industry." *Academy of Management Journal,* 1988, *31*(4), 737–770.

Hackman, J. R. "The Design of Work Teams." In J. W. Lorsch (ed.), *Handbook of Organizational Behavior.* Upper Saddle River, N.J.: Prentice Hall, 1983.

Janis, I. *Groupthink.* Boston: Houghton-Mifflin, 1982.

McGrath, J. E. *Groups: Interaction and Performance.* Upper Saddle River, N.J.: Prentice Hall, 1984.

Michel, J. G., and Hambrick, D. C. *Diversification Posture and the Characteristics of the Top Management Team.* Working paper, Columbia Business School, 1988.

Quinn, J. B. "Managing Strategies Incrementally." *Omega,* 1982, *10,* 613–627.

Rumelt, R. P. *Strategy, Structure and Economic Performance.* Boston: Harvard Business School Press, 1974.

Schein, E. H. *Process Consultation.* (2nd ed.) Reading, Mass.: Addison-Wesley, 1988.

Shea, G. P., and Guzzo, R. A. "Group Effectiveness: What Really Matters." *Sloan Management Review,* Spring 1987, *3,* 25–31.

Song, J. H. "Diversification Strategies and the Experience of Top Executives of Large Firms." *Strategic Management Journal,* 1982, *3*(4), 377–380.


## Chapter Three

Hambrick, D. C., and Fukutomi, G. D. "The Seasons of a CEO's Tenure." *Academy of Management Review,* 1991, *16,* 719–742.

Heilpern, J. D. "The Emerging Role of the CEO." In D. A. Nadler, R. B. Shaw, A. E. Walton, and Associates, *Discontinuous Change: Leading Organizational Transformation.* San Francisco: Jossey-Bass, 1994.

Millstein, I. M. "The Evolution of the Certifying Board." *Business Lawyer,* 1993, *48,* 1485–1497.

Nadler, D. A. "Managing the Team at the Top." *Strategy and Business,* 1996, *2,* 42–51.

Nadler, D. A., and Tushman, M. L. "Leadership for Organizational Change." In A. M. Mohrman Jr. and others (eds.), *Large-Scale Organizational Change.* San Francisco: Jossey-Bass, 1989.

Nadler, D. A., and Tushman, M. L. "Types of Organizational Change: From Incremental Improvement to Discontinuous Transformation." In D. A. Nadler, R. B. Shaw, A. E. Walton, and Associates, *Discontinuous Change: Leading Organizational Transformation.* San Francisco: Jossey-Bass, 1994.

Tushman, M. L., Newman, W. H., and Nadler, D. A. "Executive Leadership and Organizational Evolution: Managing Incremental and Discontinuous Change." In R. H. Kilmann, T. J. Covin, and Associates, *Corporate Transformation: Revitalizing Organizations for a Competitive World.* San Francisco: Jossey-Bass, 1987.

Vancil, R. F. *Passing the Baton.* Boston: Harvard Business School Press, 1987.


## Chapter Five

Argyris, C. *Overcoming Organizational Defenses.* Needham Heights, Mass.: Allyn & Bacon, 1990.

Nadler, D. A., and Ancona, D. G. "Teamwork at the Top: Creating Executive Teams That Work." In D. A. Nadler, M. S. Gerstein, R. B. Shaw, and Associates, *Organizational Architecture: Designs for Changing Organizations*. San Francisco: Jossey-Bass, 1992.

Perkins, D.N.T. *Ghosts in the Executive Suite: Every Business Is a Family Business*. Branford, Conn.: Syncretics Group, 1988.

Schein, E. H. *Organizational Culture and Leadership*. San Francisco: Jossey-Bass, 1985.

Tannenbaum, R., and Schmidt, W. "How to Choose a Leadership Pattern." *Harvard Business Review*, 1958, *36*, 95–102.

Vroom, V. H. "Can Leaders Learn to Lead?" *Organizational Dynamics*, 1976, *4*, 17–28.

## Chapter Seven

Ford, J. D., and Ford, L. W. "The Role of Conversations in Producing Intentional Change in Organizations." *Academy of Management Review*, 1995, *20*(3), 541–570.

Fukiyama, F. *Trust: The Social Virtues and the Creation of Prosperity*. New York: Free Press, 1994.

Winograd, T., Flores, R., and Flores, F. "The Action Workflow Approach to Workflow Management Technology." *Information Society*, Oct.-Dec. 1993, *9*(4), 391–405.

## Chapter Eight

Block, P. *The Empowered Manager: Positive Political Skills at Work*. San Francisco: Jossey-Bass, 1987.

Filley, A. C. *Interpersonal Conflict Resolution*. Glenview, Ill.: Scott, Foresman, 1975.

Fisher, R., and Ury, W. *Getting to Yes*. Boston: Houghton Mifflin, 1981.

Sherwood, J. S., and Glidewell, J. E. "Planned Renegotiation and Norm Setting." In J. W. Pfeiffer and J. E. Jones (eds.), *The 1973 Annual Handbook for Group Facilitators*. San Francisco: Jossey-Bass, Pfeiffer, 1973.

Thomas, K. W., and Kilmann, R. H. *Thomas-Kilmann Conflict Mode Instrument*. Tuxedo, N.Y.: Xicom, 1974.

Tuckman, B. W. "Developmental Sequence in Small Groups." *Psychological Bulletin*, 1965, *63*, 284–399.

## Chapter Nine

Nadler, D. A., and Tushman, M. L. *Strategic Organization Design: Concepts, Tools, and Processes.* New York: HarperCollins, 1987.

Tushman, M. L., and Nadler, D. A. *Competing by Design: A Blueprint for Organizational Architectures.* New York: Oxford University Press, in press.

## Chapter Eleven

Buchanan, R., and Sands, R. "Creating an Effective Corporate Center: The Influence of Strategy on Head Office Role." *European Business Journal,* 1994, *6*(4), 17–27.

Grove, A. *Only the Paranoid Survive.* New York: Currency Doubleday, 1996.

Werther, W. B., Kerr, J. L., and Wright, R. G. "Strengthening Corporate Governance Through Board-level Consultants." *Journal of Organizational Change Management,* 1995, *8*(3), 630–677.

## Chapter Twelve

Bliss, D. R. "Strategic Choice: Engaging the Executive Team in Collaborative Strategy Development." In D. A. Nadler, M. C. Gerstein, R. B. Shaw, and Associates, *Organizational Architecture: Designs for Changing Organizations.* San Francisco: Jossey-Bass, 1992.

Byrne, J. "Strategic Planning." *Business Week,* Aug. 26, 1996, pp. 46–52.

Collins, D. J., and Montgomery, C. A. "Competing on Resources: Strategy in the 1990s." *Harvard Business Review,* July/Aug. 1995, pp. 118–128.

Coyne, K., and Subramaniam, S. "Bringing Discipline to Strategy." *The McKinsey Quarterly,* 1996, *4,* 14–25.

Galpin, T. J. "Making Strategy Work." *Journal of Business Strategy,* Jan./Feb. 1997, *18*(1), 12–15.

Grove, A. S. *Only the Paranoid Survive.* New York: Doubleday, 1996.

Hamel, G. "Strategy as Revolution." *Harvard Business Review,* July/Aug. 1996, pp. 69–82.

McGrath, R. G., and MacMillan, I. C. "Discovery-Driven Planning." *Harvard Business Review,* July/Aug. 1995, pp. 44–54.

Porter, M. E. "What Is Strategy?" *Harvard Business Review,* Nov./Dec. 1996, pp. 61–78.

Prahalad, C. K., and Hamel, G. "Strategic Intent." *Harvard Business Review,* May/June, 1989, pp. 63–76.

Slywotsky, A. J. *Value Migration: How to Think Several Moves Ahead of the Competition.* Boston, Mass.: Harvard Business School Press, 1996.

Stalk, G., Jr., Evans, P., and Schulman, L. E. "Competing on Capabilities: The New Rules of Corporate Strategy." *Harvard Business Review,* Mar./Apr. 1992, pp. 57–69.

## Chapter Thirteen

Hamel, G., and Prahalad, C. K. *Competing for the Future.* Boston: Harvard Business School Press, 1994.

Porter, M. E. "What Is Strategy?" *Harvard Business Review,* Nov./Dec. 1996, pp. 61–78.

## Chapter Fourteen

Schein, E. H. *Organizational Culture and Leadership.* (2nd ed.) San Francisco: Jossey-Bass, 1992.

# Index

DEMCO